D1541390

PRAISE FOR *CLOSED LOOP LIFECYCLE PLANNING*

"Bruce has an uncanny knack for putting his vast experience together with the varying degrees of corporate politics and monetary and regulatory compliancy to deliver a set of objectives for business professionals with little to a significant IT background to execute against. You would be hard pressed not to find something in this book you either won't want to try and/or see a new way to tackle an ongoing 'business challenge.'"

—Tim S. Houterloot, IT Lifecycle Manager (Fortune 100 company)

"This book provides detailed processes that companies can use to effectively manage their desktop hardware and software assets. These processes have been developed over years of practical application with a wide variety of clients and have been successfully implemented numerous times."

—Anthony F. Pellegrini, Senior Vice President of Sales and Marketing (retired), CompuCom Systems, Inc.

"It is great for Bruce to summarize his years of experience helping IT customers. This book should be the guide every IT manager uses to effectively and efficiently manage technology for their company."

—Michael White, Enterprise Marketing Manager, HP Personal Systems Group

"Bruce Michelson, through his closed loop lifecycle planning methodology, has developed a very powerful approach to optimizing the desktop environment. Too often major corporations pursue optimizing their desktop environments by improving select activities (e.g., procurement, asset management, disposition). Because the activities of the desktop environment are interdependent, optimization should be approached holistically. CLLP is a proven methodology to unlock the operational efficiencies and maximize the total savings."

—Jim Kimball, HP Asset Recovery Manager, Adjunct Faculty, Endicott College

"The information technology industry has considerably matured since the early 1990's, with new technological standards and design infrastructures that in many cases severely impact pertinent, daily business activities that financially impact business survival and optimization. Bruce Michelson's *Closed Loop Lifecycle Planning* elaborates on every key technological operation, from organizational structure, hardware and software maintenance and longevity, operational streamlining and productivity, as well as exposing esoteric costs that have long-term implications on an organization's vitality. I highly recommend this book if you, as an information technologist or information officer, desire to alter or optimize the lifecycle of your existing network infrastructure."

—David Franson, Game Development Author

CLOSED LOOP
LIFECYCLE PLANNING®

CLOSED LOOP
LIFECYCLE PLANNING®

A Complete Guide to
Managing Your PC Fleet

Bruce Michelson

✦✦Addison-Wesley

Upper Saddle River, NJ • Boston • Indianapolis • San Francisco
New York • Toronto • Montreal • London • Munich • Paris • Madrid
Cape Town • Sydney • Tokyo • Singapore • Mexico City

Many of the designations used by manufacturers and sellers to distinguish their products are claimed as trademarks. Where those designations appear in this book, and the publisher was aware of a trademark claim, the designations have been printed with initial capital letters or in all capitals.

The author and publisher have taken care in the preparation of this book, but make no expressed or implied warranty of any kind and assume no responsibility for errors or omissions. No liability is assumed for incidental or consequential damages in connection with or arising out of the use of the information or programs contained herein.

The publisher offers excellent discounts on this book when ordered in quantity for bulk purchases or special sales, which may include electronic versions and/or custom covers and content particular to your business, training goals, marketing focus, and branding interests. For more information, please contact:

U.S. Corporate and Government Sales
(800) 382-3419
corpsales@pearsontechgroup.com

For sales outside the United States please contact:
International Sales
international@pearsoned.com

This Book Is Safari Enabled

The Safari® Enabled icon on the cover of your favorite technology book means the book is available through Safari Bookshelf. When you buy this book, you get free access to the online edition for 45 days. Safari Bookshelf is an electronic reference library that lets you easily search thousands of technical books, find code samples, download chapters, and access technical information whenever and wherever you need it.

To gain 45-day Safari Enabled access to this book:
- Go to http://www.awprofessional.com/safarienabled
- Complete the brief registration form
- Enter the coupon code 97JX-F5ZK-MMNF-2KKR-DYIR

If you have difficulty registering on Safari Bookshelf or accessing the online edition, please e-mail customer-service@safaribooksonline.com.

Visit us on the Web: www.awprofessional.com

Library of Congress Cataloging-in-Publication Data
Michelson, Bruce.
  Closed loop lifecycle planning : a complete guide to managing your PC fleet / Bruce Michelson.
    p. cm.
  Includes index.
  ISBN 0-321-47714-6 (hardback : alk. paper) 1. Microcomputers. 2. Computer systems—Management. 3. Business—Data processing. I. Title.
  QA76.5.M498 2007
  004.16—dc22
                                                    2007011464

ISBN-13: 978-0-321-47714-9
ISBN-10: 0-321-47714-6
Text printed in the United States on recycled paper at RR Donnelley in Crawfordsville, Indiana.
First printing June 2007

Editor-in-Chief
Karen Gettman

Development Editor
Mark Renfrow

Managing Editor
Gina Kanouse

Project Editor
Betsy Harris

Copy Editor
Keith Cline

Indexer
Lisa Stumpf

Proofreader
Kathy Bidwell

Technical Editors
Michael White, Enterprise Marketing Manager, HP Personal Systems Group

Chris Mertens

Tim Houterloot, IT Lifecycle Manager

J. Boyd Nolan, P.E.

Anthony F. Pellegrini

David Franson

Publishing Coordinator
Romny French

Multimedia Developer
Dan Scherf

Cover Design
Alan Clements

Composition
Bumpy Design

This book would not have been completed without the support and patience of Victoria Macy, Charles Michelson, and of course Bubbie Macy. Thanks for all of your insight and confidence.

CONTENTS

CHAPTER 5   Staging and Integration 71

CHAPTER 6   Installation 85

Part II and a Bonus Section are located online. Register your book online at www.awprofessional.com to access these chapters.

ACKNOWLEDGMENTS

A book such as *Closed Loop Lifecycle Planning* could not have been written without a lot of support from a tremendous team of individuals.

Vicki, Charles, and Bubbie: It is because of you three that I have been able to engage and expand my skills as a writer and practitioner. I could not have done any of this work without your support.

The team at Addison Wesley: You all are fantastic—Mark Renfrow, Kristin Weinberger, Stephane Nakib, and Karen Gettman; thanks to all of you, this book has become reality.

Chris Mertens, the best manager I have ever known, and Newton Walpert, VP leader: Thanks for providing me the opportunity and the environment to develop under your guidance. Todd Bradley, Senior VP, defines the role of a hands-on executive and also provided furtile grounding for my growth.

Tony Pellegrini: In a relationship that has extended almost two decades, I have learned more from you than anyone; thanks for investing your time in me.

For all of my HP colleagues: The past 20 plus years, you have taught me the art of lifecycle management.

Finally, to the customers, prospects, and businesses (over 600 and counting) that have permitted me to listen, advise, and study: Thank you for investing your time and energy into what has been a successful and meaningful relationship. I look forward to sharing even more in the future.

ABOUT THE AUTHOR

Bruce Michelson is the National Lifecycle Manager for Hewlett-Packard's Personal Systems Group (PSG). In this role, Bruce is responsible for engaging with Hewlett-Packard's largest and most complex accounts in developing continuous process-improvement plans and cost-savings strategies. As a subject matter expert in lifecycle and the total cost of ownership, Bruce's credentials include industry recognition for his independent research.

Bruce has been appointed and recognized as a Distinguished Technologist by Hewlett-Packard. Distinguished Technologist is a title reserved for an elite few individuals who have met a rigorous standard within three performance criteria: impact and continuity of technical contributions, leadership, and breadth and depth of knowledge.

Bruce is the author of more than 200 industry/customer white papers. He holds multiple copyrights for the research and publications he has developed. Bruce has participated as an adviser on two management textbooks. From a subject matter expertise perspective, Bruce holds multiple certifications.

Prior to assuming the role of National Lifecycle Manager, Bruce held regional positions in the high technology field, gaining expertise in the utility business model, lifecycle services, and cost management. A frequent keynote speaker representing Hewlett-Packard, Bruce has presented various lifecycle topics to a diverse group ranging from colleges and universities to senior executives.

Bruce has more than 30 years of experience in high technology, cost management, and total cost of ownership across multiple industry segments.

Bruce earned a Bachelor's degree in business accounting in 1974 from Indiana University.

Introduction

Lifecycle management has been in existence as a concept for many years. As early as the 1990s, lifecycle management was touted as an IT strategy that would streamline operations and reduce costs.

Along the way, the marketing messages were confused with the actual discipline of lifecycle management. The maturity level of lifecycle management was in its early development. The needs of IT managers were not yet fully defined and articulated. There was an abundance of providers, all of whom had similar marketing messages with a wide array of core competencies and definitions at a detailed level of what lifecycle management represented. However, in all this confusion began to rise a conceptual vision of what lifecycle management could be and an operational definition of what it would comprise.

Two clear steps were required make that vision become reality: define the requirements, and then organize to deliver the service levels that the requirements addressed. This proved to be more complicated than many IT professionals believed because, in the vacuum of definitions, silos developed organizationally for the delivery of the services. Around these silos, cultures and a "comfort" level developed; the challenges to consider and implement lifecycle management had become political, too. To adopt lifecycle management, the organization would need to become more flexible.

About the same time, other significant breakthrough developments occurred that facilitated how businesses would perceive lifecycle management. The first development was the widespread acceptance of the *total cost of ownership* (TCO). As both a concept and a deliverable, the TCO message convinces IT professionals and executives that the cost of a client device (PC) can in fact be measured and tracked.

Whereas TCO measured and reported the costs specifically, areas of potential impact were generally identified. The measurement and reporting, however, was not a plan to execute a strategy to impact the cost and service structure; that is the role that lifecycle management plays. TCO highlighted the need for IT organizations to have a defined lifecycle strategy. After all, it has become clear in the industry that the acquisition price of an access device represents a small percentage of the overall costs to support that device.

The TCO became a primary justification for the need to define a plan. From the 1990s through today, many (if not most) large businesses have had some sort of TCO validation. At times, the TCO was both a validation for change and a validation that a business was already optimized.

Y2K had many interesting long-term impacts that were not clearly understood at that time. During Y2K, end users discovered that they could add, change, or modify certain parameters including the image and software to access device configurations. In many cases, end users also discovered that IT involvement was not required (and in some cases, IT didn't even need to be notified of the changes).

Because of the scaling of Y2K remediation, end users felt empowered as competent users of access technology to enable the technology on a more personal level. This heralded the end of the casual end user. End users suddenly felt "comfortable" making changes and were not concerned with implications across the enterprise; their concern was to make the access device more adaptable for their own use.

Through all the evolution of technology of personal computing for the enterprise, lifecycle has remained constant. Interestingly, the definition of *lifecycle* depended on who was asking the question and from whom the response was sought. The belief of businesses was that if you asked six consultants the same questions regarding lifecycle management, you would get six completely different answers. Although this might seem a bit humorous, it happens to be quite true.

What businesses now seek is a practitioner's point of view and an industry definition of lifecycle management, which is the primary objective of this book. Just as with a cookbook recipe or a manufactured product, a bill of material can be defined to represent the requirements to support access devices across the enterprise. This book should be viewed as the "cookbook."

To be clear, lifecycle management is vendor neutral. A simple definition is that *lifecycle management* is the set of deliverables required to support access devices in an enterprise. Many businesses truly believe that lifecycle management is not "rocket science." I would agree. Lifecycle management represents a combination of business, political, and economic considerations. It is the combination of all these agendas that make lifecycle management challenging to deliver in the marketplace.

Closed loop lifecycle planning offers a methodology that provides businesses an opportunity to objectively assess and improve the entire lifecycle environment. Looking at lifecycle management from a practitioner's point of view yields the clearest possible insight into optimizing the client lifecycle portfolio.

Lifecycle Management

1

Closed Loop Lifecycle
Planning Methodology

INTRODUCTION

The lifecycle journey begins by looking at client lifecycle management as a loosely defined products/services portfolio potentially delivered to multiple organizations by multiple service providers (both internal and external) in a "stovepipe" enterprise model. Then the solution itself begins to transform, in a building-block approach (as discussed in the following sections), into a deliverable.

All the client lifecycle elements interrelate; decisions made in one element invariably show up and are reflected in the others. The lifecycle elements lend themselves to a model that groups the elements in such a way that tightly coupled elements are addressed as a "suite." Many businesses have addressed lifecycle in the following manner to expedite the overall conceptual plan, with these suites representing a reasonable grouping of client lifecycle-management elements:

- Commodity suite
- Value suite
- Economic suite

As you explore client lifecycle management, these broad categories may suggest the best manner to assign resources within an enterprise. You can easily make the business case for which elements belong in which category. The fundamental construct is that many decisions can and, according to *closed loop lifecycle planning,* should be made at the time of acquisition.

Many businesses have different names for the suites, but most determine that one is point of sale, one is custom, and the final is action oriented. Whatever the nomenclature, the philosophy is the same: Segment to make the conceptual framework easier to understand and execute.

COMMODITY SUITE

The commodity suite contains many of the lifecycle elements that can be identified, scoped, and aligned with the product point-of-sale decision. In fact, many of these lifecycle elements can easily become product attributes because they can be priced and defined during the acquisition process. These lifecycle elements include the following:

- Acquisition of hardware
- Acquisition of software
- Staging and integration
- Installation
- Moves, adds, and changes (MACs)
- Warranty and maintenance

Organizationally, viewing the commodity suite may present some initial challenges. The acquisition team might not have the necessary information to incorporate the lifecycle elements into the packaging of the product. If the preceding list of the commodity suite is reviewed, it could be clear that much of the information can be somewhat easily obtained or reasonable estimates of the volume or effort required defined.

In each section of this book, there is likely enough information, for example, which would permit a business to establish a reasonable set of assumptions that would facilitate packaging the commodity suite. If this is not possible, all the resellers, manufacturers, and partners could easily provide the averages in each of the lifecycle elements desired.

One of the key benefits of exploring the commodity suite is that these lifecycle elements do not require significant redefinition of the work to be performed. Therefore, the number of lifecycle decisions and scope are reduced, thus making available more planning resources to focus on the more strategic elements of the lifecycle.

An interesting observation is that in many lifecycle engagements, much time is spent on the commodity suite. It is quite appropriate to invest the time up front, of course, and define the deliverables and the service levels. What is interesting is that the same rigor is often deferred in the value suite and the economic suite that follow. Part of the observation might be that the full team is not engaged in the lifecycle discussion, or that in the initial process it is the acquisition process that defines lifecycle.

Closed loop lifecycle planning encourages a broader definition, one more inclusive of the overall definition up front.

NOTE: Many of the elements of the commodity suite represent decisions and packaging that can be embedded or a product attribute.

VALUE SUITE

This second grouping, or suite, adds value to the process, has (often) a custom set of deliverables, and is somewhat unique to every business. The value suite consists of those lifecycle elements that may have a more customized service level or may be packaged requiring a level of due diligence significant enough to be packaged or quantified separately. These lifecycle elements include the following:

- Interoperability and prototyping
- Image management
- Help desk
- Asset management
- Program management
- Management tools

The value suite represents (most likely) a combination of services both internally and externally delivered. In the value suite, it is not unusual to find that if there is consideration to externally deliver a service, it is frequently separated into a separate set of decisions or assessed by a separate process.

As always, there is no right or wrong approach. The question is to place the entire lifecycle-management portfolio into context so that the integration issues can be identified and understood. At the end of the process, having a consortium of service providers may or may not be the optimal solution.

NOTE: Frequently, the value suite is integrating the set of à la carte lifecycle elements, customizing and consolidating these elements into a solution architected for the business.

ECONOMIC SUITE

The economic suite represents the overall set of service delivery approaches and explores the action required to execute change. The economic suite consists of those lifecycle elements that have a significant bearing on the overall set of economics that relate to closed loop lifecycle planning. Although all the lifecycle management elements impact costs, these elements specifically can have an immediate and tangible impact on the overall cost.

These lifecycle elements include the following:

- Technology refresh
- Disposition
- Service delivery strategies

Many businesses attempt too early in the process to arrive at conclusions regarding the entrance and exit into certain lifecycle practices. In many instances, the internal communications are not fully clear either, which often creates uncertainty within IT and the end-user base that IT supports.

The first example is the *request for information* (RFI). The RFI is the process by which a business secures industry information, specifically information from product/service providers. To generate an RFI for client lifecycle management is basically to ignore all the research, white papers, and work performed by both funded independent and "tethered" or aligned consultants. Often, the RFI substitutes for businesses' own empirical research. Whether this is a good or bad practice is not to be determined here. The major point is that there should be *absolutely* no major surprises from a pricing/costs RFI.

Moreover, when responding to RFIs, product/service providers almost always withhold investment and pricing information until the time of an actual *request for proposal* (RFP). RFIs are generally "boilerplate" and accessible to most businesses through Internet research.

One benefit of the RFI process accrues because each business has suppliers come in and present their portfolio. From this, a business can secure a comfort level in dealing with certain suppliers. If the client lifecycle management marketplace is as mature as commonly believed, supplier presentations should not be overly customized, except perhaps for some particulars unique to a business or industry.

The second proof point is that many RFIs and RFPs just validate decisions and courses of action, and thus result in no new decisions. Instead, they simply affirm existing processes.

NOTE: The economic suite is often overlooked as a part of the lifecycle process. Because the economic suite reports and measures results, many believe it can be deferred. Unfortunately, deferral often results in the work not being performed until driven by a compelling event.

IMPLEMENTING LIFECYCLE MANAGEMENT

After the decision has been made to adopt lifecycle management, or closed loop lifecycle planning, the question becomes where to begin.

You have a number of choices, and the best advice is to do what can reasonably be achieved. Do not sacrifice the quality of the full solution in haste to get an overall program in place. The phased approach, just as in a technology refresh plan, is likely the best approach. Determine the priorities for the business and set up through the program office the plan to achieve the objectives. Therefore, establishing and empowering the *program management office* (PMO) is the first step in the process. The second step is the development and delivery of the program plan or a series of integrated project plans.

Equipped with a PMO and an approved plan, the question is, again, where to begin. Assuming that a business is global, the strategy could be, as an initial phase, to select one of the three suites discussed earlier for implementation in specific locales. A plan can be defined and a set of deliverables articulated and documented.

If a transition plan is to be developed, the transition statement of work must be scoped so that the planning process can assess the time and effort required.

Other businesses have taken specific lifecycle elements, such as help desk and asset management, and defined teams to define the local workflow and transition to the new process.

Depending on the ability to absorb change, an enterprise can adopt practices quickly by converting to certain suppliers. Some changes are quite easily accommodated, others are not. The commodity suite requires the least investment of time and resources. The key is that the empowerment model the commodity suite is structured around be a standard product and point-of-sale portfolio. On a global scale, this should be accomplished by ensuring ratification by all the business units.

In general, value suite implementation requires more planning, resources, and senior management support. Participation should not be optional, and the value suite should be an integral part of the overall enterprise agenda to improve service levels and reduce costs. In most cases, the adoption of the help desk and asset management sets the tone for overall lifecycle management. Although the other functions and operations can continue or change to new suppliers/processes, without the support of these two critical functions, the client lifecycle-management approach could fail.

Phasing in the help desk is always a solid idea; building on existing success is much easier than trying to manage multiple implementations globally, or even nationally across multiple business units. The "Stealth IT" is much easier to identify and address if the phased approach is taken.

Asset management is challenging because of the informal manner by which many business units address this issue today. As mentioned earlier, the implementation might depend on potential benefits for the business. Often, asset management is viewed solely as benefiting IT. Although asset management can be implemented in a phased approach, this approach might then be viewed by some as optional. Asset management can also be handled in a "big bang" manner—thus providing the processes and workflow, installing the agent, and enabling the examination of *all* network hardware and software.

Many lifecycle elements can be implemented in a co-terminus manner. In this approach, multiple teams work on the projects under one PMO. This tactic expedites the overall adoption rate.

The next section provides sample closed loop lifecycle planning timelines. These guidelines are based on general studies/research. Activities are listed, followed by the estimated time for such processes. Some of these actions might overlap in time, but are provided separately here to establish expectations. The scope of the lifecycle engagement is the key determining factor, so these guidelines must be tempered with that judgment. Even if a decision is made to continue internally and to adopt best practices, many of the timeline elements apply.

LIFECYCLE ACTIVITIES

The following table presents a potential timeline for lifecycle activities. Of course, based on management direction, the timelines can be expedited/changed.

Timeframes in this table frequently reach the maximum listed when costs do not align or when service-level results fail to meet end-user expectations. Each business handles the process internally somewhat uniquely.

Closed loop lifecycle planning drill down	1 month
Response to lifecycle considerations identified in the drill down	3 months
Decision to move ahead with lifecycle as an approach for the enterprise	12–18 months
RFI	2 months
RFP	3 months
Select supplier(s) and negotiate terms and conditions	2 months
Staff and define PMO	1–2 months
Develop and deliver transition statement of work	3 months
Develop overall statement of work	3 months
Deliver proof of concept, or first phase	3 months
Begin production transition	6 months

The message that a business can conclude from this brief chart of guidelines is that the activities (from deciding to explore the approach to executing the strategy at some level) that define lifecycle management require 12 to 18 months.

Note that the majority of the 12- to 18-month window is dedicated to internal activities within a business to prepare for lifecycle management. In many cases, the timeline is informal; businesses explore lifecycle as a normal part of the day-to-day rigor in service delivery strategies. At some point, however, the dialog always becomes serious, and the topic is explored.

Most lifecycle management approaches begin under the initiative of a cost reduction or a compliance/risk issue. As businesses become more aware of the practices, the timelines will decrease; but today, 12 to 18 months appears to be the reality.

NOTE: Closed loop lifecycle planning timeframes scale easily. The timeframes can be expanded or contracted based on resource availability.

THE MAP

If client lifecycle management is a journey, closed loop lifecycle planning is the map. Like all maps, no one single approach goes from one point to another; there are decisions to be made. The analogy can be carried even further. Like all maps, there is a target destination: the future state.

Don't confuse the future state with the final state; there are always new roads being built and new modes of transportation. It is important in client lifecycle management that clear objectives be defined and quantification of those objectives be clearly stated. The cost-reduction, cost-avoidance, and service-level agendas must be clearly articulated and defined. From these objectives stem implications for end-user satisfaction, customer satisfaction, retention, and the flexibility that comes from planning.

The logical next step in client lifecycle management is user segmentation, an emerging practice. In somewhat vague terms, user segmentation has already been referenced in this chapter. User segmentation depends on lifecycle business practices being at a sufficient level to diversify the portfolio.

A sense of urgency exists regarding the combination of client lifecycle management and user segmentation because the market is changing rapidly. Although the access market itself is changing, the regulations, laws, and governance are not changing. If the governance model is changing at all, it is only increasing, not simplifying. Access device selection now represents one of the core decisions that a business must make.

NOTE: Each discipline of closed loop lifecycle planning can be delivered as a suite or separately.

DISTRACTIONS ON THE ROAD

Distractions from lifecycle management will always occur—perhaps another project competes for scarce resources, or perhaps a business unit working on a niche project tries to solve lifecycle issues on their own. Distractions will also occur simply because of the focus required to perform lifecycle management in a planned manner. The trade-off is speed and quality.

As indicated in the table earlier in this chapter, implementation of lifecycle management can reasonably take 12 to 18 months. During that time, businesses might become impatient and attempt to expedite the process. Although speed-ups are possible, you must still build the appropriate plan and execute it.

Earlier in this chapter, I identified senior management support of lifecycle management as a crucial success factor. As lifecycle plans are being developed, including the timeline, it is crucial that senior management understands and buys into the timeline and the process. The worst-case scenario is an impatient senior management demanding that the timeline be expedited. At that point, the mid-course correction becomes highly visible, and the Stealth IT can become a factor.

As in all journeys, anticipate the distractions and objections. A timeline of even 6 months might prove to be a challenge. Seek out the small wins in lifecycle planning early in the process and trumpet them. Report frequently and do *not* let end user, Stealth IT, managers, and support teams "guess" where a project is at in terms of progress. Your marketing and communications teams should also be aligned with the lifecycle management program.

Equally important is to recognize when an objection or competing program or other initiative is more than a distraction. Senior program managers understand that priorities can change and business objectives can shift. Consider, for instance, that a lifecycle program is in progress when a major acquisition occurs. In this scenario, priorities may shift immediately based on board approvals. Any existing lifecycle management program should be leveraged (to the extent possible) with the new business acquired.

You can think of lifecycle management as an executive "sale." Not a sale from the perspective of a supplier, in this case *sale* means that lifecycle management is a strategic initiative. Although businesses may have many attempts at beginning and ending certain lifecycle elements, there is generally only one opportunity to deliver the strategic solution. The executive sponsor of lifecycle management can "make or break" the program through the empowerment and support provided (or withheld).

In lifecycle management programs, the program manager generally reports to the *chief information officer* (CIO). So, the program manager should always have access to the CIO. Distractions in the process should be brought to the attention of management in regularly scheduled program reviews, but also if there is a sense of urgency about the concerns. It is preferable to identify issues, even if they're out of the cycle, if they are significant enough to impact the overall program. Escalation is not a sign of weakness. It can be and often is a sign of maturity.

NOTE: Many companies use some of the processes of closed loop lifecycle planning, but treat the lifecycle elements as standalone functions. As the improvement process moves forward, those people best suited to manage the integration of the processes will become known and may constitute the PMO.

CLOSED LOOP LIFECYCLE PLANNING: THE "LOOP"

Because many people think in terms of pictures, Figure 1-1 shows a diagram that represents closed loop lifecycle planning. This is the recipe, the bill of material. You might have heard before that if a strategy cannot be presented in one slide, it might be too complicated to implement. Although I'm not certain that is true, what is true is that the overall bill of material for closed loop lifecycle planning can be expressed in a single diagram.

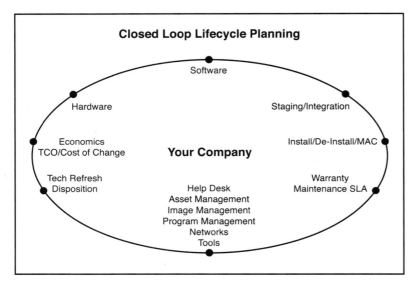

Figure 1-1   The closed loop lifecycle planning bill of material

As you will observe, beginning with the hardware portion, the diagram moves clockwise with the content of this book. This diagram also presents the commodity, value, and economic suites in a relevant manner so that you can see how the lifecycle management vision can be established.

This approach mirrors the discussion in the data-gathering sections. First, the current state, or stable state, is discussed. The costs to provide the service levels are defined, and the workflow provided. The next step is to discuss the potential future state in the lifecycle element. This is where the experience level of the practitioner and the architect comes into play, as they seek to establish as an objective a reasonably attainable future.

It is not unusual for the future state to be defined in such a manner that it is truly a "vision" of the future state, not a deliverable easily achieved. Although academic in its construct, management within most businesses does not want to spend time on theory. Remember back, for instance, when *total cost of ownership* (TCO) was all the rage, and businesses were exploring the benefits of being at 100 percent (or so) practice levels (and counting on funds that could be available in those circumstances). As soon as it became apparent that these were academic or hypothetical figures, enthusiasm waned. By no means did this waning interest diminish the value of the TCO, only the position it plays in businesses today.

From this basic methodology, the fundamentals for user segmentation, risk cycle, cost of change, and appropriate incumbent behavior were developed. The methodology has been proven to be effective in more than 200 engagements and has consistently been successful in identifying the 10 percent cost-reduction and cost-avoidance objectives that businesses have sought.

The road map analogy mentioned earlier is based on this design concept. When conducting research, I learned that many businesses used this model as the deliverable that they provided to their business units, and that the deliverables were all about process and the quality of that process. After all, the bill of material structure of the "loop" enables a business to create their deliverables against the backdrop of this image.

As you can see in the closed loop lifecycle planning model, successful architecting of the approach requires several things. These requirements complement the critical success factors discussed throughout this book; these points focus on data gathering, crafting, and assessing the potential gap in the business model today. The requirements include the following:

- Ensure that each lifecycle element has input from a subject matter expert in the scope contemplated by the business
- Ensure that content experts have access to information about how the business currently delivers services (service-level attainment information)
- Identify the implications and interdependencies within a business on each lifecycle element
- Secure relevant information that will assist in identifying practice levels (including asset management information, help desk statistics, headcounts to deliver specific service levels, and any cost benchmarking or subcontractors currently delivering services)
- Identify which lifecycle elements are in scope for changes and which are not subject to changes
- Define the organizational model in effect in the current state and any potential changes open to discussion

- Define the processes in effect in the current state and any changes contemplated

- Discuss any impediments to secure information or known objections to embracing lifecycle management

- Identify any changes that can be discussed, such as mergers, acquisitions, and divestitures

- Identify all the toolsets in place and whether the continuation of any or all of those toolsets is a firm requirement of the architecting

- Ensure that the information is covered under a nondisclosure agreement so that the free flow of information is not compromised

Often I'm asked whether a checklist exists that can be used for lifecycle management in general and closed loop lifecycle planning in particular. The short answer is yes; of course there are checklists. Experience has taught, however, that it is not the level at which one probes or the questions that provide the best insight into lifecycle and practice levels, it is the follow-up questions that invariably define the environment.

This is comparable to the early days of the TCO (1990s), when almost everyone who read an article or other text became adept at asking an open probe. The actual (and often overlooked) challenge was determining how the open probe relates to the business, identifying the potential benefits of answers to the open probe, and deciding whether further research (staff, teammates, or otherwise) was necessary to seek out answers.

Lifecycle management is quite similar in that respect. For instance, you can consider the lifecycle drill down discussed earlier in this chapter as a series of sessions with subject/content experts that follow lines of questioning from an open probe to the quantification of potential benefits for the business. Generally, these drill downs are conducted in a series of half-day sessions that are basically probing and second- and third-level follow-up inquiries. The end of this process results in a set of concerns related to the information gathered.

Using the loop as a basis, a set of questions in each area can be formulated depending on the scope of the lifecycle management contemplated. A typical drill down might take as long a week, so the number of questions asked can become quite large. The intention of this book is to provide you enough information in each part so that you can formulate the questions relevant to your business requirements.

SUMMARY

Closed loop lifecycle planning is a unique methodology that examines the bill of material required to address end-user needs in supporting client and other access devices. The rigor of the methodology is captured in the planning and the implementation phases of the program.

Unlike TCO and similar approaches, closed loop lifecycle planning is based on extracting specific business information that can then be used in formulating how the bill of material can be modified and adjusted to meet end-user requirements.

The basic data collection can be leveraged for the drill down, user segmentation, risk cycle, and the cost of change processes. The difference is in how the information is analyzed and assessed from different discipline perspectives. The methodology has been widely used and is rapidly becoming accepted as a standard part of lifecycle management.

2

Overview of Closed Loop Lifecycle Planning

INTRODUCTION

As mentioned in the preceding chapter, closed loop lifecycle planning represents the overall bill of material that defines what IT needs to fund to support the client environment.

Total cost of ownership (TCO) represents the results of inputting information into a toolset that compares input to the industry averages and averages of other similar businesses. The result is a measurement output that suggests areas of improvement. The analogy that can be used is that, as a measurement strategy, TCO can identify where to go "fishing" for savings; lifecycle identifies how to "catch" the fish.

At the time of Y2K, networking and other IT policies were not as mature as they are today. The regulatory environment and management toolsets then were not as advanced either. As a result, unsecured end users could add, change, and otherwise impact what might have been intended to be a locked-down (secured) environment. For the best example of this, compare the number of application titles in an enterprise back then with the number of applications in use today in the enterprise. Whereas much of that growth has been organic (required by the business), much more of it has likely resulted from end users exercising the flexibility of the access environment.

In the late 1990s, lifecycle was mentioned in most manufacturer and service provider portfolios. However, no consistent industry definition addressed the full range of IT and business requirements to provide businesses a "playbook" from a practitioner's perspective.

The methodology presented in this book is proven. Closed loop lifecycle planning has been embraced by many businesses as a building block of the overall lifecycle-management plan itself, as evidenced by more than 200 white papers (and counting) and its implementation in more than 500 unique businesses (and counting).

The table of contents (and hence the chapters, or structure) of this book presents a menu of closed loop lifecycle planning elements. These lifecycle elements inter-relate and operate within all enterprises, regardless of size. The lifecycle elements include the following:

- Acquisition of hardware
- Acquisition of software
- Staging and integration
- Interoperability and prototyping
- Installation
- Moves, adds, and changes (MACs)
- Warranty and maintenance
- Asset management
- Help desk
- Networking
- Project management
- Technology refresh
- Disposition
- Management tools
- Total cost of ownership
- Service delivery strategies

Closed loop lifecycle planning includes user segmentation, cost of change, and appropriate incumbent behavior. This book addresses each of these topics. User segmentation and the cost of change are distinct disciplines. Properly implemented, these elements will ensure end users get what they need and do not act independently.

WHAT IS AN ACCESS DEVICE?

Closed loop lifecycle planning is based on the access computing model: how end users obtain data and information from a corporate repository. The bill of material described previously identifies the elements required to support an access device used to obtain such information.

Just a few short years ago, the definition of *access device* would have been quite straightforward: a desktop or a laptop computer. However, the technology workers now use to perform their jobs has changed dramatically. These changes have not been driven solely by business requirements, which traditionally drive behavior; they have also been driven by the consumer market and the rapid adoption of various new technologies.

NOTE: The Bonus Section of this book, "User Segmentation: A Complement to Closed Loop Lifecycle Planning" (located online), covers the overall role of technology in lifecycle management.

The important point here is that end users access information to perform their jobs in a number of extraordinarily variable ways. To manage lifecycle today means a focus on the following devices, just to name a few:

- Desktops
- Laptops
- Tablet PCs
- Handheld devices
- Smart phones
- Home devices
- Printers
- Thin clients

Access device diversity creates both actual and potential complexity. For end users, the diversity could mean more flexibility. The balance between device diversity, control, and flexibility will challenge most businesses. Do businesses strive for more control or more flexibility? A plan that allows end users flexibility while meeting company security and other controls (such as data backup and protection) is optimal, but always a challenge to define.

Today, when personal privacy issues, intellectual property protection, and regulations hold businesses and individuals more accountable for managing corporate information, device diversity could add more complexity, cost, and risk, making the decision process more difficult than anticipated. And as part the overall context (and complexity), most businesses are trying to constrain or reduce their IT expenditures.

One metric often used to indicate how well a business manages lifecycle is the ratio of PCs to end users. Obviously, the goal is to get to as close to a 1:1 ratio as possible. However, the real metric today should be the ratio of access devices to employees. This subtle difference recognizes the fundamental change in the client lifecycle management discipline and the fundamental change in discussing end-user access within a business.

Lifecycle costs and risk associated with a diverse portfolio of access devices drive changes in IT. Today, many businesses do not include the full range of access devices in a single portfolio. As a result, costs, risk, and resources are commingled with other expenditures and are difficult to isolate.

New technology may also alter the traditional separation of IT and network infrastructures. The demand for mobile access, for instance, is resulting in hybrid technologies that combine both IT and networking disciplines. For example, is a remote handheld device that has access to email a device that IT should manage or is it a device that the networking team should manage?

NOTE: Security is the number one priority in the twenty-first century. Even the smallest security leak can prove devastating. A security breach is now potentially a new form of global terrorism.

The organizational roles and responsibilities could begin to become blurred as mobility becomes standard within businesses.

PCS ARE NOT A COMMODITY!

One cogent business position holds that access devices in a business enterprise are not commodities. Others believe that the pricing of the device itself makes it a commodity, and to some degree that is correct. The big picture suggests however, that a PC is not a commodity.

You might be asking, if PCs are *not* a commodity, why is there so much governance regarding how a device is configured and deployed? And, if PCs *are* a commodity, why is there so much concern about their support costs? Another question is this: Why is there such concern about cleansing the information on the device before disposing of it.

The answer is simple: After a standard PC has been customized in any way, it loses all the characteristics of a commodity. That customization can even include the placement of the device within a business infrastructure.

The definition of *commodity* is often confused with *consumable*. This confusion inhibited lifecycle practices with regard to access devices for a long time. The idea that access devices are commodities suggests that you can take one device and, without change (or very minor changes), transfer the device just by changing where you the plug it in. In a business, however, users (and their access devices) have a profile, an image, retained data, and personalization that must be considered. Transitions are complex. Therefore, PCs (and other access devices) should not be considered merely commodities. Many businesses have yet to accept this fact, and therefore access device governance is perhaps less than it would otherwise be.

PRICE DOES NOT EQUAL COST

One principle of lifecycle management holds that price does not equal cost. Typically, PC manufacturers and access device manufacturers price their products within a narrow bandwidth of other manufacturers' prices. However, the manner in which the devices are acquired, deployed, managed, retired, and so on (all factors of actual cost) may be unique to the *class* of device.

IF A LIFECYCLE-MANAGEMENT CHANGE CANNOT BE QUANTIFIED, IT WON'T HAPPEN

Lifecycle management in an organization requires that any proposed change to an existing stable current-state environment must be quantified; this quantification is necessary to get senior management to buy in to the change and support it in practice. Further, the quantification must be expressed in terms that reflect true dollar impact (that is, the balance sheet and income statement impact).

Many businesses sincerely believe in productivity gains, downtime measurement, reduced risks, and the benefits of end-user satisfaction. However, in actuality many businesses consider these types of impact "soft" costs. Soft costs cannot be directly related to the IT budget and financial statements and so are often overlooked. As a result, most business justifications that are based heavily on "soft" costs are not embraced as quickly as those that are based on a firm dollar relationship to the budgeting process.

Even in this area, perspectives are changing. It is now understood that productivity, downtime, risk, and other costs traditionally considered "soft" can be quantified, tracked, and measured. Due diligence is required to make a business case, but that is generally understood. Administrative regulations, laws, and corporate governance have all elevated the role that these "soft" costs play in justification of a business case.

Senior management generally tends to discount business cases in which "soft" costs are the predominant driver. If the "soft" costs are explained in terms of cost reduction and cost avoidance, however, this complementary positioning adds considerably to the business case. After all, cost reduction and cost avoidance still represent the cornerstone of most business cases for change.

In closed loop lifecycle planning, the focus is on "hard" cost impact: cost reduction and cost avoidance. Cost reduction shows up on both the balance sheet and income statement. Cost reduction impacts both the capital and expense categories of the IT budget. Cost avoidance focuses on those costs and expenses that might continue or might increase if change is not embraced. Cost avoidance is the category in which many of the entrance and exit costs show up.

It should be clearly understood that cost avoidance is not a "soft" cost; instead, it is similar to a cost reduction. Cost avoidance represents the financial impact and service level impact of not making certain lifecycle decisions (in other words, retaining the status quo).

One example of cost avoidance is a business decision not to acquire a management tool for imaging, but to continue the manual process of loading an image. If the requirements or volume increases, the alternative is generally to increase staffing. The increased staffing becomes a cost-avoidance categorization.

In a general context, many lifecycle elements can be addressed by "throwing more resources" at a problem area. The increased resources represent real costs and should be identified as a conscious decision not to avoid costs, but to increase the expense to address a certain issue.

Together, cost reduction and cost avoidance underlie the business case for lifecycle management. After these elements have been quantified, management must validate the reasonableness of the numbers so that the plan can be put into place to address and effect change.

Only after cost-reduction and cost-avoidance quantification has occurred does the impact of service levels and "soft" costs become fully relevant. In many cases, a higher service level can be achieved for less cost. In other cases, the service level may be modified to reflect the end-user requirements (as in the case of user segmentation).

Note, however, "soft" costs are playing a bigger role in the overall justification of more and more business cases. Businesses are learning that the "soft" costs can be more than merely subjective. This understanding reflects as much of a cultural shift as a business shift.

IS LIFECYCLE MANAGEMENT A "BEST PRACTICE"?

Best practices are generally defined as the processes followed to optimize service levels while minimizing risks and costs. Although few would disagree with this definition, there is often an assumption that "one size fits all" as relates to best practices in general.

Experience has taught, however, that a logical threshold determines whether a business can fully adopt best practices. Most important perhaps is whether a best practice can scale according to the complexity, size, and scope of a business. Most companies, for example, need different service levels for different types of users, and IT must be able to meet this requirement.

One way to put best practices into perspective is via an employee count or a count of the end-user population. Based on my experience, the following scaling perspective will help you understand best practices.

Number of Employees or End Users with Access Devices

Fewer than 5,000

5,000 to 10,000

10,000 to 20,000

More than 20,000

If viewed in this context, lifecycle management can be more easily adapted to the unique requirements of businesses based on the criteria of scope, size, and complexity. The fewer the number of employees or end users, the more likely that the processes will be manual and that lifecycle management will have more of a high "touch" perspective. Affordability, as it relates to investing in lifecycle management, will factor highly in the "fewer than 5,000" category. Although automation, TCO, lifecycle management, and risk are important issues to these businesses, cash flow just might not suffice to address these issues at a high level yet. And so, these businesses put off addressing these issues until profitability and investment priorities are compatible.

Management tools and predefined processes for this size of business are being scaled to make things more affordable for these companies. The market has recognized their growth potential, and so this segment will clearly get favorable attention. Even as of this writing, investment dollars are focused on scaling solutions for those businesses in the "fewer than 5,000" employees or end users category. After all, the risks and liabilities are as important (some might say more important) to this business category as to any other.

In the "5,000 to 10,000" category, the perspective of lifecycle management is that the scaling is such that manual intervention and resources required suggest a higher level of best practices. This implies more tools and more well-defined strategies going forward. Businesses in this category often believe that they are on the cusp of requiring more sophistication as it relates to best practices. Although not scaled to be fully manual, and perhaps not sized to have a large, robust IT department, many of the processes and resources are stretched. The "5,000 to 10,000" category tends to be more resource intense and expense constrained.

The "10,000 to 20,000" category is a clear area where best practices can be scaled and are more easily defined. The governance is extraordinarily relevant, and the expectations are clearly higher. Accountability is necessarily high in this category because the scope of what needs to be managed becomes much more complex, simply because of the number of end users impacted. In this category, it is not unusual to find that businesses are growing organically or through acquisition. In this scenario, lifecycle management becomes a critical discipline that can impact how competitive the new organization can be in the market. Information is a key and critical asset. IT plays even a more pivotal role in the new enterprise.

When a company has more than 20,000 employees or end users, lifecycle management really becomes non-negotiable. Without doubt, to comply with regulations and governance, these businesses must fully embrace best practices relevant to the size and scale required.

The overall message in this section is not that best practices are inflexible or inadaptable; it is that best practices must be viewed in context. Scaling and scoping are key factors to consider. The fundamental work to be performed does not necessarily change, but how that work is accomplished will certainly vary. Lifecycle management, therefore, is a custom solution.

Lifecycle management itself is a best practice!

WHY DOES IT OFTEN TAKE A COMPELLING EVENT TO INITIATE LIFECYCLE MANAGEMENT?

According to closed loop lifecycle planning, a *compelling event* is an occurrence that triggers a review and potential change in access devices and support strategies. Such events are common and occur frequently. Another helpful term to understand is *business as usual*, which describes the stable state of a business.

In the client computing environment, having or anticipating an event can be enough to trigger an evaluation of lifecycle management. The events and scenarios listed here are types of business-as-usual activities that might trigger a lifecycle review. Each of these topics is covered in detail in various sections of this book. A compelling event might be any of the following, among others:

- Technology refreshes
- Software compliance audits
- Cost-reduction initiatives
- Acquisitions/divestitures
- New management
- Related industry developments
- New technologies
- New facilities
- Regulatory/legal requirements
- Risk-reduction initiatives
- Policy or governance
- Personal privacy protection
- Intellectual property protection

Any of these compelling events by themselves could be the catalyst for lifecycle management to be explored in earnest. In each of these compelling events, lifecycle as a solution becomes the lynchpin of the approaches to secure benefits (whether it is to reduce costs, avoid costs, mitigate risks, or improve service levels).

One common element in all of these compelling events is that they suggest change.

In today's business-as-usual environment, most of these compelling events are considered the norm, not an exception. This change in the definition of a compelling event could be one reason why lifecycle management has remained constant and periodically seems to elicit renewed vigor with regard to the discipline.

"IT TAKES A CHANGE AGENT"

To implement lifecycle management, someone must act as a "change agent." The change agent will be, simply put, a very unpopular person for a period of time; after all, change to many implies that something is "wrong." The dynamics of change and the cost of change are discussed more fully later in this book. The reason to raise this point here is that in all organizations, there needs to be a focal point to establish and effectuate the vision.

Don't confuse the role of the change agent with that of a program or project manager. The roles differ significantly, and to a large degree are unrelated. The change agent addresses the organizational, emotional, political, and cross-business issues relating to lifecycle management. The project or program manager provides very specific deliverables in terms of process and procedures relating to work actually performed. Depending on the size and structure of a company, someone on the staff can be given direct responsibility to implement the vision; this person is the change agent.

Lifecycle management will always require support at the executive level. Without this commitment, only portions of lifecycle management may be delivered. For many companies, a partial approach might seem adequate, and so not all businesses will fully embrace integrated lifecycle management. However, partial implementation ensures suboptimization. And although the business case for lifecycle management might have been effectively created and accepted, the cost of entry (in both political and economic capital) might entice some businesses to attempt a partial implementation.

One role of the change agent is to determine what the vision (solution) is at the governance and policy levels. The next step is to determine how this vision can be executed within the organization. Without executive sponsorship and a champion, however, no vision can be effectively implemented (or behaviors changed). One would logically look to the chief information officer (CIO) and chief technology officer (CTO) as key sponsors for change within the enterprise. The CIO, chief organizational officer (COO), chief financial officer (CFO), or CTO generally champions change within an organization. Any or all of these executives can be considered senior management change agents.

The staff person driving the change must be empowered by the executives and have their full support. If not, the changes are difficult (if not impossible) to implement. Experience has suggested that change agents have a high turnover rate due to the significant pressures; frustration and "burnout" are symptoms commonly expressed.

A change agent is a highly sought and a highly valuable resource. The role is so critical that it does relate to how competitive a business can be in its industry.

PILOT AND PROOF OF CONCEPT

The terms *pilot* and *proof of concept* are often used interchangeably in the industry. For lifecycle management, these terms have specific meaning and are not the same. It is important to understand the differences between the two terms as another foundation for lifecycle management.

A pilot is the testing to determine whether a technology works. Product specifications are provided, speeds are defined, networking connectivity is defined, and so on. Pilots are a technical evaluation process and are generally performed in a lab environment. The persons performing the evaluation are the engineers and architects. The objective is to ascertain whether the specifications provided perform correctly and the functionality is as presented. Piloting is a critical task within lifecycle management and is covered in more depth later in this book.

Proof of concept, on the other hand, is a business proposition. A proof of concept takes the approved technology (validated technically in the pilot phase) and rolls out the technology along with the support processes in a scaled production environment.

Lifecycle management should be viewed in a proof-of-concept perspective. Many businesses consider the proof-of-concept phase the initial phase of the overall deployment of lifecycle management practices. The thinking is that if the proof of concept is executed as expected, the policy, process, and procedures can be adopted.

The distinction between pilots and proofs of concept is critical. Lifecycle management is not a pass/fail proposition. Many of the business support decisions regarding the proof of concept should be made in this phase.

In summary, a pilot and a proof of concept are two different things, each with its own unique criteria: one technical and one business. These two lifecycle elements should not be confused.

CONTINUOUS PROCESS IMPROVEMENT

Lifecycle management is not a one-time-only event or activity. Dynamics are constantly changing (a great driver, in general, for our economy). The billions of research and development dollars spent on innovation and new technologies and tools is a cornerstone of lifecycle management. Those businesses that take advantage of technology innovation differentiate themselves from others and thus accrue a competitive advantage.

End users expect a continuous process-improvement plan to be in place. Many times, end users are unaware of the plan, and this can lead to concern. For example, suppose an end user has an older PC and does know when the device will be replaced. At some point, the end user might call the manager, the help desk, or some other support resource. If the end user knows about and understands the continuous process-improvement plan, however, that inquiry might not occur. (And, don't underestimate the emotional impact on the end user of not knowing what is going on.)

A key element of any plan in lifecycle management, including the continuous process-improvement plan, is communication. If the plan itself is not broadly known, the value of the plan is lessened.

THE IMPACT OF THE CONSUMER MARKET

In the past, as client technology was developing, there were "casual" users. These individuals avoided technology unless absolutely necessary. The skill set and training was at a very basic level because technology was something to be avoided, if at all possible. The consumer market has changed this dynamic. In contrast to the past, innovation in the consumer market is driving enterprise changes.

Today it is virtually impossible to think of any industry that is not impacted by client technologies and the innovation that sector has initiated. Simply put, today you cannot buy any goods or services that are not directly related to client technologies. The consumer market impacts everything from how you bank (ATM), to how you buy groceries (electronic scanners), to how you listen to music (MP3), to how you rent cars (automated checkouts), and even to the basics of how we communicate day to day (cell phones/smart phones).

At the crux of the technology is a simple proposition: how you access information or content that you want. This is the similar proposition in businesses: how to access relevant information.

As a result of these market dynamics, the consumer market has resulted in an overall rising of awareness of client technologies and a fuller understanding of how devices can work. Therefore, the "casual" user no longer exists; after all, having a PC at home is the norm in many households.

The demise of the casual user has an important impact on IT and lifecycle management. Recognizing this shift in competency is key to lifecycle management going forward. Many IT departments remain skeptical that end users can "handle" PCs. But, this skepticism is misplaced. Many of the end users might have home systems set up that are more complex those they work with at the office. With regard to PCs, therefore, much of the mystique surrounding IT (and its access devices) has diminished. In some cases, a lack of trust develops between IT support and end users. When this occurs, a "Stealth IT" organization might perform lifecycle management work informally.

Another fundamental shift is occurring as a result of the consumer experience: Employees expect the business experience to be at least as robust as they have at home (or experience in their day-to-day activities). This translates into expectations regarding service levels, the types of access devices available, and how support can be delivered. One of the many metrics IT uses is end-user satisfaction. If a business is several generations behind in how its employees can access information compared to the consumer experience, it is not unreasonable to assume that end-user satisfaction may decline considerably.

Although financial, operational, and logical differences between the consumer experience and the business experience will always exist, the gap between the two is narrowing considerably.

Access devices are viewed by employees as productivity tools. Productivity is often considered a "soft" cost, not directly traceable to the financial statements. However, just as other benefits, technology may be considered part of the investment a business makes in its employees.

It is now time to bring in the topic of lifecycle management specifically. Access devices are not considered an entitlement. However, whatever the access devices are, it is expected that the lifecycle-management solution behind them is more than adequate to ensure their effective use.

Self-service support has been available for several applications for many years, but the adoption rate is low. It is anticipated that because of the consumer experience, self-service adoption will increase as end users become more comfortable with that service-delivery alternative. Again, the mystique will be gone. After all, these are the same end users who know how to download music from the Internet to their MP3 player; they can likely change a password.

Remember this old adage: A rising tide raises all ships. This is the impact that the consumer experience is having on lifecycle management.

WHAT ABOUT THOSE REGULATIONS?

It seems as though not a day goes by without the media reporting on issues of identity theft, personal privacy, intellectual property, and other technology- and lifecycle-related topics. How data and information is used and how secure it is remain critical issues.

The objective of regulations, governance, and laws is to protect the confidentiality and secure the correct focus.

IT has a daunting challenge. The myriad access devices and the number of ways that information can be inappropriately obtained from these devices is obviously a concern to everyone. In fact, IT might not even have control over access devices that come into an organization. Disposal of the various devices is also a recognized challenge.

All the regulations, governance, and laws have one principle in common: They hold businesses (and in some cases, individuals) accountable for the information and its access.

Regulations, laws, and governance are perhaps the easiest and most compelling rationale to adopt lifecycle management. A strong lifecycle management practice is the best way to protect the information. Those businesses that have not embraced lifecycle management are at a considerable disadvantage.

We all conduct business with many companies that handle and use personal information. We expect that this information will be appropriately used and secured. In many cases, the law requires it. As consumers, we fully expect businesses to have a lifecycle management program that ensures that their access devices (and more specifically, the information they could contain or have access to) will be handled in a manner that poses the least risk. This is yet another reason that lifecycle management is no longer optional.

MAKING LIFECYCLE MANAGEMENT DECISIONS CONSCIOUSLY

A recurring theme in lifecycle management is that decisions are made both consciously and unconsciously. Because of the proliferation of access devices, many businesses defer decisions and provide a de facto "best effort" service level for certain devices. In other words, the business decides not to make a decision. Best effort service level, experience suggests, almost always leads to dissatisfied end users; regardless of the service level provided, it is often considered too little and too late.

Decisions need to be made consciously! De facto standards, support, service levels, and expectations become established when end users are left to assume that what they are leveraging is correct. In lifecycle management, benign neglect is a concern.

IT may or may not be able to approve or reject end users or organizations; however, tacit agreement in today's highly regulated environment is simply not a good idea. Many businesses today, for example, provide "best effort" support for certain categories of handheld devices. The initial conclusion, therefore, is that the handheld devices are an acceptable company standard, and that IT is prepared to support these devices.

In lifecycle management, the implications from decisions that are made are often as important as the initial decisions themselves. In the example just cited, at what point does the best effort apply if the overall population of devices becomes significant and IT simply cannot deliver an acceptable service level? At that point, a predicament arises; after all, IT cannot go back and suggest that the devices were inappropriate in the first place.

Businesses defer lifecycle decisions for a variety of reasons, but all of the dynamics discussed in this chapter clearly suggest that decisions should be made consciously, because the information and data to be accessed is still the same.

SUMMARY

Now that the basics have been introduced, the journey begins. It is important to remember that all of the lifecycle elements presented in this book are interrelated.

Remember, it is not the initial questions that are necessarily important; we must consider the full implications of those decisions and their impact on other lifecycle elements, too. Like any journey, this trip might seem long and arduous. It is. The problems that lifecycle management addresses are not simple. You won't find a "one size fits all" solution. Every business will have its own complexities and culture. However, some commonality will exist, and so the ability to create the vision for your business will be greatly facilitated.

So let's begin.

3

Acquiring Hardware

INTRODUCTION

Lifecycle begins with a product decision, so the closed loop lifecycle planning methodology begins at this point. All the policies, processes, and procedures revolve around the support of the product. This chapter addresses the lifecycle management surrounding the product acquisition, sometimes referred to as product fulfillment. Ultimately product includes both hardware and software. Closed loop lifecycle planning addresses these topics separately, recognizing the importance of both elements.

Many businesses view this initial step in the process as a basic lifecycle element, and there is a tendency to minimize or dismiss product acquisition as a less-complicated step in overall lifecycle management. Minimizing the acquisition phase would indeed be an oversight, however, because product fulfillment can prove quite complex. Product acquisition requires due diligence and has a defined rigor to execute well.

This chapter addresses the following lifecycle considerations for determining the product-acquisition plan for a business. These topics represent significant decisions for businesses to make in the determination of an overall strategy. Topics include

- Sole supplier versus multiple suppliers
- Direct and indirect order channels
- Standards versus a price list
- Ordering in advance of demand
- Third-party peripherals and options
- Point-of-sale services
- Integration of suppliers
- Global fulfillment
- The need for a forecast

SOLE SUPPLIER VERSUS MULTIPLE SUPPLIERS

The decision to go with a sole supplier or a multiple suppliers has as much to do with corporate culture as with the maturity of the market. Both sole-supplier and multiple-supplier decisions can be effective if expectations are established up front. The decision to go with a sole supplier or multiple suppliers for client devices is one of the first decisions to be made. A strong business case can be made for both alternatives depending on the circumstances.

A sole supplier works effectively when the core competencies and culture of the supplier aligns well with a business. A sole supplier relationship requires a high level of trust and both supplier and buyer maturity.

It is a natural instinct to be cautious about a sole-supplier relationship because of the commitment the decision represents. Businesses that focus on pricing as a measure of the relationship will likely have a difficult time in a sole-supplier relationship. The feeling will be that there is always a better price that could be obtained; this can strain the sole-supplier relationship. A sole supplier relationship should not be based solely upon pricing.

A sole-supplier relationship permits the incumbent supplier to invest in an account well beyond the pricing. To many businesses, this investment is critical to the overall success of lifecycle management.

The breadth and depth of a technology manufacturer's product line represents a significant factor that should carry some weight in the sole-supplier versus multiple-supplier decision. Combined with service capabilities, the business case might be quite compelling. If a company moves forward in a sole-supplier relationship, leveraging the full portfolio of all the goods and services that could be provided seems to be a logical step.

Having a multiple-supplier base for access devices is comfortable for many businesses, and several logical tactics can effectively separate the client technologies. Typically, desktops and laptops are in one category, and there can be various other categories such as tablet PCs and handheld devices. In making this type of decision, the business elects not to seek an investment model across the enterprise, but to limit the provider's roles.

Another tactic is to have a primary and secondary supplier for all client devices. In addition, it is not unusual to include the server supplier in the consideration of the supplier mix. Services can also be a determining factor in the decision to go with a single supplier or multiple suppliers.

Although closed loop lifecycle planning focuses on client and access computing, note that server computing requires a unique skill set and specialized support. When seeking a sole-supplier relationship, core competencies and solutions must be fully considered.

Having multiple suppliers generally suggests a belief that the client technologies must compete to be price effective. Whereas on the surface this might seem logical, a number of valid pricing methodologies available could address the concern over competitiveness.

Often, a purchasing (also known as sourcing or strategic sourcing) initiative drives a *request for information* (RFI) or a *request for proposal* (RFP). In many scenarios, the competition is part of the governance model. The key in this scenario for both supplier and buyer is to truly understand the objectives of the process.

It is not unusual for the process previously described to be leveraged to influence pricing only, not necessarily to provide overall competition. When this scenario occurs, time and resources are invested by the buyer, which might instead be better invested in improving the lifecycle business practices themselves.

Another driver of a multiple-supplier scenario is the balance of trade. Do not confuse balance of trade with the legal issues regarding the restraint of trade; these activities are completely different. Balance of trade suggests that customers and suppliers may very well share a common trust, a common culture, and a rationale for working together based on open requirements.

CAUTION: Always be aware that the balance of trade can play a significant role in IT decisions (and in business in general). The balance of trade works for both the buyer and seller and should be disclosed to all competitors as a factor in the decision criteria.

In general, the balance of trade can be "walled off" and effectively separated so that there is no appearance (or reality) of inappropriate behavior. The balance of trade should be openly discussed with all competitors in the product-acquisition process so that the playing field is truly level. This important part of the overall disclosure leads to a more trusting and collaborative relationship required for lifecycle management.

When exploring a sole-supplier or multiple-supplier relationship, businesses should consider defining the criteria that makes either business case compelling. When requesting bid responses to an RFP or an RFI, businesses should proactively ask respondents to provide the compelling rationale. Before asking, however, a business should decide whether any rationale would drive internal decisions one direction or another so that the respondents can focus on a response that truly assists a company in moving forward with lifecycle practices.

As mentioned earlier in this section, investment is optimized when an incumbent supplier has to focus less on the cost-of-sales effort to retain an installed base and instead focuses on leveraging the knowledge transfer regarding lifecycle management. The importance of including this commentary in the product-acquisition phase is that the true value in a relationship may reside in the transfer of knowledge just as much as in the product pricing and configuration.

If industry trends remain consistent, product pricing in most cases will continue to be competitive, with only a small gap between supplier prices. Under this assumption, the investments take on a greater relevance.

The actual product represents only a small portion of the overall costs, and therefore should be placed in that context. Incorporation of a product into a business environment may enhance the value of a product for a business, with the product now an integral part of an overall solution.

Regardless of whether the sole-supplier model or multiple-supplier model is selected, considerable effort should be expended in discussing and capturing the exit strategy if a change in supplier is contemplated. A well-defined, contract-based exit strategy that can be implemented is crucial.

Often, exit plans are informal and do not specifically address exit and cost-of-change costs. Because many businesses have an installed base with multiple makes, models, and manufacturers, addressing potential change can help avoid disruption and mitigate costs during any transition. Although this discussion might be a bit uncomfortable, this is a normal part of the rigor.

DIRECT AND INDIRECT ORDER CHANNELS

The PC industry has matured considerably over the years. The ordering channels, direct and indirect, are both very mature. The *direct order channel* is defined in this book as having a fulfillment relationship between a customer and the manufacturer. The *indirect order channel* establishes a fulfillment relationship with a third party (the reseller or partner), with the indirect channel dealing directly with the manufacturer. A hybrid model is also frequently used.

The hybrid model has a defined role for manufacturers and for resellers, or partners. In the hybrid model, the work to be completed may occur in multiple locations and may be performed by different groups. As this text discusses global lifecycle management, it is the hybrid model that is most prevalent.

Another school of thought suggests that in all scenarios when an indirect channel is engaged, the manufacturer remains engaged and has a role in driving the relationship. Although this might be correct in many circumstances, there remains the reality that the channel partner is the focal point to the business, and their relationship will be more than procurement and related-service tenders. The concept of scaling across a broad portfolio of enterprises suggests that the indirect channel become an integral part of the relationship.

It is important that the direct and indirect channels not compete for the same enterprise mindshare; it might confuse the messages. Although manufacturers and indirect channels will frequently compete (and they should), it is important to recognize that the optimal model that best achieves the enterprise's objectives should be the driving alternative.

As the market has matured, the conflicts between indirect channels and manufacturers have been significantly minimized. The level of collaboration is much higher than ever before.

NOTE: The enterprise benefits greatly when indirect channels and manufacturers are in sync with the overall enterprise strategy and account relationship.

Given that the ordering of product seems to be fundamental, when would a business select one model over the other?

The direct channel and the indirect channel are generally governed by a service level referred to as a *statement of work*. In many instances, there may be pricing differences between the two fulfillment models. In channel strategies, pricing has become less of an issue across the board. Both direct and indirect channels can provide a wide array of services. These services are often quite robust and range from imaging all the way through disposal.

Given all the obvious similarities, what are some of the differences? Many of the differences are subjective, such as the decision about where a company wants to have its fulfillment reside. Each of the alternatives has a unique set of pricing and investment models that accrue to the approach that is taken for fulfillment. Another consideration is the leverage secured by a relationship decision. After a series of subjective decisions have been made, any number of criteria can be considered to differentiate the channel strategies, including the following:

- **Size**

  The size of a fulfillment partner might permit some mitigation of risk associated with the supply chain. A channel strategy may be scaled based on the level of business or the overall number of end users.

- **Multiple manufacturers**

  One advantage of an indirect channel strategy could lie in the fact that they can represent more than one manufacturer and multiple product lines, thus adding potential flexibility to the business model.

- **Global reach**

  The ability to perform global fulfillment is a key criteria. The scale of the global fulfillment is an important point to consider. Remote, low-density global locations will be a challenge for any model.

- **Outsourcing relationships**

  If a business has outsourced lifecycle management, assuming that fulfillment is in scope, there may be a preference for channel direction.

- **Core competencies**

  If there are services beyond product fulfillment in the scope, the core competencies relating to each of the channels may be a differentiator.

STANDARDS VERSUS A PRICE LIST

Many businesses pride themselves on having a set of defined and widely communicated standards. *Standards* in this book are defined as a concise set of part numbers available for order fulfillment. Standards generally apply to the make and model of a client device. It is generally believed that the higher the standardization, the lower the overall lifecycle costs. Note that standards include the hardware and the software products.

For a variety of reasons, end users in many businesses enjoy a high degree of flexibility and autonomy with regard to options outside of the standard—perhaps because of the consumer experience, where expectations have already been established. The options can range from personalization to unique software tools. To end users, this flexibility is always desirable. To IT and the enterprise, however, this flexibility might create significant and unanticipated implications. In many cases, the greater the flexibility, the greater the issues of compliance and complexity. At some point, if end users are allowed to add on and modify the base configuration (the standard), the overall configuration will become custom, or nonstandard. Although the core might remain the same, after the options have been added and then deployed into a custom enterprise infrastructure, the support costs will likely increase. At this point, many of the benefits of standardization may be lost.

Many businesses find themselves in a position where once the flexibility is provided, it becomes an entitlement or part of the culture. When this dynamic occurs, it is difficult to change. The perception is that by reducing the pricing list, IT is taking away end-user choice. Emotions and politics play an important role in this scenario.

It is critical for the enterprise to understand the financial impact of the pricing list approach and determine whether the cost-benefit relationship is one to be consciously supported.

ORDERING IN ADVANCE OF DEMAND

In many scenarios, products (PCs et al.) are ordered in advance of demand. Often, this is a result of a business wanting deployment to the end user in such a tight timeframe that the only way to accommodate that level of service is to retain inventory. Another rationale is that there is a need from a business to have a "safety stock" plan in case a manufacturer or partner has a delay or problem in delivering its agreed-upon service level.

In some situations, the safety stock also provides "hot backup" or a "spares" inventory. The on-hand inventory is then leveraged for service purposes.

Whatever the rationale, which could include just wanting a comfort level that on-site inventory provides, businesses need to consciously understand the implications of business-owned inventory in advance of demand. In making this decision, a business enters into the operations of fulfillment. The entry means that a business in essence becomes an internal reseller or provider of inventory. The policies, processes, and procedures (and the management and reporting) need to be established to address this operation.

Warehousing, real estate, and security must be a part of this portfolio if a business is to effectively manage this operation.

An additional implication of ordering in advance of demand is that the warranty window begins at the time of shipment, as a general rule. If a device is in inventory for 30 days, a business does not recapture those 30 days when the device is actually deployed. If a device is in inventory for an extended period, the implication is clear. This lifecycle consideration is a very good discussion to have between manufacturers, resellers, partners, and the enterprise.

To be truly effective in ordering in advance of demand, inventory management should be at a mature level from a practice perspective.

And, remember, software licensing, version control, and maintenance is often contractually established based on a high-water mark. Therefore, devices in inventory might have to be included in the final device counts.

Many businesses believe that on-site inventory is a cost of doing business. It is not unusual to see a robust infrastructure be established to accommodate on-hand inventory. One rationale often cited is the lack of confidence in the ability to comply with service levels. However, this raises a much larger question of service-level management. Realistically, no major manufacturer and reseller would enter into a service-level agreement if they could not meet or exceed the parameters.

It is more often an emotional comfort level than one based on performance history. (Of course, exceptions prove the rule.)

When ordering in advance of demand occurs and an infrastructure has been created, it becomes difficult to exit such an operation. At this point, the investment becomes part of the culture, and a new "silo" is created.

The scope of the on-site inventory is of key importance. If there is a change in product mix or if there is a change in technology, the inventory might not turn over as fast as desired, and the product mix could be subject to a level of obsolescence.

Generally, inventory on hand remains in stock typically not more than 30 days (less is desirable). Depending on the technology-refresh strategy and the overall installed base, the quantification and financial impact of the inventory can easily be derived. The price of the products and the cost to warehouse the inventory are known.

Another consideration when ordering in advance of demand is to have the channel partner warehouse the inventory on behalf of its customer. This is a specific allocation of material.

The business case for just-in-time inventory often makes businesses anxious. It is reasonable, therefore, to expect product suppliers to share their plans to meet demand.

A final rationale for retaining inventory in advance of demand is that there will be periodic nonforecasted demand, such as an unanticipated new hire. Generally, businesses can anticipate hiring some new employees, but sometimes not, and so the business position clearly has its merits.

NOTE: Remember that as far as ordering in advance of demand goes, there simply is no right or wrong answer. Do not confuse the questions and considerations discussed in this section with a rebuke of the strategy. Instead, these questions and considerations are just a recurring part of the rigor when assessing the strategy. (After all, conscious decisions must be made.)

Businesses that consciously decide to conduct inventory management operations may want to consider a more formal approach to the process. Leveraging Poisson distribution logic or a much simpler minimum, maximum, reorder-point logic would seem to be required. This is even truer for businesses that significantly scale and have considerable inventory in advance of demand. Automated inventory management would seem to be an appropriate expectation to effectively control this investment.

THIRD-PARTY PERIPHERALS AND OPTIONS

In many circumstances, the suppliers of desktops and laptops differ from the suppliers of components, peripherals, and third-party options. The consumer experience might have a significant impact in this area. Most, if not all, manufacturers and resellers have a core competency to supply a wide range of third-party products. It is assumed for purposes of this section that the pricing is in a narrow bandwidth, and so there is no pricing rationale to select one channel over another.

Based on the core competency, this presents an opportunity for a conscious decision to potentially consolidate suppliers. This could provide additional leverage for a business and an opportunity to simplify the processes, and thus reduce the complexity.

Suppliers and their customers must fully understand core competency in this area. As costs and pricing of the actual desktops and laptops continue to decline, the options become a larger percentage of the total expense.

Third-party components, options, and peripherals lend themselves to standardization. Businesses should consider exploring all the alternatives available and look at minimizing the number of makes and models to be supported in this area, just as they do for access devices themselves. The types of devices are significant, and they play an ever-expanding role in IT support for the business. This following list identifies just some of the components, peripherals, and options. This list is far from exhaustive, and is included here only to highlight the number of decisions that may be required:

- Printers
- Scanners
- Faxes
- Copiers
- Disks
- Thumb drives
- Memory
- Cameras
- USB adapters
- Wallpaper
- Personal software
- Security cards
- Network cards
- Routers
- Wireless LANs
- Encryption (including embedded features, third-party software, and programming techniques)
- Monitors
- Graphics cards
- Cell phones
- Handheld devices

In some businesses, the third-party content is a large portion of the total IT dollars spent. The governance and policy vary from business to business. Standardization will play a key role in addressing support issues that could arise.

NOTE: Third-party peripherals and options represent a critical success factor in most deployment projects. In many situations, the third-party options and peripherals are as important as the actual access device itself.

Without a standard strategy, end users could acquire such a wide array of products that, theoretically, each device would be, in essence, a unique implementation.

POINT-OF-SALE SERVICES

You might think that a discussion of services as a part of the product-acquisition phase is out of place, but there is an important market dynamic at play. All the major channels have developed a portfolio of services that can be implemented at the point of sale. In effect, these services are a point-of-sale transaction themselves, and the tenders could become a part of the product itself as an embedded feature.

The services portfolio can be quite comprehensive. Historically, warranty and upgraded versions of warranty were the initial tenders. Today, the portfolios can include a full lifecycle-oriented portfolio for a business to consider. Having these tenders available early in the lifecycle decision process permits businesses to begin the lifecycle discussions during the initial phase of the process.

The inclusion of services in the dialogue suggests that the lifecycle approach has matured to the point where standard deliverables can be identified.

NOTE: In many instances, point-of-sale services are underscoped and undervalued. Many enterprises defer the services discussion until a later point, only to discover that the cost to achieve a defined service level is much more significant than anticipated.

There is a wide range in point-of-sale service tenders and ability to deliver. Acquisition decisions about the point-of-sale services should not be driven exclusively by pricing. A lower acquisition price at the point of sale might indicate quality and breadth-of-services concerns regarding the tender.

INTEGRATION OF SUPPLIERS

No review of product acquisition would be complete without a discussion about the integration of suppliers. When a business makes the decision as to who they will be moving forward with in terms of products, a new set of dynamics should begin. When a sole-supplier decision is made, those suppliers not selected should clearly understand the rules of engagement going forward. The company's resources must then focus on executing the relationship selected.

In a multiple-supplier relationship, the rules of engagement must also be clearly articulated by the company making the decision. In both the sole-supplier and multiple-supplier scenarios, after competitors have been notified, the rules of engagement should be communicated. Quite often, only a win or loss is effectively communicated.

As a result of the lack of direction, the selling processes may continue. This, if not properly managed, reflects on all parties involved. At some point, suppliers need this level of integration to be effective for the business.

I have always found it interesting that at the beginning of the process, there are meetings to discuss timing, criteria, processes, and so on, but post-process expectations are seldom defined. A solid lifecycle-management plan requires that processes should be fully defined and articulated, and that this communication should be open.

Do not understand this section as a suggestion to cease a relationship or as a signal to a channel not to invest. Instead, this section seeks to remind you to define and set reasonable expectations.

GLOBAL FULFILLMENT

Simply stated, global product fulfillment is complex. Lifecycle practitioners know this to be true. The reasons for this complexity *could* include, among other things, the following:

- Local country kits
- Local part-numbering strategies
- Power supplies, keyboards, and adapters by country
- Component and peripherals
- Local taxes
- VAT taxes
- Lead times in country and to country
- Customs
- Reporting requirements
- Coordination and expediting
- In-country fulfillment requirements
- Direct and indirect engagements
- Variable service levels
- Region-specific release dates for software
- Region-specific requirements for regulations

This short list is by no means comprehensive, but is provided as evidence of the complexities of global fulfillment. A level of sophistication is required to address the many issues that occur in a global fulfillment relationship. A key consideration includes the escalation path when issues develop. Global product fulfillment should be driven by a detailed statement of work. To some degree, the overall life-cycle statement of work would contain this as a subset of the entire program.

The more detailed the statement of work, the more positive the overall experience for all parties. One of the most difficult issues to address in global environments is low-density locales. Often, larger businesses (more than 20,000) are perplexed by issues that arise with regard to remote locations and global locations, particularly when the overall volume between companies is significant.

The solution is actually quite simple: One size *does not* fit all. Further, volume in large metropolitan areas is just different when viewed globally. Density in North America, for example, does not facilitate or really have any bearing on the experience globally. The converse is also true.

The conclusion is that fulfillment will be somewhat variable and should always reflect the reality, not what a business would like the reality to be. This should not suggest a lessening of service levels, but more of a planning to correctly calibrate how to accomplish acceptable service levels. Metrics should be established to track the results of global fulfillment so that the experience can be improved and to anticipate challenges.

NOTE: For a business, having experienced global support is a requirement for success.

THE NEED FOR A FORECAST

Every business faces a question of how best to anticipate the number of PCs to acquire annually. Whether you are a buyer, seller, support staff, budget manager, or play any other role within a business, this information is important for all the parties involved. Interestingly, this question of whether to forecast is one that often results in a "debate." The initial scrutiny might ask: Because service agreements that have no committed volumes are already in place, why is a forecast necessary or helpful?

From the supplier side, the response generally agrees with the premise of this question regarding the commitment to meet or exceed the service level. However, at least a request to share expectations of volume and timing is important so that a plan can be developed. Businesses benefit from the added predictability in the overall planning process by translating the forecast into service levels to meet end-user requirements.

Suppliers can use a number of techniques to estimate demand by a business, including the following:

- Account knowledge
- Historical ordering
- Planned projects

Every business has an IT budget, which is typically a fixed amount. The IT budget includes funds allocated to acquire new technology. Some businesses are quite comfortable in sharing the budget number and projections (not commitments) in the normal course of business. However, many businesses are not comfortable and decline to share this level of detail. Perhaps it is the belief that the supplier would then take the business for granted or that the suppliers simply do not need to know. Whatever the case, there are clearly two distinct behaviors.

It is believed from a lifecycle perspective that it is in the scope of the relationship to share this level of information. If by this sharing the supplier can execute better, it is reasonable to expect the investment to reflect this from the supplier. The supplier should share their planning assumptions, too.

If in the course of a relationship, components or peripherals become constrained, for example, or if unforeseen logistical issues arise, the capacity (of all parties) to respond is enhanced if the volume and timing are known.

The sharing of the forecast is perhaps a reasonable barometer of the level of collaboration between businesses and their suppliers.

SUMMARY

Acquiring hardware is usually the initial step in lifecycle management. Businesses invest much time and resources in acquisition decisions. However, acquisition pricing has been the focus of many of those decisions, in many situations to the detriment of other lifecycle elements.

Product-acquisition decisions and processes have cost and service-level implications that are not readily visible to a business. Many businesses use the term *lifecycle,* but then proceed with a focus on acquisition price as the key criteria. These businesses are beginning to understand that the acquisition price is just a percentage of the total cost and that the implications are greater than the assumed impact of the acquisition price.

4

Acquiring Software

INTRODUCTION

Software products represent a significant portion of the lifecycle costs for client technologies. Many believe that if all the costs were properly accounted for, the cost of the software would easily exceed the cost of the hardware product. Yet despite the significance of the software costs, it is not unusual to find a significant variation in how businesses track, manage, and control software costs. The more detailed the recordkeeping and tracking process, the easier it is to reconcile and to harvest licenses as part of the disposition process.

Many businesses are now just beginning to appreciate the financial impact and compliance risks that software represents. The recognition is due, in no small part, to the maturity of management tools and the ability to establish measurable, enforceable governance models.

This chapter addresses the issues and principles surrounding the costs and related services required to develop the lifecycle management plan for software. The closed loop lifecycle planning methodology approaches the lifecycle planning for software in a similar manner to the hardware product, except that issues specific to software are identified.

In addition, critical dependencies exist between lifecycle elements. One of the principles in closed loop lifecycle planning is that the implications of decisions impact several lifecycle elements. This point is particularly true in the software element.

This chapter addresses the following lifecycle considerations in determining the software-acquisition plan for a business:

- Business PC or personal PC?
- Software licensing
- Purchasing cards
- Software maintenance
- Dependency of asset management
- Software version control
- Patch management
- Compliance
- Audits
- Resources to reconcile

BUSINESS PC OR PERSONAL PC

It might seem basic or simple, but is a PC an exclusive business device, or is it a device that contains both business and personal software? The actual answer might surprise you. Most companies have a policy or governance model that restricts PCs to business use, and perhaps occasional personal use. Generally, a provision requires reasonable usage; however, *reasonable* is a difficult standard for enforcement. Many businesses understand this point, but do not define a governance model that is clearly understood by the end users.

NOTE: The decision determining whether a PC is a business device or a personal device cannot be ignored and must be communicated.

The formal and informal home office and the resultant telecommuting model will add a significant level of complexity if users mix business and personal software on the same device, a common occurrence. The commingling of business applications and personal applications has long been a source of contention in businesses. Now that there are formal and informal home offices, the distinction is becoming gray.

Many times, businesses simply do not address the issue and assume stewardship will occur and that the number and nature of titles does not represent any potential conflict.

In the absence of viable enforcement of a governance model, titles will likely proliferate. It is also likely reasonable to assume that if a business owns the asset, the business is responsible and liable for the information and the applications residing on that PC. Based on the risks and costs, it is interesting how many businesses do not have a more aggressive governance model.

NOTE: Without a strong governance model for software, cost and risk significantly increase.

In discussing this with many businesses, I have found several different perspectives that are prevalent.

Through policy or actual programming, the end user is thought to be in essence "locked down." A locked-down device suggests that only business applications reside on the device. It is also widely accepted that a locked-down device represents the least-cost scenario from a total cost of ownership (TCO) perspective.

Businesses must be able to assess which applications are on a PC and determine whether their presence is appropriate. Reasonable management suggests that there be a tool that can be used for determining the software in use and its applicability for business use.

It is important to remember that if the devices are indeed business PCs, it is the business that is liable for its proper use, the software compliance, and other related issues. Businesses today are finding it difficult to distinguish between proper and improper.

A distinction exists between "personal software" and the "improper use of software." Businesses may allow applications that are innocent in nature, provided that these applications are passive (such as certain "wallpaper").

Many businesses track the use of devices to inappropriate sites or certain and competitive sites (such as a job search at a competitor).

In many respects, the business usage of software may be more of a judgment call by a business, which is why a clear definition and governance model in place is a necessity.

Many businesses have a misconception that software titles in the business devices do not represent significant risk, cost, and exposure. This perception is incorrect; software does represent a substantial investment and impacts risk and cost.

Many businesses assume that there are certain privileges after a software title has been installed on a PC and has been included in the installed base. Software is copyrighted, and permissions are required to use almost all commercially available software. Although exceptions apply, businesses are liable for the appropriate, legal registration of software titles and their usage. The laws and regulations are not ambiguous about this, and most businesses should be aware because, as consumers, most end users are cognizant of the music industry challenges similar to those with software.

Culturally, end users require support and want the flexibility of selecting software just as components and peripherals. The general feeling is that there is employee stewardship that will govern the behavior to ensure that the policies are followed.

An opposing view is that the PC is not a personal-use device and should not be commingled in its usage. Businesses may go to great lengths to lock down the image and application suite. For these companies, the devices represent the businesses' response to job requirements exclusively. In closed loop lifecycle planning, businesses determine the core application set that all end users will have on an access device; this determination represents an enterprise commitment to standardization.

Between the two extremes presented here is likely the middle ground where the business use of the device would have some nominal level of "personal" use such as Internet browsing or use of other approved applications. From a lifecycle management perspective, the devices are business PCs. The day might arrive soon when the distinction becomes blurred, but at the time of this writing, it seems clear that regulations, governance, and existing agreements suggest that if the business acquires the physical asset, the business owns the complete use of that asset.

In many lifecycle engagements, there are discussions regarding the applications suite. In many cases, the applications are separated into four broad categories: core applications; unique, departmental applications; preference software; and personal software. The key is identifying the software and categorizing it so that reports can be provided to the businesses.

CORE APPLICATIONS

Core applications are a part of the corporate core image. The image represents the applications tested and approved within the enterprise. The licensing and relation lifecycle management disciplines focus on the core applications.

UNIQUE, DEPARTMENTAL APPLICATIONS

These applications are built after the core image, or in some cases added to the core image during deployment. Management tools today permit the addition of the unique, departmental applications remotely if desired. These applications address specific department, division, or business unit requirements. Quite often, these applications are fully tested and supported. The key to this category is that not all the enterprise end users require these applications.

PREFERENCE SOFTWARE

Many businesses have preapproved software packages identified on the intranet within their business or otherwise published. Assuming that whatever the approval process is within a business occurs (usually via the immediate supervisor), an application can be acquired by an end user through the defined process.

PERSONAL SOFTWARE

This category contains a host of applications. This category also includes downloads from Internet websites. In this category, the IT organization and the business itself are not involved. The titles often do not reflect the content, so it might be challenging for IT and the business to identify them, but it should be done.

OPERATING SYSTEM SOFTWARE

One of the first decisions a business needs to consciously make is which operating system access devices will run; this is a strategy for the enterprise.

Many businesses have multiple operating systems as a result of planned and unplanned technology-refresh strategies. The operating system software may or may not be a part of the criteria. Closed loop lifecycle planning holds that the operating system is part of the compelling event that must be considered.

Just as the decision relating to whether a PC is a business or personal device, a business needs to determine which operating system(s) will be the standard. Other business, departmental, and global applications must operate in concert with the standard operating system.

Multiple operating systems add complexity, risk, and cost to a business environment.

The operating system is linked specifically to the acquisition of the hardware, as discussed in the first chapter of this book. As more manageability features are included as a part of the operating system and the hardware products, the linkage between the operating system and the hardware will become more pronounced.

The operating system software follows a separate set of criteria from other software applications and needs to be examined by an enterprise as a separate exercise. The adoption of operating software must be a consciously made decision.

NOTE: Operating system software should not be confused with the business application suites. Operating systems are closely linked into an overall platform decision.

Operating system decisions are at an enterprise level according to closed loop lifecycle planning and should have IT governance to support the determination. Businesses should closely manage the number of operating systems in place.

SOFTWARE LICENSING

Software licensing is the process of acquiring and providing support for software titles. Sometimes businesses review both software titles and software suppliers as key indicators in lifecycle management practice.

When looking at the core applications, which are generally enterprisewide, software licensing agreements relate to end-user count, employee population, and other metrics to establish a "high-water" mark to set the threshold for software licensing costs. Generally, core applications are licensed over time with an annual "true up" (or reconciliation).

Software licensing, just as hardware products, can be acquired directly from software suppliers or indirectly through resellers. In either case, the service levels are similar, and the contractual agreements require businesses to provide a level of governance and control of the software licenses in the enterprise. Depending on the size of a company, software licensing can be highly centralized or decentralized. In the core applications, the norm is a centralized model.

It is in the unique, departmental applications where there is a level of crossover in the centralized versus decentralized model. The effectiveness of software license management, to some degree, depends on the level of resources that can be applied to manage titles and suppliers. Many businesses are implementing automated requisitioning to address the workflow.

Preference software is, perhaps, where the real challenge begins when addressing the various software titles. The same behavior that elicits a price list of available hardware products is similar in the software lifecycle. The difference is that as difficult as it is to manage the hardware aspects, the software licensing is even more challenging because we are dealing with intellectual property, not tangible, physical assets. Recordkeeping is a must, but is not consistent in this category, particularly when the transaction might be viewed as a one-time-only expense.

Personal software presents yet another level of challenge. From a title perspective, it just might not be easy to identify and categorize this software. However, in many cases, the answer is obvious.

Many businesses generate reports for software suppliers and software titles but are not quite certain the most effective way to manage the volume. Businesses are generally quite surprised when they are apprised of both the number of titles and the number of suppliers.

A number of logical steps can be taken to address the software lifecycle licensing. It is assumed that a management tool is implemented that can be used to generate reports for titles and suppliers. A report can be processed, and a listing obtained. Most businesses merely have generated lists providing names and perhaps the cost center, department, or division. More often than not, no direct linkage back to the end user exists in these reports.

During the initial reporting out, the output report should be cleansed of obvious errors or flawed content. The rationale for this high-level review is that the overall credibility is weakened if the data contains obvious flaws.

The next step is to categorize the software by definitions such as core, department, preference, or personal. Then, in separate pages, summarize the output for review. In some cases, reports are sent to the management team for review, which is always desirable. Most important, a reporting process should be implemented so that the review and reconciliation does not become a fully manual effort. It is not unusual for businesses with more than 20,000 seats to have well over 15,000 titles.

At the heart of the matter is a fundamental question: Whose software is it? It is generally conceded that on a business device, it is the business that bears the ultimate responsibility for compliance and support. The conclusion is that the contents on the device are held at the business level, and that if personal applications exist, they do so with the tacit approval from the enterprise. In other words, the business is responsible.

The expectation regarding software licensing is that businesses will strive to be compliant and will quickly address any known material weakness in the reporting. This is a high standard, but is completely reasonable.

CREDIT CARDS USED TO ACQUIRE SOFTWARE

Many businesses have adopted corporate credit cards and purchasing cards. These cards permit employees to pay for and acquire certain business IT assets, supplies, and services. For certain items, such as supplies or known deliverables, this approach is quite feasible and optimal. More and more, businesses are restricting the use of such cards, prohibiting software acquisition.

Many businesses define specific processes that address how to acquire software. In the past, shrink-wrapped or off-the-shelf software was considered an ancillary cost, similar to peripherals. However, businesses quickly discovered that the governance model leads to the propagation of titles and suppliers.

Whereas quantity "1" of a software package might not seem significant by itself, if a large population of end users adopt the independent-acquisition approach, there would be little a business could do, and de facto standards could be created. This is one of the key drivers for a more centralized acquisition model.

SOFTWARE MAINTENANCE

Just as lifecycle in general, there are implications from decisions that are made that influence and impact other disciplines. Software licensing does not always include ongoing software maintenance. This maintenance could include software maintenance from the software manufacturer, but could also include internal IT support. There could be some crossover between help desks.

Businesses have developed policies regarding the software-maintenance strategies enterprisewide.

Maintenance could vary but could include ongoing support (access to toll-free numbers outside of the help desk), version control (to be discussed in subsequent sections), software fixes, and other service levels. Clearly, a level of maintenance is always required, including warranty. The key is determining at the time of acquisition what maintenance strategy, if any, is desired. By acquiring software autonomously, the end user makes the decision, as in the preceding purchasing card scenario.

Ultimately, IT needs to incorporate service levels into the portfolio. To do that, centralization is required to make decisions consciously. Titles can be aggregated, and an overall support plan developed. Many businesses focusing only on software licensing may be missing a large portion of the cost picture and may find themselves with multiple support plans in place.

SOFTWARE VERSION CONTROL

One of the most significant indicators of the maturing of the software elements of lifecycle management is the number of versions of existing software titles. There can be many root causes of the multiple versions, including some of the following rationales:

- Lack of centralized acquisition, so that the end user or ordering process might not be aware of existing versions.
- Lack of reconciliation before acquisition of "new" titles.
- Business applications built around older, prior versions.
- No upgrade budget allocated.
- No perceived value in managing versions.

There is no general right or wrong answer in these explanations, only rationales of the root causes.

Version control could impact the ability to support a software package. Help desk calls and personnel need training on multiple versions to be familiar with differences. The number of versions adds to the complexity of the support plan.

More critical is that some of the older versions of software might not be compatible with new operating systems, antivirus software, and other applications. This scenario could create issues regarding the ability to participate in technology refreshes and expose the enterprise to viruses. In such cases, older technologies might need to be retained.

From a lifecycle perspective, each version of software supported represents a unique title. Simply put, the costs for multiple versions are higher.

Businesses that have centralized the software-acquisition process are now proactively seeking to review multiple versions as a part of the process.

Another tactic that is often effective is an enforceable governance model that states that only current or certain versions of a software package will be supported. Similar to hardware products, this is in essence the creation of a standard.

DEPENDENCY ON ASSET MANAGEMENT

Software titles should be related back to the number of end users with that software to properly license and maintain them. To deliver the service in this area, an accurate accounting and a reasonable practice level in asset management are required. Businesses often assume that they may be overlicensed when asset management is not at a priority practice level. This assumption is at a high-risk level. Many businesses still regard asset management as a hardware-oriented discipline. To believe so may lead a business to underinvest in software asset management. Experience suggests that the impact that the software asset management presents is just as, if not more, significant than hardware asset management. A business needs to invest in both disciplines.

The thinking is that the licensing is set at a high-water mark, and there is less harvesting (recapture) of licensing during the lifecycle. Unfortunately, this may or may not be the case. "Educated" guesses may present cost and risk exposure, and may not be appropriate.

To gain perspective, one can create a scenario. If a business has 15,000 PCs in its installed base, there might be a "shrink-rate" factor. The shrink rate represents the number of devices that cannot be accounted for at any particular moment.

For many companies, a shrink rate may vary from 2 percent to 5 percent. Using simple arithmetic, we arrive at the following shrink rates for a business with 15,000 PCs:

- 2% equates to 300 PCs.
- 3% equates to 450 PCs.
- 4% equates to 600 PCs.
- 5% equates to 750 PCs.

One implication of the shrink rate is that it is unknown for certain which titles are retained on the "unaccounted-for" devices. When real numbers are viewed rather than percentages, the actual exposure may seem more real.

Another point relates back the discussion about ordering hardware products in advance of demand: Do these devices add to the high-water mark of the software licensing and support plans?

NOTE: If software asset management is not at a high competency level, can the other related dependencies—such as patch management, compliance, version control—and other lifecycle elements be optimized?

Cascading (reuse of inventory) is yet another consideration in the software licensing picture. The number of devices that are in process represents incremental unit counts to the installed base.

The bottom line is that the software lifecycle for client computing has a direct and relevant correlation to the practice level of asset management. Many businesses can generate voluminous reports, but because of the weaknesses in asset management, the best that could be performed in reconciliation is 10 percent or less, potentially depending on the accuracy of the various lifecycle elements. A 10 percent gap in software could be significant in terms of cost and compliance.

Another reasonable question to ask is this: If asset management is at a less-than-optimized level, what assumption can a business make regarding software compliance? The answer suggests that all the practices be viewed in context so that the asset management, license management, patch management, and reconciliations can be placed into a context. The general rule of thumb is that the threshold may be in the 10 percent to 15 percent accuracy level. Many agreements provide a percentage of deviation for compliance and true-up reconciliations.

PATCH MANAGEMENT

Patch management is defined as the capability to provide updates, including versions, fixes, and security. Patch management is generally accomplished through remote-management software tools. Some businesses still retain very manual processes, which may or may not be optimal. Predominantly based on the size of the installed base and the resources to apply, businesses make the decisions to approach patch management.

Note that the cost and resources required to automate this function have significantly been refined so that they are indeed scalable for lower seat counts. Patch management software is generally part of a larger, more comprehensive overall suite of management tools, but the market has dictated a more modular approach so that businesses can adopt relevant portions.

Typically, patch management provides the updates and upgrades for all end users who are on an enterprise network. Just as in software licensing, asset management is a key dependency. It is important to know which end users are on a network, and how many are not. It is reasonable to state that patch management should be accompanied by asset management. The two elements are that tightly linked.

The question is this: Is it enough to say that an enterprise has upgraded and updated all end users, without knowing specifically which end users? A follow-on question could be this: How many end users remain to be updated?

For most businesses, patch management provides a comfort level that asset management is being performed. This may or may not be correct.

The patch management tool, however, presents the optimal approach to deploy fixes, updates, and upgrades. Those businesses that remain manual or more of a hybrid, using desk support, should, given the maturity in the market, consider reevaluating that approach. This is true regardless of the scale.

COMPLIANCE

Closed loop lifecycle planning assumes the basic premise that all businesses want to be compliant in all matters related to software elements. Grounded with this assumption as the starting point, the question becomes this: How does a company become noncompliant?

The answer to the question is quite complicated and has several causes, which is not unusual in lifecycle management (as you have seen previously). The following list identifies potential reasons that compliance issues arise. Note that this list reflects some of the topics already covered in the software section (and so this should revalidate just how interrelated the lifecycle elements truly are linked).

Compliance issues could arise from, among other things, the following:

- Asset-management reporting
- Quantifying noncompliance
- Lack of software reporting
- Lack of reconciliation resources
- Multiple paths for software acquisition
- Centralized or decentralized controls
- Basic order-agreement confusion
- Acquisitions and divestitures
- Other compelling events
- Users sharing software

ASSET-MANAGEMENT REPORTING

It has been well documented in this book that asset management is a key dependency for software compliance. Software compliance should be viewed as one of the reasons to pursue asset management as an integral part of overall lifecycle. Reporting software is not an easy thing to do—the reports can be quite voluminous and the task daunting. However, the payback in terms of reducing costs and risks clearly outweighs the effort.

If there are factors relating to the number and profile of client devices, the overall number needs to be a part of the business case in determining what the high-water marks should be.

QUANTIFYING NONCOMPLIANCE

As mentioned earlier in this book, one of the basic premises of closed loop lifecycle planning is that impact must be quantified to be considered. Impact needs to be stated in terms of balance sheet and income statement impact. This is done via cost-reduction and cost-avoidance figures.

Many businesses have difficulty articulating what the penalty or other financial impact is of noncompliance. In many instances, the impact is significant. Given the knowledge in the industry of the impact and what is contractually committed, it would seem to be a basic task to define exposure and its relevance to the enterprise. However, there still seems to be hesitation to account for risk until it happens.

When the scenario occurs, then there is generally a full accounting, and penalties, if any assessed. As a general rule of thumb, businesses are likely aware of where the gaps in practice are and the potential impact of those gaps. The question is one of priority and true financial impact.

LACK OF SOFTWARE REPORTING

Although a number of businesses have adopted sophisticated tools for reporting, it is quite another thing to have those reports reduced to exception reports so that persons can work on the reconciliation. Large, detailed reports that cannot be sent out to business units or IT resources to be effectively reconciled may have the same impact as not having reporting in the first place. It is a simple task to generate volumes of reports that pass the "plop" test (the sound of all the paper makes as it hits the tables top); it is another to generate and edit reports so that they are actionable. After all that is the intent of the tools and reporting in the first place.

Software compliance suggests that the reporting should be devised so that the responsible entity, whether it is IT or another team, can effectively use the output. The more pages or cleansing that must be performed, the less useful the reporting.

NOTE: Having reports available is not enough; resources need to be assigned to examine and ensure that the reporting is actionable. The reports should enable the relevant persons to identify and reduce nonsanctioned software, multiple versions of software, similar-functioning software, or any other specific category and to validate compliance. The financial impact of not performing this activity is increased risk of compliance, costs of extra licensing, and an overage of software titles.

LACK OF RECONCILIATION RESOURCES

Many (most) businesses want to be compliant, but they might not be able to allocate resources to effectively work on reconciliation in a business-as-usual environment. To effectively work exceptions and consolidate licensing and versions, resources need to review output and then determine whether there is a business basis for exception items.

In many instances, end users do not have access to an overall database to see whether anyone already has acquired software or if another package in the environment may exist that can address the requirements prompting the end user to acquire software. Without applying resources, IT likely accepts most business cases because rejection suggests a resource to work the exception.

Resources in the software lifecycle area can be self-sustaining. This suggests that most businesses require optimization to the point where at least one head count can address the reconciliation. Even if the head count expense is not covered, the risk of being out of compliance clearly exceeds the cost of the resource. It is surprising the number of businesses that avoid the issue by not assigning resources or claiming that there are no resources on board to reconcile the licenses. Under this premise, why generate the information in the first place? The answer is clear: There is the intent and desire to work the reconciliation. It is a matter of priority.

MULTIPLE PATHS FOR SOFTWARE ACQUISITION

In most businesses today, software suppliers and titles enter into the installed base in various ways. When an operation is at a mature level, the options are fewer. By categorizing, the software businesses can aggregate demand to leverage the basic software agreements and move closer to compliance. Increasing the number of alternative acquisition paths does not equate to more end-user flexibility. In fact, it might create more effort because end users need to assess and determine the software capabilities and functionality.

Businesses often wonder why there is a Stealth IT group within the enterprise. Part of the answer might lie in the software-acquisition and -support discipline. In this scenario, the potential for informal peer-to-peer support and incremental IT assistance can be clearly understood.

CENTRALIZED OR DECENTRALIZED CONTROLS

A number of lifecycle elements lend themselves to an enterprisewide approach to scale effectively; software is clearly one of these areas. Centralizing the approach is clearly suggested to optimize the software elements. Centralized support can be sustained over a longer period of time and is not subjected to other priorities if assigned.

NOTE: Closed loop lifecycle planning maintains that centralization of the software lifecycle element is optimal.

Decentralization seems to go contrary to the ability to create a core suite of software and support to be applied consistently. Decentralization encourages empowerment of the end user in an area where the business requires specific knowledge and expertise that might be lacking elsewhere. End users would not be expected to know, research, or even care about existing titles and suppliers.

IT needs to develop support plans so that the end users and business units do not feel compelled to reach out unilaterally. For compliance purposes, the matching of the capabilities required by the end users should permit IT to properly address software-acquisition and -support issues. This is the basis for the service level.

BASIC ORDER-AGREEMENT CONFUSION

Software agreements between software manufacturers, resellers, and business entities are quite comprehensive. Generally, these agreements are negotiated and are not simple to understand without knowing the content of the full agreement. Pricing, volume thresholds, support, maintenance, right to new copies, version control, updates, and so on are governed by the agreement.

Intellectual property, copyright protection, source code ownership, and so on add complexity. The terms and conditions, although often negotiated, are likely only fully understood by a few persons within an organization (generally purchasing, legal, and IT). A level of due diligence is required when adding or subtracting suppliers and titles.

Contract language exists for express and implied warranties, penalties, compliance definitions, and many other terms specific to software. In addition, annual reconciliations are the norm, generally under an umbrella set of terms and conditions. Sometimes source documentation acceptable for reconciliation is defined. With all this as background, it is not reasonable to expect end users or business units outside of a centralized function to be aware of all the details.

The conclusion, therefore, is that responsibility for and accountability of the software lifecycle element needs to reside where it can be effectively managed and optimized. In part, this is the rationale for centralization, but also why without this discipline it is easy to fall out of compliance.

ACQUISITIONS AND DIVESTITURES

Acquisitions and divestitures are unique from other compelling events because the impact can easily be highlighted and more directly defined. Both the acquiring company and the divesting company have changes in literally every aspect of the software lifecycle element. Every aspect of software lifecycle management would likely be altered. Agreements would need renegotiation, processes, and procedures; governance would need to be reviewed (and likely modified); and acquisition would need to be redeveloped. Certain industries are known to grow through acquisitions, and the ability to commence the "business-as-usual" model quickly is a key criteria for integration success.

Often, restructuring funds are allocated in large acquisitions and divestitures to address many of the one-time-only changes, and clearly this lifecycle element represents one of the particularly impacted scenarios. The basic question is whether the restructuring funds include this aspect of the acquisition. In the case of an acquisition, there are two agreements for a period of time. It is important to decide which contractual terms and conditions apply.

The acquiring company has more leverage, whereas the divesting company may have less. It is not unusual for businesses to have a defined period when the most favorable conditions apply to both companies during a transition period.

OTHER COMPELLING EVENTS

A host of other significant and compelling events often trigger a review of software business practices. Sometimes, as discussed elsewhere in this book, business-as-usual rigor in and of itself is the catalyst. Sometimes it is simply a new manager or executive who just wants an inquiry to be comfortable that compliance is not an issue.

The following list identifies a few examples of other compelling events:

- Audits, contractual compliance reviews
- New management
- Reorganizations
- User segmentation
- Downsizing
- Outsourcing or out-tasking
- Regulations (new and existing)
- New operating systems

- New business applications
- New technologies
- Contract renewals
- Technology-refresh cycles
- Sophisticated end users

A WORD ABOUT AUDITS

At some point in time, most businesses will be asked to perform and participate in a software audit of some type. Whether internally or externally driven, it is important to understand that the goal of any audit is to ensure that the appropriate rules are adhered to in the particular scenario.

For software, the process should be straightforward. There is an agreement, there are purchases, and there are transitions within an operation to track change. The results and impact of an audit are likely easily understood because most of the software agreements address this issue up front.

Businesses of all sizes and scope should assume that at some point there will be a need for reconciliation. It is best to assume that this will occur annually so that if there are any complications they will not extend beyond one fiscal year.

The larger the business, the more significant the risk and exposure to software management. It is incumbent upon IT to proactively report any concerns to management so that there are no surprises in this area given the potential risks involved. During an audit is the wrong time to reconsider those resource priorities that could have reconciled the software licenses and titles.

OTHER LIFECYCLE DEPENDENCIES

The software element of lifecycle management does have a significant impact on all other lifecycle elements, directly or indirectly. Software licensing plays a substantial role in the overall complexity of a business.

In the past, it was widely believed that software was easily separated from other functions and was "walled off." The impact of this belief was to create "silos" that focused on the acquisition price solely and not on the overall IT implications.

Now that the cost of software is equal to or greater than the overall cost of the hardware, the basic dynamics have changed, and IT needs to take more control over this lifecycle element than ever before. Software acquisition, just as hardware acquisition, represents an entry point into lifecycle and the enterprise.

GLOBAL

When the scope of the software element is global, the complexity increases. Just as in the hardware portfolio, there are in-country considerations for acquisitions, and applications will likely have aspects unique to each country.

For example, licensing and contracted services, such as updates and versions, must be adopted globally. And, obviously, language needs to be included. Does each language represent a new version? In the reporting aspect, how licenses and related support will be tracked globally must be defined so that the volumes are included.

The impact of licensing on a global basis cannot be minimized. The cost and risk are significant enough to imply that an enterprise should focus a significant amount of resources and tracking to software licensing. In many businesses, the challenge is one of reporting/identifying the devices that the software resides on. The ability to create an actionable set of reporting is a key building block to successfully managing the lifecycle of software.

New versions of software might not be universally available. Many businesses assume that applications are available globally at the same time and are surprised to discover that this is not necessarily the case (which happens frequently). It just cannot be assumed that an application is available globally and will function seamlessly in all regions of the world. This situation results in more interoperability and prototyping, which is a lifecycle requirement.

"Harvesting" Licenses

When assets are disposed of at the end of life, software licensing should be "harvested." The *harvesting* process means that the retiring devices have an accurate accounting of what software resides on the device, and then the records are updated.

The accounting is not just for the title; an array of information should be secured, including title, version, serial number or end user, location, and the more traditional information. This information is shared with the appropriate staff, and is also used to update the asset records so that the software database reflects the change.

Harvesting the software is one of many activities in the disposal process that are covered in depth in this book.

CUSTOM OR PROPRIETARY SOFTWARE

Most businesses have some level of custom, homegrown, or proprietary software. Closed loop lifecycle planning uses these terms interchangeably. In some cases, the software is owned completely by the business. In other cases, the software is built upon the core of software, perhaps shrink-wrapped software or other software. It is important to understand in the software environment how much of the software is truly customized and how much is based on other commercial-based software.

The custom software still resides in the context of an operating system and other business applications. Another important question to ask as the software around a custom application changes is this: Does the change to the custom application require other applications to also change?

At some point, all businesses want to move away from custom applications if they can. Future growth equates to investment dollars; and the more custom the application base, the more complex the environment. Skill sets are unique to support the custom applications, as are the programmers and documentation writers. There will likely be some customization required, but these customizations may take the form of a front or back end to an existing package.

In the area of software, the determination of off-the-shelf applications, proprietary applications, or an adoption in between represents a conscious decision that a business needs to make. A business case can be made for proprietary applications that are based on what is on the market. This represents a traditional "make versus buy" scenario that businesses frequently see in the manufacturing process. The software lifecycle element is complex, and these determinations represent part of the complexity in making the optimal decision.

Custom applications also require the ability to recover and back up source code, all of which is more complicated without a shrink-wrap or defined software base. The availability of accurate source code may be an issue.

Based upon this, businesses are either transitioning or are looking at enterprisewide applications to manage their business operations. These applications have matured and are now feature rich, so much so that they can address most business requirements. The challenge to some degree has become the transition costs from a highly custom environment to a more standard-driven state.

TECHNOLOGY-REFRESH CYCLE

The technology-refresh cycle often plays an important role in the software aspect of lifecycle. Regardless of what drives a technology refresh, the questions are what software and version are deployed.

Whether the technology refresh follows a phased approach or a "big bang" approach, the question to be asked is this: Must multiple images and versions be supported? Technology-refresh cycles are a normal part of the business-as-usual model, but have such a significant impact on software it is not possible to conduct a technology refresh without fully understanding the software implications.

As discussed earlier in this chapter, the operating system of the enterprise plays an integral role in the technology-refresh process. In fact, the operating system and the ability of the enterprise to support certain operating systems may in fact drive a technology-refresh cycle.

SUMMARY

Experience has demonstrated that the software that resides on a PC may represent more cost and risk than the device itself. The software-acquisition phase establishes the framework and expectations for the services that can be provided to end users.

The application software, including the operating system software, represents an initial conscious decision that the enterprise needs to make. If not managed effectively, software costs will increase; it is that simple. IT and finance need to establish a strong and enforceable governance model.

Subsequent chapters explain how management tools enable enterprises to address many of the discipline issues, including software, that they might encounter.

5

Staging and Integration

INTRODUCTION

After hardware and software products have been determined, the next step in the bill of material that is closed loop lifecycle planning is to put all the pieces together in a meaningful configuration. Staging and integration is the lifecycle element in which the hardware and software are combined and prepared for the deployment to an end user.

The staging and integration processes over the past few years have significantly changed. Businesses now have a wide array of choices and alternatives that can be scoped to reflect new economies, philosophies, and cultures. Businesses can now apply management tools, service alternatives, and new rigor.

One of the basic starting points in understanding the staging and integration role is to focus on the actual work to be performed, just as in all the lifecycle-management elements.

Staging and integration easily lends itself to a definition contained in a statement of work. Unfortunately, some businesses focus first on who does the work rather than the work itself. When the sequence is reversed in this manner, emotions and politics may become apparent.

In general, as a part of the overall lifecycle rigor, emotions and politics should play a nominal role in decision-making criteria. Emotions and politics could be a symptom of a larger issue relating to the cost of change.

Senior management needs to be aware of issues beyond the assessment criteria and determine the root causes and weight that the enterprise will assign to these issues. The enterprise could fail in optimizing the environment if the emotional criteria lead to a nonoptimal solution.

NOTE: One thing I've learned from applying closed loop lifecycle planning is that you can't use business logic to address an emotional issue. Instead, senior managers and decision makers need to validate the reality of issues and concerns.

Some businesses believe that staging and integration is a function that should be held close to the business. They therefore conclude that the "who" question is as important as the work itself. Such thinking results in the retention of business operations long after the market may have shifted to other alternatives.

When exploring the staging and integration lifecycle considerations, these basic questions, among others, should be answered:

- What is the actual work to be performed?
- What skill set is required to perform the work?
- What effort is required to complete the work?
- What tools are available to assist in the performance of the tasks?
- What is an image?
- What certification is to be performed?
- What customization needs to follow on to the staging and integration script?
- How are components and peripherals to be handled?
- What service-delivery alternatives are available?
- When is the work to be performed?

After these and other related questions have been asked and responses received, a business can comfortably answer who performs the work and where that work can be performed. As always, these decisions need to be consciously made and reviewed regularly.

WHAT IS THE ACTUAL WORK TO BE PERFORMED?

The work to be performed in the staging and integration can be documented in a *statement of work*. This statement of work is often referred to as the *staging script*. In such, the work to be performed is defined, along with the sequence in which the work is to be completed.

This staging script should also define the core image (the operating system and suite of enterprisewide applications) that is to reside on all business PCs. For many businesses, the staging script loads the core image, business applications, and antivirus software, as well as any remote agents.

More complexity can occur if the staging includes local business applications at the departmental or division level. In many cases, these applications layers are loaded during the installation.

Staging and integration could include the kitting, or consolidating and aggregation, of other devices and a level of bench testing for DOA (dead on arrival) or completeness of the imaging. Third-party components and peripherals could be added in this phase.

The following list represents just some of the different elements of integration work that could occur in this phase of lifecycle management:

- Desktop or laptop (or any access device)
- Network cards
- Graphics cards
- Encryption software
- Security cards/software
- Printers, fax, and scanners bundled
- Cables
- Locks
- Operating system software
- Enterprisewide applications (core image)
- Local, division, or departmental applications
- Asset tagging
- Testing components
- Updating repository records
- Shipping and packaging

- Documentation for logistics
- Documentation updates, both usage and technical and new help desk scripts

This is only a partial list, but you can understand from it that the number of tasks within this lifecycle element make it more complex than most people think.

WHAT SKILL SET IS REQUIRED TO PERFORM THE WORK?

If the staging script is well documented and the work defined, the skill set to perform the work is not overly complicated. The key is the planning and design, so that the staging is scalable and repetitive.

WHAT EFFORT IS REQUIRED TO PERFORM THE WORK?

The amount of effort required is a key metric in understanding staging and integration costs. If the staging script includes assembling the components (or opening the packaging, if not done by the manufacturer), loading a gold disk image and related software (preset) through a disk or tool, and then testing, the basic loading can be achieved in 30 to 45 minutes (or less in many cases).

The key to optimizing staging and integration is often a function of how many devices can be staged and integrated over a period of time. The "benching" of devices for staging and integration is a variable in the overall cost of the function. Just as in the discussion regarding acquisition of hardware products, the setting of a minimum and maximum is usually an important consideration. The minimum represents the least number of devices that can be staged that yields an optimal set of economics. The maximum represents the highest number of devices that the capacity would permit optimally to be staged. The scaling of the effort required for staging and integration may introduce capacity constraints for the resources performing the work. The staging and integration should consider the work to be performed, the resources required, and the facility (space) necessary to fulfill the requirements.

WHAT TOOLS ARE AVAILABLE TO ASSIST IN THE PERFORMANCE OF THE TASKS?

Staging and integration is facilitated today by myriad automated tools that enable the loading of software and much of the staging and integration remotely.

Even for those businesses that do not want to perform remote staging and imaging, the ability to load software through tools is a breakthrough in the lifecycle paradigm. Before the development of these tools, significant manual effort was required. If businesses today were to compare the effort required today to stage and integrate an access device with the effort required to stage and integrate for Y2K, they would see that the gap is significant.

As businesses migrated from Windows 2000 to Windows XP, the effort was clearly more automated and less intrusive from an end-user perspective (and from the IT perspective, too). Management toolsets, scripts, and the manufacturers', resellers', and partners' core competencies have all been enhanced.

New operating systems will further embrace automated management tools.

WHAT IS AN IMAGE?

An *image* is the software set that resides on a client device. An image typically includes the core image, which is the operating system, antivirus, and specific business applications. The core image is applied across the entire enterprise. The core can also include the firewall and additional items such as encryption and other security features.

At the next level, the image can include certain business applications unique to the department, division, or other segment of the organization. In some cases, these applications are known at the time of staging, sometimes they are not. The choice is this: These applications can be loaded in the staging and integration area or deferred until the installation process. (Although proven processes and management tools facilitate addressing this in the staging and integration area, many businesses defer until the installation.)

The definition of an image may be in a transition. Because images can be built through management tools, some customization can now be scaled that required a manual effort in the past. Therefore, the concept of an "image" may very well be redefined as the core application suite, including the business applications, delivered by an enterprisewide tool.

WHAT CERTIFICATION IS TO BE PERFORMED?

The first step in the imaging process is to define the image. After that, the image must be certified. The *certification* is a joint, formal process between the enterprise and IT (or its agent) validating the content of the image.

Often the engineering team (not necessarily the same team described in Chapter 20, "Interoperability and Prototyping" [online]) is engaged.

WHAT CUSTOMIZATION NEEDS TO FOLLOW ON TO THE STAGING AND INTEGRATION SCRIPT?

Depending on the local applications that might be configured during the staging script, a number of local business applications may be loaded in the field during the installation process.

Businesses should view staging as a repetitive function performed outside of the end user. As the process becomes more customized, the duration of the process is extended.

HOW ARE COMPONENTS AND PERIPHERALS TO BE HANDLED?

In staging and integration efforts, components are usually, if not always, added to the configuration. The configuration is then tested to ensure functionality. The components are defined as memory, disks, networking cards, graphics cards, and middleware that add to the overall configuration. Components are embedded and become product attributes.

Peripherals include monitors, cabling, printers, and scanners (and other similar devices). These are not embedded, but are attached to the client devices. In the interoperability and prototyping phase, the testing included any drivers and compatibility required. The objective is that when the devices arrive at the end-user location, no more testing is necessary.

Accessories are yet another category that can accompany the devices. They can be kitted and jointly packaged and shipped so that the end user sees a bundle for the client device.

After the decisions have been made regarding the scope of the work to be performed and how comprehensive the scripting might be, a business then focuses on who performs the work and where the work is to be performed. The alternatives, generally summarized in a statement of work, must represent conscious decisions based on details.

WHO DOES THE STAGING AND INTEGRATION WORK?

In some businesses, staging and integration elicits strong emotional responses. Although the work to be performed can be well defined, relinquishing control over staging and integration might pose a potential challenge to a business. The staging and integration is the first lifecycle step that has end-user exposure in terms of the IT value add. The staging and integration must be performed correctly; after all, an incorrect staging and integration will reflect negatively on IT. Therefore, there is a tendency to overmanage the effort.

Retaining control, however, should not be equated with doing the actual work. A balance must be struck.

Entrance and exit costs for staging and integration are significant. Besides labor, these costs include real estate, logistics, shipping, and other costs. The question that businesses need to ask is whether staging and integration is a substantial value-add proposition that must be delivered in-house, or a repeatable set of deliverables that could be managed.

Several viable alternatives exist as to who actually performs the work in staging and integration. A business case should be developed for each, reviewed periodically, and then the optimal alternative selected. Among the alternatives are these:

- Internal (insourcing)
- Contractors (on-site)
- Manufacturers
- Resellers/partners
- Consultants (outsourcing)
- Hybrid (combining delivery alternatives)

Internal (Insourcing)

Many businesses believe that the staging and integration process needs to be retained in-house and performed by its own resources. Part of the rationale is the belief that the complexity is such that it is beneficial to have the operation occur in-house.

For some businesses, it is a question of affordability. If adequate space and security are available, and the resources are skilled internally, a strong business case can be made for insourcing.

Contractors (On-Site)

Some businesses recognize that qualified contractors can perform the required work for staging and integration. The use of contractors validates that the scripting has been adequately completed and the interoperability and prototyping performed, which means the work can be managed. Many businesses manage their headcount by using contractors who can perform lifecycle-management functions.

Contractors can be trained and well scripted to perform the work required. The decision to make, however, is whether to use internal resources (or possibly increase internal headcount to create those resources) or leverage contractors. The logic would seem to be that if contractors can be used, retaining the staging and integration function in-house is essentially out-tasked. This then raises the overall question of building an internal infrastructure.

Manufacturers

All the Tier 1 manufacturers have developed a strong core competency in staging and integration. This core competency often includes ISO certification and compliance with audits and security provisos.

The manufacturers recognized that the market required them to enter this operation and excel. The staging and integration can be very basic, from the loading of a gold disk through full customization of the devices. Given this broad range, businesses need to determine the level of engagement that is desired.

Resellers/Partners

Many of the same business drivers that led manufacturers to develop competency in staging and integration have prompted resellers and partners to develop similar capabilities. The determining factor for going with this approach could be the multivendor aspect, plus the potential stocking in advance of demand or other relevant service levels.

The size/capacity of a reseller or partner is a valid consideration. Most resellers work in harmony with the manufacturers, and vice versa.

Consultants (Outsourcing)

Consultant service providers (outsourcing) clearly have proven expertise and competency to perform staging and integration. If a business has outsourced or is using consultants for other lifecycle activities, it is logical that the staging and integration be considered as an integral part of the services to be provided.

The service-delivery strategies of out-tasking and outsourcing are discussed later in this book. In this section, it is important to understand that the out-tasking model does not prohibit bringing the staging and integration in-house or elsewhere even after the practice has been established.

Outsourcing is a formal exit from an infrastructure, such as the staging and integration function, for a defined period of time, usually in a five- to seven-year range.

Hybrid (Combining Delivery Alternatives)

Lifecycle management is often reduced to a comfort-level decision. Therefore, it is not unusual to see a mix of strategies and alternatives in place for staging and integration. Often, between user-segmentation and geographic considerations, a combination of insourcing, out-tasking, and outsourcing is the optimal solution to consider.

WHERE IS THE STAGING AND INTEGRATION WORK PERFORMED?

At this point, you know what the work is and who is performing the work. The question now is this: Where is the work to be performed? Like other lifecycle disciplines, this, too, has several alternatives, each with its own set of drivers and benefits. The answer to where the work is to be performed needs to be a very conscious decision. Each scenario has its advantages and disadvantages, and the alternatives include the following:

- On-site
- Manufacturer location
- Reseller/partner location
- Off-site
- Hybrid

On-Site

Having the staging and integration work occur on-site provides advantages but also risks disadvantages. On the plus side, the devices are close by, and access is often easier. Spot demand is facilitated. The downside is that the space, security, and inventory tracking may represent significant cost.

On-site suggests that the product can be delivered to a central location, usually a business facility. On-site inventory might seem optimal if space is available and the cost is minimal, but this is not the case for all businesses. It is more likely that space is at a premium (and secure space even more so).

Security is not to be taken lightly. Inventory shrink rates often begin in this space, where accommodations might see devices earmarked for net new being used as hot spares. This commingling can be effective, but the practice needs to be at a reasonably mature level.

The ability to track inventory (and keep effective account records of such) is a requirement for on-site staging and integration. Resources need to be allocated based on availability. Finally, the overall capacity needs to be considered in terms of on-site staging and integration.

Manufacturer

The industry trend is to have the manufacturer do as much in the manufacturing process as possible. This reduces the cost and enhances consistency of the deliverables.

Scaling is generally not an issue, and the work processes can be easily standardized and changed.

Resellers/Partners

Resellers/partners often have their own space or warehouse that can be used for the staging and integration. The advantage is that this is usually scalable and provides easy access. This alternative to on-site inventory enables businesses to leverage their resellers'/partners' inventory-management core competencies.

This approach makes sense when the reseller is stocking in advance of demand, because space is already allocated for the inventory. Although there is a difference in finished goods and work in process, most resellers and partners would have this capability and space availability.

Off-Site

Some businesses simply want staging and integration to be performed off-site. Part of their rationale is that they want any desktop or laptop in the enterprise to be ready for deployment.

Some businesses have formal warehousing strategies so that the work is physically separate from the enterprise.

Customizing the Service-Delivery Approach

Hybrids in staging and integration often result from the decision to not make a decision. To some degree, this reasoning could apply to any of the hybrid decisions.

In terms of where the staging and integration is performed, it seems logical to select a strategy that can be adopted enterprisewide. A hybrid decision is often suboptimal.

Business-as-Usual Approach Versus Project Approach

A pronounced difference exists when staging and integration is incorporated as part of business as usual (and supporting the day-to-day operations) versus when staging and integration is considered a project and the business "breaks" the business-as-usual infrastructure for staging and integration.

Projects require extra capacity, and the work is performed off-site and through the manufacturer, reseller, or partner as much as possible. This is often the only way that projects can be effectively scaled.

Many businesses have followed the project approach to staging and integration, and as a result have decided to review any further staging and integration on a business-as-usual basis. The project, a compelling event, forces a business to relinquish the staging and integration process for a period of time. As a result from that break from staging and integration responsibilities, businesses begin to ask this question: As a business, do we need to have core competency in staging and integration?

The questions of who, what, and where are brought up as a matter of due diligence.

GLOBAL STAGING AND INTEGRATION

Staging and integration becomes more complex as the global aspect is considered. Businesses need to consider the available service-delivery alternatives and assume that one approach might not necessarily be the right approach throughout the whole enterprise.

The more remote the location or the less dense a global site, the greater the risk that resources cannot be easily applied. These nuances of lifecycle are truisms throughout this book. The key to understanding global staging and integration is breaking the work required (as described in this section) and applying business logic to discover the optimal way to deliver services to the end users or local IT.

Global staging and integration cannot be performed without due diligence that engages the locations impacted. Assumptions are often made. Not understanding whether local manufacturing, local resellers, partners, or service providers are engaged makes staging and integration a challenge. There is no reasonable shortcut for performing due diligence.

The staging and integration operations are being changed fundamentally by the emergence of management toolsets. Many of the functions that required a "touch" of the device may now be completed remotely, during installation, or even by the end users. Because of this change, as more and more businesses seek to standardize on processes globally, it will be the management tools that introduce an enforceable and repeatable process to the staging and integration process.

WORK TIMING

Many businesses no longer have a shutdown period (as was the case in Y2K) and care must be taken to avoid interfering with business-as-usual activities (or business events such as board meetings, client events, and so on). At a minimum, these events should be taken into consideration as part of an overall plan.

The timing of the work needs to be a planned function. Within an enterprise, it should be widely known that change will be occurring and that the planning and readiness is in the preparation phase.

Timing issues become more critical when the scope is global because there are much more complicated schedules to adhere to and a higher degree of coordination required.

WORK DURATION

The duration to deploy a new configuration, including staging and integration (and the interoperability and prototyping), is a significant issue for enterprises to address. It is not unusual for the entire process to have a planning horizon in excess of 90 to 120 days. This lead time, combined with the refresh cycle itself, can impact the installed base in excess of 12 months, on an end-to-end basis.

The related impact is that the cost to stage and test defers the benefits of standardization and adds a fair amount of complexity to the infrastructure (an unintended consequence).

End users often believe the process "takes too long." Although this might be an oversimplification, the issue is real. The duration that it takes to certify and deploy may impact downtime and market competitiveness. It should be assumed that there is a change because there is a business driver; if an enterprise cannot take advantage of that driver, there will be a cost implication. The business needs to view this aspect as another economic consideration of lifecycle management.

NOTE: The timing and the duration of the new configuration is not viewed by many businesses as an economic proposition. Closed loop lifecycle planning holds that shorter cycle times create optimal financials.

SUMMARY

Staging and integration represents the scaling of the business-as-usual environment. Taking the results from an engineering team, the IT staging and integration team then certifies and scales the configuration for the enterprise.

The details of the work to be performed, who performs the work, where the work is to be completed, the timing of the introduction to the business units, and the duration of the activities represent to IT the first significant execution challenge of lifecycle management. The readiness and adoption must be planned carefully so that there is no end-user downtime.

The cost of delaying the staging scripts must be quantified so that the proper focus can be assigned to this activity.

6

Installation

INTRODUCTION

Installation carries a different definition than moves, adds, and changes (MACs) and is therefore presented and discussed separately. Installation is defined in closed loop lifecycle planning as the deployment of net new devices added to the PC fleet. A MAC derives from the existing installed base and has its own set of economics and deliverables. MACs are discussed in the next chapter.

Installation takes the device after it has been staged and integrated and deploys the device to the end users work space. Installation can be represented by a statement of work defining the actual tasks to be performed, including the following:

- Coordinating with staging and integration
- Coordinating with end users
- De-installing the existing device
- Migrating data
- Physically installing new device
- Accepting the new devices
- Preparing the prior system
- Managing the project

COORDINATING WITH STAGING AND INTEGRATION

For an installation to occur, the installation team needs to know when the product will be available. It is assumed that the staging script would be completed in advance. This implies a level of coordination between the installation team and the staging and integration team. In some cases, there is an electronic notification, through the help desk; in other cases, the notification is a bit more informal. Often, the process is more manual; the product is received by the shipping and receiving function and then passed on to the installation team.

The coordination is a significant part of the role of the installation effort. The coordination needs to be defined so that the resource allocation can be appropriately planned. Decisions need to be made in the help desk role, the manufacturer's/reseller's role, and the staging team's role.

Regardless of the channel selected, there needs to be a way to track the product through the installation process, much as a work in process tracks in a manufacturing operation.

Generally, a coordinator within a deployment team is the primary interface with the various constituencies that need to be made aware of the planned installs.

COORDINATING WITH END USERS

The installer needs to tightly establish the timing with the end user, both the end-user availability and the optimal time to perform the work. Specific times are established, minimizing the wait time of both the installer and the end user. Wait time is downtime to the end user and is an important consideration in the overall planning process.

Depending on the assignment of the end user, the installation might need to be completed off-hours. A determining factor is whether the end user is revenue generating, mission critical to the business, or otherwise considered essential personnel. An off-hours install might prove particularly impossible if training, navigation, or orientation is required as a part of the installation process.

DE-INSTALLING THE EXISTING DEVICE

Unless the end user is net new to the organization, which implies a new hire, for every installation there is a de-installation of the existing device. During the installation, the existing system is unplugged and positioned so that the device can be removed from the present location. A typical installation takes less than one hour. The key variable is the data migration.

Even though the de-installation might not be a time-consuming effort, it is important to define the process. After the device has been unplugged and removed to a secure location, asset tracking needs to occur to retain control over the asset.

Many businesses overlook part of the required rigor, and as a result often discover devices cannibalized for parts, cascaded, or otherwise missing. The de-installation process is important because the de-installed devices might retain software licenses and data on the drives.

MIGRATING DATA

Data migration represents an important variable. Most businesses assign the responsibility for data backup to end users, but they also understand that the end users rarely, if ever, back up their data. (This has held true in most of the studies performed in closed loop lifecycle planning.) Businesses need to consider the policy or governance and define a technique to back up as required, remotely if necessary. Some businesses consider assisting the end users' pre-installation process. Depending on the size of the data to be migrated, the time required for this task in an installation usually ranges from 30 to 90 minutes.

Regardless of the governance model in place, one of the constants is that IT will likely own the responsibility to restore if a problem arises. This is particularly true if the user segments are assessed in advance. It is important to remember that the software packages on the device are likely part of the data migrated, so if the profile is changed, this presents an opportunity to remove noncore or unauthorized software (or at a minimum identify the packages).

The key point is for businesses to have a governance policy for backup (which in reality might not be followed) and to define the responsibilities and implications when that policy is not followed.

NOTE: Installation represents a time window of potential exposure. Data is exposed during various functions that occur during installation. Businesses need to be mindful of this and ensure that the data is protected and that the overall process is tightly managed to reduce risk.

PHYSICALLY INSTALLING THE NEW DEVICE

Just as the actual de-installation portion of the process, the physical installation is usually not complex. After all the parts have been kitted during the staging portion, the installation is facilitated.

More and more devices can actually be physically installed by the end users. It is the data migration and customizing that may require support. Even the data migration and level of customization are being driven down to the end users.

An emerging model is for the end user to unplug the existing device, set it aside for the facilities or IT team to secure, and physically install the new device. Often, color-coded cabling and attachments ease the installation. After the physical installation has been completed, the help desk can load applications remotely, or the desk-side installation team can support the process.

The end-user involvement in this process is possible because end users are comfortable with such tasks due to their experiences in the consumer market (a theme you will read much about in this book).

ACCEPTING THE INSTALLATION

The installation now needs to be accepted. *Acceptance* is a formal signoff that the installation, de-installation (if required), and data migration (if required) have all been successfully completed. A best practice is to have end-user signoff. The acceptance signifies that the service has been successfully delivered and the scope was complete.

Many businesses go even further and initiate a customer-satisfaction survey through the IT team as follow-up to this process.

PREPARING THE PRIOR SYSTEM

De-installation requires more than previously discussed in this chapter. After the system has been set aside and readied for the logistics team to remove to a secured area, the device needs to be updated in the asset-management reporting system as work in process, or as an available system. This begins the return or restaging process in terms of planning and reporting.

Generally, a "quarantine" period is allowed, during which the original device is secured until the end user accepts the new access device and IT and the end user are confident that all information has been correctly migrated to the new device and that user settings are accurate.

MANAGING THE PROJECT

At some point, installation activities scale to become a project. The work to be performed may be scaled and essentially the same, but project management skills are required because of the coordination required.

At the low end of the spectrum in terms of support, project management can be basic coordination and milestone tracking. Usually, the forecasting, scheduling, and planning for resources and access are key requirements. In terms of a larger-scale installations, at some point those installations become "deployments." Typically, installations evolve to deployments when a plan needs to be executed according to facility access, required work, and impact on end users.

Business-as-usual installations do not, generally, rise to the level of a project.

FUNDAMENTAL INSTALLATION CHANGES

Installation activities have changed significantly in just the past few years. Consider, for example, the effort expended in Y2K deployments. In contrast to those highly manual and IT-based efforts, remote management tools and even end users themselves help in the installation processes. Even when desk-side support calls are used, end users do more with the software than just manually load CDs.

As a result of these installation changes, the required skill sets have changed, and the time required for installation has decreased. In the future, we are likely to see even more remote- and end-user-focused installation as mobile devices change the basics of the support model. (I believe that these changes will become the norm in the near term, and that the skill sets required will differ from what they are today.)

END-USER SATISFACTION

Installation might be one of the few IT functions in which IT presents its "face" to its end users, their customer. General opinions of IT may be formed on the basis of this initial contact. It is important to have an installation script so that the experience is repeatable and the satisfaction level is representative.

BUSINESS-AS-USUAL INSTALLATION VS. PROJECT DEPLOYMENT

Business-as-usual installations vary in scope. If the installation is a single end user (small scale), the cost to deliver will always be higher than a larger-scale installation. After all, an economy of scale applies when installations are aggregated. This applicable scope in any installation reflects the technology-refresh strategy as much as the installation lifecycle element.

When the scope of the installation makes it a project, installation takes on a tenor of deployment, and deployment might imply tasks that require coordination.

DESKTOPS VERSUS LAPTOPS

Installation may be, and often is, different for desktops and laptops. With desktops, devices are staged, integrated, and shipped to a site in a traditional manner for installation. Because of real estate and logistics, desk-side support calls are the norm for installation of desktops devices. Although much of the work might be the same, where and by whom devices are installed remains a fundamental difference in the operation.

Laptops present a variety of alternatives for installation. A laptop can be fully configured and shipped to the end user or IT for self-installation. Many businesses have more robust profile and segmentation information on laptops than on desktops. The rationale for this seems to be that laptop users are often part of larger segments, such as the sales force, and can be more easily profiled remotely.

Shipping out the laptop often occurs in such a manner as to "overpack" the device, so that the previous device can be returned. This assists in the disposition practice addressed elsewhere in this book.

As a technology, laptops lend themselves to an "event" strategy. The best example of the event strategy is the sales force, although any consolidation of locations or business functions could be leveraged. Many sales teams have an annual meeting, for example, where all the sales teams meet and prepare for the next selling season. Most sales personnel bring their laptop devices.

Once at the event, the sales force could "turn in" the existing device to IT. During the meetings, IT migrates data as required, sets up the new laptops (if required), and otherwise prepares the new device for the sales professional. At an appointed time, the sales professional receives the new device; IT retains the older device for decommissioning.

Whether the "event" model is effective, the point is to demonstrate that for laptops, there are alternative ways to install the devices, ways that takes advantage of the technology form factor. In effect, laptops and mobility have introduced an alternative installation service-delivery model that might also be applied to the floor of an office building, a user segment, or any other defined category.

The key for the laptop installation is the planning that occurs prior to the work being performed.

NOTE: A trend in the industry suggests that laptops can be remotely readied in a manner that requires little, if any, end-user intervention.

SELF-INSTALLATION

The consumer experience has resulted in an increasing number of end users who can install devices themselves. Manufacturers even have color-coded cabling and provide step-by-step instructions that can be integrated with the company's help desk support to assist in the installation process. Because many end users have PCs and other access devices at home, and they have everyday contact with technology, the scripting of installation is not out of question.

Self-service is an emerging model that will likely be adopted because of the dramatic improvement in service levels and the cost impact. This trend and level of service is very likely to expand in the near term.

In the past, self-service has been an option for some of the IT portfolio. The attach rate was variable based on the business (but generally low). Installation may become one of the drivers for change in the adoption of management tools because the local end users can perform work that previously could be done solely by IT.

The challenge in all of this remains, as mentioned elsewhere, managing the "Stealth IT" costs so that the business in the field does not become an extension of IT in terms of duplication of responsibilities. The focus should be on encouraging end users to adopt the practices or formally respond as to why an approach might not work in their situation.

NOTE: With end users becoming more able to handle technology issues, many businesses are providing self-installation as a viable alternative to IT resources.

HIGH "TOUCH" ENVIRONMENT

Through conscious decisions, many businesses allocate (invest) IT resources and infrastructure to installations. The decision to have a high "touch" environment is based on establishing a one-to-one IT relationship. This positive contact generated in a desk-side support call is believed to result in a significant level of goodwill. This goodwill becomes an integral part of the IT relationship in a corporate culture.

In many businesses, a clear line of demarcation exists between central/corporate IT and end users. Such personal contact may be invaluable, and it is considered an added value in the justification of the practice. Quite often, overall end-user satisfaction is developed from the "touch."

The costs associated with the high "touch" environment are also high; representing the most expensive approach that can be used. The desk-side support call (in this case, installation) represents a financial commitment to the field. In terms of rough order of magnitude in comparison to a self-installation or an installation led by the help desk, the cost of the high "touch" could be as much as four times the cost or more. The ability to provide more and more remote support and self-service through management tools will likely widen the gap.

The costs and staffing implications are substantial in a high "touch" environment. Remember that casual end users exist no longer, so adoption rates will become greater. As help desks perform more of the lifecycle-management functions, and as the resolution rates become even higher, the service-delivery models will evolve to other alternatives. In fact, contractors are being used more and more in this installation lifecycle element.

One concern that arises during this evolutionary phase of remote support is whether certain lifecycle functions are becoming too automated and the personal interface too removed. In the consumer market, we have all experienced and observed this phenomenon.

Although this perspective certainly has merit, and represents a strong argument, the cost itself will likely drive consumer (in this case, the business) behavior. As responsibility accounting expands, and end users potentially pay for consumption, the gap between remote, automated support and a desk-side support visit will widen. Desk-side support might even ultimately become cost-prohibitive. Be observant of these trends. A company needs to consider where to invest its capital and resources. The cost and skill set required for a desk-side support call are changing also, and the trending is for a lower-cost visit.

Migration to remote services and self-help tools may trigger an internal dynamic in businesses that today have a high "touch" model. Businesses must understand that the migration might initially face hostility because of end users' sense of entitlement (to desk-side support). Therefore, businesses must be aware that expectations will have to be altered.

If the costs are explored, the perspective relating to change becomes much clearer. To be clear, "touch" will always be part of the IT arena. The question will be this: What will the scope be, and how will it be delivered? Installations will likely be one of the final lifecycle elements to be fully embraced remotely because devices still require a level of physical delivery in the case of desktops.

With regard to desktops specifically, and considering the scale and scope of the work necessary, the duration of a local visit could be shortened. The laptop environment augurs this fundamental shift.

NOTE: Many businesses determine that the high "touch" model is optimal based on their assessment of end-user capability and the role that the enterprise defines as an IT role. Most businesses defer to a high "touch" model if the end user is required to do anything that might impact the imaging of the access device.

THE IMPACT OF OTHER ACCESS DEVICES

As desktops and laptops are complemented (or supplemented) by other access devices, installation itself might be redefined in the near term. As the technology footprint becomes smaller and consists of multiple access devices, there is an opportunity for the business to bundle the various access devices. The scope could include cell phones, handheld devices, and options. After a governance model has been established, this becomes more of a service-level discussion focusing on how to consolidate demand. This process will become more common.

STEALTH IT

In one business-delivery model, central IT performs the initial work, but the field either completes the actual installation or contracts a service supplier to do so. For many businesses, this model is both logical and serviceable. Be aware, however, that this model may raise a number of concerns.

For instance, if the field is to complete the installation, businesses must invest in any needed infrastructure to allow them to do so. After all, resources must be assigned or hired.

Introducing this model into an enterprise is relatively easy when compared to exiting (or controlling) this strategy. This model, unfortunately, may lead to informal IT (or Stealth IT). Informal IT and related resources are difficult to identify/quantify. Installations are likely to be just one of the tasks the field performs, but that task requires local business unit (internal) resources that must be identified, quantified, and allocated.

The field, branch, division, or other non-IT entity exercises some degree of control over resources. And, although it is possible to quantify the resources necessary, that quantification might be considered subjective and lead to political/emotional issues within the business unit (or between the business unit and the central organization). This implication applies to all industries, but is especially prevalent when clear differences exist between the field and the central organization.

Power/control issues may also arise: Who funds the resources? To whom do the resources report (for performance appraisal)? In general, agreement about the work to be performed (by both the field teams and IT) is the easy part. The other issues discussed in this section must also be considered and their resolutions formally documented to help set reasonable expectations.

SUMMARY

Installation is a basic lifecycle function that on the surface seems to be straightforward and not overly complex. However, the traditional, more manual approach to installation is changing. Driven again by centralization, manufacturers' core competencies, management tools, and the core competency of end users, more of the installation script can be performed remotely.

Ultimately, the work is performed remotely in terms of the content, and the work done in the business unit is likely the remaining manual steps of the physical install. And, it is clear that the more the installation and preparation is done remotely, the less disruption there is to the end user.

Exposure is a risk associated with data migration. Therefore, businesses should be mindful to encrypt information, control access, and de-install. Businesses need to be aware of potential exposure during the installation process and make certain that the project plans and investment model identify and mitigate any exposure.

Installing a new access device inevitably leads to other lifecycle operations, such as de-installation and data migration. To be comprehensive in a practitioner's approach, under a closed loop lifecycle planning methodology, the installation of new access devices should be considered as a suite of related operations.

Moves, Adds, and Changes (MACs)

INTRODUCTION

MACs differ from installations both by definition and by the work required. Moves are the relocation of client devices (PCs), adds are the upgrades in the field, and changes are typically defined as hardware swaps. MACs involve existing installed base technology and do not involve net new access devices.

The actual work to be performed in a MAC generally falls into one of two categories: formal or informal. There is potential for installation-type work, but those events tend to be captured as cascaded (redeployment; or more specific, scaled moves). From a closed loop lifecycle planning perspective, how the work is categorized relates directly to who performs the actual work.

NOTE: Integration into asset management is a critical success factor in effectively performing MACs.

IMPACT OF TECHNOLOGY

It is not unusual for technologies that enhance end-user flexibility to require more "back-office" support. For example, as wireless connectivity becomes more and more available, the impact of MACs will become a greater challenge for IT and the network teams. Not only must the access device be tracked, but the suite of wireless accounts and addresses must also be effectively managed and administered. And it is important for network-access requirements to be part of the MAC script that defines the work to be completed so that end users do not experience significant downtime.

Business may, for purposes of MACs, also consider the bundling of the suite of access devices that leverage the same wireless accounts. The work performed to effect a MAC must, therefore, include addressing the bundled wireless account associated with either the device or the end user.

In the near future, IT and the network teams find challenges that differ significantly from traditional desktop and laptop MACs. Historically, desktops and laptops were "standalone" devices in the sense that the actual device represented the access point. Now, with the wireless network and related infrastructure playing such a significant role, MAC activity can become more complex.

Just as with installation, MACs are frequently underscoped or thought to be simpler to perform than reality eventually proves.

MOVES (FORMAL)

Moves are the relocation of an access device, typically a desktop or laptop. The relocation can be from one office to another, one building to another, and so forth. Most businesses today have offices networked, so a physical relocation from point A to point B is not the significant effort that it might have been in the past. And, because cable plants are included in most office designs, offices are typically enabled for and ready for traditional PC access.

As new technologies such as wireless hubs and Voice over Internet Protocol (VoIP) are adopted (as examples) and deployed, businesses must ensure that the cable plant and the infrastructure are in place so that business-as-usual activities are not constrained.

For desktops, the moves may require (and typically do require) support for placing the desktop on a cart and relocating it. This organization or business unit generally takes the lead for these tasks, not IT. After the desktop has been unplugged and the cables disconnected, asset-management information can be updated. (A move, just like an add or change, is treated like a cycle count of inventory.) A help desk ticket, or other request, triggers the event to occur. Tracking of the assets is an important consideration and should be part of the rigor. Whether assets are assigned a location, or to an individual, MACs represent an opportunity to capture the information.

Formal moves require the same discipline as any other lifecycle element. The work to be performed can be presented and defined in the format of a statement of work or a service level.

Often, moves are aggregated so that there is an economy of scale associated with the function. Many businesses require a minimum number of moves before the work is actually performed. The number depends on the business requirements themselves. Other businesses select a specific day that moves are to be performed and decide whether the moves are to occur during business hours or after hours.

At some point, the scope and volume of a move becomes a project. If the move, for example, is to a new facility, a level of coordination may be required. The move needs to have the coordination of the facilities unit personnel, the end user, the help desk, and IT. In many cases, access (personal or with an escort) is required if the persons doing the work are not formally authorized to perform work in the building.

MOVES (INFORMAL)

All businesses have day-to-day exigencies that require responses to end users outside of the established service levels, and sometimes outside of defined processes. These informal moves might not follow the same procedure as a formal move. (For example, there might not be a help desk ticket to initiate the process.) Nonetheless, the work is performed. Note that this informal move does not preclude the post-updating of the asset repository or other information.

Informal moves are often performed by the Stealth IT team or the facilities unit in the normal course of business. Informal moves are generally not a concern except when the number of informal moves becomes significant enough to represent a need to resource plan or when the moves suboptimize other lifecycle functions. There will always be an informal mechanism to assist end users day to day, and this is a good thing, but the recordkeeping and accountability needs to align with the overall governance model so that the lifecycle plan remains effective.

ADDS

Adding to an existing configuration in the installed base typically involves adding disk, memory, access cards, and so on. The "add" portion of the MAC acronym has become increasingly more a part of the technology-refresh planning process. In the past, device upgrades were in the mainstream. With the prices of access devices declining, the question increasingly becomes this: Does adding components make economic sense? The answer, of course, depends on the available budget and the number of years the technology is to be retained in the fleet.

When the full cost of additional components is considered—labor, parts, end-user impact, inventory, logistics, and so on—a question arises as to whether the remaining useful life of the asset is truly extended. If the device is in the second year of its useful life (assumed to be three), for instance, do the additional components make economic sense? The trade-off is the full cost of the upgrade compared to the full cost of a new, properly configured device.

If the budget does not allow for new devices, upgrading is the answer. However, these types of decisions represent an incentive for business units or organizations to consolidate technology budgets so that they can avoid making decisions that cannot be applied across the enterprise.

CHANGES = CASCADING

A *change* is defined in closed loop lifecycle planning as equivalent to cascading. Depending on the scope, cascading may or may not be a practice for a business to consider. A business needs to consider all the implications of a cascade. The following example, based on a hypothetical scenario, identifies the decisions that must be made and the work that must be performed. Understand, however, rarely does one organization or business unit make these decisions; instead, they are distributed among several groups within an enterprise. Therefore, conflict is a potential implication when teams or business units make different decisions regarding cascading.

Step 1. An end user receives a net new device. This net new device may be a part of the planned refresh cycle or may be out of cycle. Nonetheless, assume that a net new device enters into the installed base.

Step 2. IT and the business unit review the device that is de-installed. To IT, the question is whether the device is compatible with the IT standards and configuration status to be acceptable. The other question is how long it remains in the useful life of the existing asset, if any.

To the business unit, the replaced device, whether or not fully depreciated, is now "free." Therefore, the redeployment or cascading is a desirable event.

Step 3. The group in control of the PC budget generally wins the argument whether to return or redeploy the devices. (In step 2, the end user's device is simply de-installed.) The device is set aside so that it can be transported to a staging area to be reconfigured.

Step 4. The device identified will be moved to a secured location so that the system can be returned for disposition, or transported, if required, to staging areas. The device is then cleansed of previous information (wiped) and re-imaged and configured as appropriate for the next user. This presumes the next user is known at this time. In some scenarios, the device is just cleansed and returned to inventory.

Step 5. The device is now installed at a new end user, where the previous decisions made in the preceding steps are repeated. Ultimately, it is the oldest device with the least residual value that is disposed of by the enterprise.

For businesses that embrace cascading, it is not unusual to observe two or three devices that are cascaded.

To effectively cascade devices, businesses must be at an acceptable practice level in asset management. The asset repository should be updated, and an ability to track asset movement is required. Cleansing and data retention (which underlie security throughout all the steps) are key elements to understand.

Decision makers must also be aware of the economics involved. The assumption that cascaded devices are "free" is not valid. Cascading might prove to be the best alternative, but to make that decision consciously requires an economic framework.

Cascading lends itself to a logical series of questions that can be asked. Together, the answers to those questions can identify implications of concern. It is not unusual for cascading to be an informal practice, and quite subjective. In smaller environments, the approach can work well; in larger enterprises, however, the governance needs to be very clear.

The following are just some of the detailed inquiries that can lead to the decision to cascade within an enterprise:

- What is the fully loaded cost of the cascade, and what is the work to be performed?

  The costs should include de-installation, security of the device, transportation to and from, real estate for storing, re-imaging, the wipe or cleanse of the device, license harvesting, the update to the asset repository, and the repetition of the overall process for devices impacted by the decisions.

- What is the incremental network cable plant or hubs requirement?

  With the emergence of new technologies, the requirements for connectivity might have changed since the last relocations.

- What group pays for the work performed?

  The objective is to capture the cost of the work performed and to identify any Stealth IT costs. In several lifecycle elements, one of the key drivers of the practice levels is who specifically owns the assets. Nowhere is that more relevant than in this cascading element.

- Does the cascade extend the useful life of the asset?

  If the asset ages beyond the manufacturer's warranty period, what are the potential costs?

- What risks are associated with retaining older devices in the PC fleet?

- How many cascades are to be permitted? How many cascades occur as a result of the initial cascade?

- Are the help desk and IT engaged in the process?

- Who makes the decision to cascade, and is the decision a joint decision?

- Does cascading result in an informal spares pool, or are all assets returned ultimately so that the net new equals the net decrement?

- What is the infrastructure enabled to deliver the services required to cascade?

- Does part of the criteria to cascade include a roadmap into the new applications, including operating systems and product futures?

  Cascaded devices are most logically the devices that may be upgraded after they have been redeployed. Obviously, this makes economic sense.

  Real estate is often overlooked in cascading, which is important because the devices may contain proprietary information that requires security. How are real estate considerations captured?

- What is the residual value of the devices?

  It is interesting that the residual position of the asset might not be a consideration by those making the decision to cascade devices.

As you can surmise from this preceding list, cascading is not for every business. Some companies establish strict and formal guidelines for cascading. Some businesses have determined that when all costs are considered, cascading merely adds to the complexity of the environment and excludes the reuse and redeployment of devices. What is certain is that the criteria is variable, and the decision to cascade depends on which organization or business unit owns the net new product budget and whether any charges are incurred for the cascade itself.

When a business decides to cascade in a large scope or as a mainstream operation, it is in essence a decision to enter into operations associated with internal resellers or remarketers of used equipment. Headcount, skill sets, infrastructure, cost alignment, business case, and investment are required. If the scaling is effective, this could be an extraordinary opportunity. When assessing the business model, service-delivery models should be compared.

As discussed with regard to all lifecycle services, if a business enters into the cascading operation, in particular, it will be a difficult operation to exit. If the operation is scaled, the commitment is significant. Given what we are all observing in the field of access devices, if fundamental shifts in profiles and technologies occur, this could be a significant and compelling issue to deal with in building the infrastructure. For example, if the desktop and laptop profile changes the product mix, is the decision criteria the same, and therefore does the volume cascaded change?

High employee turnover is another driver of cascading. In these cases, cascading is a part of the culture, and processes are often very well defined.

NOTE: Many businesses believe that cascading, as a business practice, is the most cost-effective alternative. Closed loop lifecycle planning suggests that cascading proves beneficial only if the asset-management function is mature and supported by a governance model and toolset that is effectively in place and maintained after cascading.

DESKTOPS AND LAPTOPS

The MAC environments have also been impacted by technologies they support. As you learn throughout this book, the move and add functions relate more to desktops than laptops. Mobility has changed the nature of moves and adds. One criterion when entering and performing these operations is the product mix. For laptops, moves are not required (although one could make the argument that the docking station might result in the same rigor).

Adds for laptops are likely less, too, because the overall lifecycle tends to be less than desktops.

Cascading is another distinct area. Many businesses consider three years for desktops the preferred term. Because of financial considerations, however, many desktops remain in PC fleets beyond three years. The longer the lifecycle term, the more likely is a cascade.

Laptops, as a general rule, are cascaded less often because of residual values, pricing, changes in form factors, and the user profiles. Criteria for cascading laptops are generally applied more aggressively.

HOW MANY MACS?

One basic question asked when assessing the maturity of business practices and to secure a better understanding of the business is the level of MAC activities. It is not unusual to see estimates of at least one MAC per end user per year as a baseline assumption. Regardless of who performs the work, MAC volume and cost will set the tone for the stability of many of the lifecycle operations in the installed base.

Many businesses do not track MACs. A prevalent assumption holds that resources that perform the work would remain in the headcount, so the work performed is not truly incremental. MAC is perceived to be a small part of the overall assignment or contract. The volume can easily scale in this type of environment without IT or the business being aware of the dynamics or cost impact.

Some businesses relocate frequently, typically as their workforce, customer base, or real estate strategies evolve. If these are relevant variables, the MAC activities will represent a significant investment.

The number of MACs may be a good indicator of the overall stability of the installed base. Note also that businesses deliver MACs in sometimes fundamentally different ways, such as a centralized model, decentralized model, and remote model.

CENTRALIZED, CAMPUS MODEL

A centralized, campus model permits the scaling of the service delivery. Whether internally or externally provided, the service level is much easier to attain when there is density.

The service metrics and the service delivery teams should be defined and managed in this environment by IT and the facilities unit.

DECENTRALIZED MODEL

The more decentralized a business is, the more local resources and Stealth IT becomes. This is not necessarily a negative, because it is difficult to make the economics positive for less dense, lower-volume sites.

REMOTE MODEL

The true remote model represents challenges for any service or IT organization. Quite often, activity is event driven and not easily planned. The density is clearly lacking, and the ability to scale in any way may be hindered by logistics involved.

In these circumstances, businesses need to adopt other strategies that might be more effective, such as aggressive sparing or a hot-spares relationship. Another important point to understand about the remote model is that downtime is measured in terms different from the other two models.

ROLE OF THE END USERS

Just as in installations, the role of the end users may be changing. With more and more end users capable of installation, any MAC becomes less significant as an event. After all, most enterprise PC users have home PCs, too. Specific IT-centric work will still need to be performed, but the desk-side time might be shortened.

Add tasks will likely continue to be performed as in the past: For integrity purposes, IT will not likely have end users or unauthorized personnel (which may include the Stealth IT) loading, erasing, or adding disk or memory to an enterprise PC. In addition, to mitigate risk and costs, IT must constantly monitor any cascading.

WHO PERFORMS THE WORK?

The MAC should be viewed in the context of skill sets required. So that the actual work required is well defined, follow-on questions should include the statement of work or scripting. MACs are customer (end-user) facing and represent the IT organization, regardless of who delivers the work.

Deciding who should perform MAC work is often deferred or handled informally. Closed loop lifecycle planning suggests that even though the work might be repetitive, and because MACs are end-user facing and subject to scaling, the IT organization should be accountable for the work performed. After all, image corruption (during the re-imaging process), device security while they're being restaged, and data migration are IT issues that might not be fully understood or appreciated outside of the IT discipline.

You cannot apply a "one size fits all" model to MACs; such a model doesn't exist. However, the three models discussed in this chapter identify viable options for MACs.

MACs are critical functions, but are often overlooked or their importance ignored. With regard to asset management, a common refrain is this: "We have control over the acquisition and installation, it is all the points after that where control is not strong."

SUMMARY

MACs represent one of the most challenging aspects of lifecycle management. At the heart of a MAC is the requirement to report and track all the activity on an access device. As mobility and wireless solutions expand, MAC process improvements will be required. The lack of asset-management maturity will be exposed in those enterprises that cascade as a part of the business-as-usual model.

MACs may require significant IT support, but not necessarily. Businesses need to determine the level of IT support and how the work is to be performed and the skill set required. If a MAC becomes a cascade, the effort is significant, and it does become an IT-driven event upon repurposing the access device.

As technology and tools continue to change, the work associated with MAC will undoubtedly change, too.

8

Warranty and Maintenance

INTRODUCTION

Quite often, warranty and maintenance is combined under a broader category of break/fix. Such a consolidation usually results in a suboptimizing of both lifecycle elements. Warranty and maintenance is significantly different.

Warranty and maintenance is a fundamental lifecycle operation, and the work to be performed is generally straightforward, or is it?

Warranty is a product attribute, maintenance is not. Warranty has a defined service level embedded into the product and is amortized along with the product. Maintenance is highly customized and has a set of larger, significant implications associated with the maintenance decision.

A manufacturer's warranty may, or may not, satisfy the service level required by an end user. Higher service levels bring higher cost and must be part of the overall evaluation. Extended warranty is another option that can be added to cover the life of the product. Whether these options are added to all products must be weighed against the ability to track by device/end user. In addition, financial conditions within a company may change over time, requiring a new look at the intended life cycle versus what current business conditions may support.

An important step in closed loop lifecycle planning is to understand the implications of the decisions made in one lifecycle element. The warranty and maintenance elements are often simplified, perhaps even trivialized, but yet, they are indicators of larger, more strategic decisions.

NOTE: The key differentiation between warranty and maintenance is in the inclusion of the service level as a product attribute in defining warranty.

WARRANTY IS A PART OF THE PRODUCT ITSELF

Warranty is a defined product attribute. Because of this, warranty is an embedded feature embraced by all manufacturers of desktops, laptop, and other access devices. The reimbursable costs include parts and labor, and are always contractually predefined. Warranties are expressed in terms of service levels, represented by call windows and repair times. All manufacturers use these standard metrics. Because of the defined metrics, performance against the service level is one of the easier lifecycle elements to track. One of the clear benefits of warranties is that to a high degree, product quality is reflected in the warranty offer.

Every manufacturer can provide warranty statistics, as can the vast majority of resellers and service providers. Reporting should be defined early in the lifecycle relationship.

Many businesses with a low practice level of asset management sometimes have difficulty reporting the serial numbers for warranty purposes. Given the number of warranty events, the reimbursements may or may not be the significant reason for capture; more important is any trending information that can be secured.

NOTE: As an embedded product attribute, warranty is amortized along with the actual PC client itself. There is no separate expense stream or specific identification of warranty dollars embedded.

Although warranty levels may vary periodically, the market ensures that tenders are in somewhat of a narrow bandwidth in definition and costs. Service levels may vary at particular times as new offerings are developed and brought to market. Different access devices will have unique warranty definitions.

A direct link exists between warranty to end users and end-user satisfaction. Warranty, therefore, must be tracked as an indicator of satisfaction.

SELF-WARRANTY AND SELF-MAINTENANCE

A number of businesses on both ends of the scaling spectrum of size and complexity have made a conscious decision to enter the warranty and maintenance operations. As in other lifecycle elements, it is important to remember that there is no right or wrong association with the decision to enter or exit an operation as long as the decision is a conscious one.

Many businesses have entered into the warranty and maintenance operations because of the belief that quality and service levels were lacking from manufacturers, resellers, service providers, or partners. To address this perception (or fact), an internal infrastructure was crafted that permitted a business to perform its own warranty and maintenance.

Conditions that drive change often change themselves. If at the time the decision was made to enter the self-warranty and -maintenance operations, the perception of quality and service was lacking, the question becomes this: What happens if the quality and service issues dramatically improve? Recent statistics tend to suggest that year to year, stability and overall quality have improved.

Two other key dynamics should be considered as a part of the ongoing dialog: more sophisticated end users and changes in the product mix. As stated elsewhere in this book, the casual user (as known before) really no longer exists. When a PC problem occurs, most help desks can readily define and identify the root cause remotely, determining whether there is a hardware problem or a software problem. This process makes the dispatch much easier to address. As a result, and because PCs are becoming more and more modular, end users can often handle what is referred to as "field-replaceable" items. This is fundamentally correct until a device itself needs to be opened and a disk, memory, or another similar upgrade is identified; these still require certification and specific skill sets.

Increasingly, hardware break/fix issues are not identified as a top ten help desk issue. When dispatch does occur, the event is of a shorter duration, and likely the technician dispatch can easily determine the issue. With the first-call resolution rates in most help desks approaching 70 percent or better, the number of field events are on the decline. Hardware warranty and break/fix are becoming straightforward, with access devices increasingly capable of self-diagnostics (and thus giving the end user more of a role in event resolution). Typically, however, end user will not be permitted to address issues that require imaging of the device or opening the device to perform repair.

The other fundamental change is in the product mix and how the mobility devices have changed strategies for service delivery for warranty and maintenance. With mobile users, the warranty and maintenance strategies are often hot spare and replace from a prestaged and ready inventory. The value of entering that operation could be somewhat diminished because the support, regardless of who provides it, is remote from the end user.

The point to be made here is not whether to enter or exit the self-warranty and maintenance operations; the true question is this: How frequently does the due diligence occur to revalidate decisions previously made. Warranty and maintenance by themselves—without including desk-side support, installation/ MACs, and other lifecycle-management services as a part of the self-support portfolio—might not be terribly compelling. After all, manufacturers, resellers, and partners would find it challenging to be a warranty- or maintenance-only provider. This is one of the reasons that those portfolios have expanded.

THE EVERGREEN STATE

In an *evergreen scenario,* it is assumed that all PCs are under warranty, even if the access devices are actually outside of the warranty window. The objective is to never have a conversation that questions warranty status, regardless of who is participating in the conversation: end users, the help desk, the service providers (internal or external), or the manufacturer. The objective is actually quite simple to view the entire installed base under a single service level for categories of break/fix.

To achieve an evergreen state in an enterprise where the installed base is under a single service-level umbrella, the relationship between businesses and their suppliers must be defined both in concept and through agreements. Service providers and manufacturers generally know the mean time before failure (MTBF), but even if not, the business itself can leverage help desk statistics to guide the discussion. Manufacturers generally do not publish or share MTBF figures because configurations, usage, and reporting may vary and may lend themselves to multiple interpretations. MTBF information is usually considered confidential because it directly impacts the competition, and engineering changes occur frequently enough to render information less relevant.

To achieve an evergreen state, a simulation might need to be developed to approximate the costs so that the economic impact can be assessed and mirrored. When an evergreen state is achieved, much end-user (and IT) frustration will be eliminated. A collaborative relationship is necessary to develop this type of model between all members of the team. A parallel is in the leasing business, where "like for like returns," once thought to be impossible to develop, is now a common term.

Warranty, when effectively executed, is a net zero function, fully reimbursable.

DESKTOPS AND LAPTOPS

Desktops and laptops have different warranty strategies, as do other types of access devices. With regard to warranty, it is important to consider the product mix in the business to make the exploration relevant.

Desktops generally have a call window and a next-business-day repair; whereas laptops are generally mailed in and part of a spare program. Product mix quickly becomes an important variable in the overall satisfaction and support structure. As mobility continues to grow, the warranty and service portfolios will undoubtedly change and grow, too.

Desktops

Warranty for desktop devices is usually straightforward. An end user calls the help desk (or desk-side support), depending on the local processes. In any case, a call should also be placed to the manufacturer. The help desk has traditionally been the focal point of the call, but this centralized approach does vary between businesses.

The ability to perform and sustain a mature diagnose-before-dispatch (DBD) capability is a critical factor in delivering a successful warranty experience. The DBD rigor should be performed in such a manner that the warranty provider shows up at the end user with the right part and the right skill set to successfully close the incident. To ensure this occurs, manufacturers generally leverage their own DBD before dispatching resources. Multiple warranty calls for desktops can be and should be avoided. When situations do occur, desktop warranty calls should be a short event in duration.

Laptops

By its very nature, laptop warranty differs from desktop warranty. Typically, the process requires the device to be shipped to the manufacturer (or partner). In advance, a similarly configured device is shipped to the end user to minimize downtime. Often with laptop warranty, safety (spare) stock is inventoried for just such situations. With this warranty strategy, the objective is to avoid as much downtime as possible.

Because of the nature of laptops, the normal wear and tear (and sometimes more) causes more warranty events to occur than occur on desktops. For this reason, among others, laptops should remain in a PC fleet for a shorter duration than desktops. Businesses should not assume the same service warranty for desktops and laptops.

NOTE: The strategy for warranty or maintenance differs for desktops and laptops, and for different user segments. There is no "one size fits all" approach.

THE DEPOT

To hedge against potential downtime and to invest in customer satisfaction, businesses frequently find that they need to invest in a depot, or safety stock, strategy. A *depot* is just a holding area for preconfigured desktops or laptops. Sometimes this inventory is leveraged for spot demand and for critical-servicing scenarios.

It is important to remember the initial business case and justification. If the safety stock level is a hedge against warranty issues, commingling business agendas might result in a lack of availability if warranty issues develop.

Entering into a depot strategy suggests a conscious business decision to enter inventory management, either directly or through a partner. Inventory management reporting is important to ensure that units have availability. Many businesses just assume that a depot inventory or a spares pool does not add to the high-water mark in licensing, for example. This might be an incorrect assumption.

It is not unusual for a business to invest in a spares or depot strategy at a 1 to 2 percent level. Many businesses are surprised to learn that the depot stocking levels exceed that initial level. Depots often result from ordering in advance of demand, technology refreshes, and from other rationales. Caution needs to be exercised so that the costs do not exceed the benefits.

DEAD ON ARRIVAL

Dead on arrival (DOA) is defined as a desktop or laptop that simply does not work. These devices are quickly returned and should be tracked. These devices should be reported separately but included in the overall report card for the manufacturers and partners. In a DOA scenario, a desktop or laptop should not be entered into the installed base. If a device is defined as DOA during an installation, a predefined return program should be escalated.

DOAs should not be commingled with warranty—not to make warranty look better, but more to highlight the importance of the event. It can certainly be included, but needs to be accounted for as a critical-quality item up front.

YEAR-FOUR AND YEAR-FIVE WARRANTIES

Manufacturers offer a fourth- and a fifth-year warranty option as part of the overall warranty portfolio. Although this does demonstrate a response to the market, businesses need to look beyond the tender and consciously make the decision about just how long desktops and laptops are to be retained in the PC fleet.

If a business decides, for example, to retain desktops for four years, a fourth-year warranty makes sense. Warranty should be a "sum zero" proposition. Desktops' MTBF are such that many businesses are willing to retain desktops beyond the three years and warranty expiration. If an incident arises, rather than incur a maintenance event, the device is replaced. In this situation, it is important for businesses to track events and capture the number of incidents that occur. Otherwise, a perception of how well the devices are functioning will drive behavior, and perhaps in the final analysis lead to a conclusion not supported by the events.

The experience with laptops will not mirror the experience with desktops. The number of incidents will be more (and with more frequency) with laptops due to how the devices are used.

Most businesses find it difficult to capture data about the age of a device when it is out of warranty. A manual effort (a serial number search, for example) is often required to determine the age of the device. Because of this difficulty, assumptions are made that influence technology-refresh cycles, disposal, cascading, expense dollars, and costs. Closed loop lifecycle planning suggests that if devices are retained in the PC fleet beyond three years, specific tracking of the events should be measured and reported.

It is interesting that processes are not frequently established to track such events when the cost impact of the decision to extend the useful life is predicated upon an economic proposition of acquisition costs and maintenance, balancing out economically.

NOTE: There is a trade-off in exploring year-four and year-five warranties. With new and more powerful security and product features on new technologies, the business will need to assess the quantification and impact of the decision.

ROLE OF USER SEGMENTATION

The profiles you create for end users (including the criteria of campus, remote, or decentralized models) will define many of the parameters to determine whether warranty levels are adequate for the end users. Warranty itself is very egalitarian because it is product specific. The geography and service-delivery strategy can significantly impact whether warranty as a standard offering is adequate.

An example will help you understand the importance of warranties. Assume, for instance, that a segment of end users is deemed "mission critical" or "essential personnel" (executives, managers, researchers, customer-facing personnel, and so on). These essential personnel literally expect a service level with no downtime.

The manufacturer's warranty might not be adequate for this segment. This type of scenario encourages the sparing and inventory of devices outside of the warranty, with warranty being perhaps only a building block. In this environment, warranty often occurs after the fact when replacing the access device. In essence, this becomes a hybrid situation, where metrics must be established and cost parameters defined. Stealth IT may develop in response to the service expectations.

Uplifted Warranties

In part to address user-segmentation requirements, in part driven to acknowledge the reality of extending the useful life of a PC, or as a result of the conclusion that "one size does *not* fit all," manufacturers have developed uplifted warranty levels. To some degree, the uplifted warranties can address some of the issues identified in the preceding section, with an objective of reducing response times and shortening windows for action and repair.

The recognition that there is a requirement for uplifted warranties and coverage suggests that downtime is a critical issue and can be quantified. Uplifted warranties should apply to crucial segments and be represented in user-segmentation analysis.

Uplifted warranties potentially represent the expectations of end users who are more technology dependent in their assignments. Increasingly, delivery of warranty is a function of the diagnostics tools and logistics that a manufacturer and partner are able to leverage.

In summary, the uplifted warranty of today may very well be the standard warranty of tomorrow. The market is moving that fast in this area.

MAINTENANCE AND OUT-OF-WARRANTY EXPENSES

Under closed loop lifecycle planning, *maintenance* is the out-of-warranty support for desktops and laptops. Unlike warranty, which is a product attribute, maintenance represents an expense stream. Maintenance brings with it its own set of economics and service-delivery considerations. Simply put, maintenance is more costly than warranty. This statement is quite logical when viewed in the context of labor and parts reimbursement that are a part of warranty and which are not a part of maintenance.

Without the reimbursements, maintenance could be as much as 2 to 2.5 times as costly when compared to warranty. The maintenance costs need to include the related lifecycle implications such as inventory, inventory tracking, residual decline, and so on for a full and fair economic comparison. Many of these factors are frequently overlooked because these are reported in several cost centers and are not aggregated.

Many businesses find themselves engaged in maintenance strategies as a result of the decision to retain PCs in the fleet beyond three years. By retaining PCs in the fleet beyond three years, the implication is, by default, maintenance. Although the hardware might be perceived to be "free" (as it relates to the capital budget of the funding organization), there is still the matter of the ongoing support, including maintenance.

Businesses have devised various strategies for maintenance (some formal, some informal). At time, costs are difficult to aggregate and account for because cost centers, centralization, and charge backs might not be in existence or appropriately defined to capture the costs.

Quite often, the implications of the decision to retain devices past the warranty period is not fully thought out, leaving IT to address the impact of the decision. If the support is internal, inventory positions need to be maintained. If the support is provided by a third party, there is a cost to be incurred. If there is no viable chargeback solution in place, IT must bear the financial impact of these decisions.

If the decision makers face no financial impact, and the cost impact is neutral to their business, it will be challenging to convince anyone that retention and a maintenance strategy is not an optimal strategy to consider. Only when a business can view the proposition holistically can the decision be effectively made. The decision might still be the same but, in this scenario, with the appropriate level of detail to quantify the impact.

In this section, the following maintenance strategies are explored in detail:

- Sparing
- Cannibalizing
- Cascading
- Inventory

SPARING

Sparing is the retention of older devices for maintenance purposes. Retaining older devices requires a level of rigor to ensure that the assets can be accounted for in the installed base. Sparing requires a logistics plan, secure real estate, and an infrastructure to support the devices. The infrastructure must be skilled to perform the work of re-imaging, cleansing, and redeployment, among other related lifecycle activities.

Security plays an important role in sparing to ensure that inventory remains available. The considerations and the work to be performed all represent elements of the maintenance plan for the devices. The cost of the labor and related expenses should be captured.

CANNIBALIZING

Often, older devices are "cannibalized" for parts. These devices are harvested for the parts themselves, not for a system-to-system replacement. This often presents a challenge when the overall installed base has the need for parts for older devices but when the funding organization might not be IT.

Cannibalizing older devices ensures that the remaining configuration has little or no value. It is not unusual for these devices to have a cost associated with disposal.

CASCADING

When devices are on a maintenance strategy, there is *cascading*. Cascading refers to the redeployment of used equipment within an enterprise. Even if devices are swapped out as replacements, the practice of cascading occurs. Maintenance generally occurs in month 37, so cascading is an immediate implication of that decision.

INVENTORY

To be in the maintenance business requires a maturity of inventory management and an inventory-management toolset. Older devices need to be located, and the logistics to support these devices are a prerequisite of service. If IT defers these tasks to the businesses, Stealth IT is encouraged and may lead to political/economic conflicts.

MAINTENANCE IMPLICATIONS

Maintenance impacts several lifecycle areas, as previously mentioned. Maintenance needs to be viewed in the context of the other decisions that are impacted by the initial decision set. This section further explores three impacts: obsolescence, technology refresh, and costs.

Maintenance strategies relate to obsolescence by having a "new" definition of obsolete client devices. The definition is not necessarily based on IT configuration specifications, operating systems, speed, warranty, costs, and so on. Instead, it is based on the ability to reuse the device without additional capital outlay.

The definition of *obsolescent* should be a corporate governance decision that should apply to all businesses and not necessarily subject to a lot of discretion. Many businesses suddenly find themselves at risk when protective software such as the antivirus, firewall, or other software cannot be as effective on an older device. The counterposition to obsolescence is true, however: The devices still work.

Maintenance strategies often result in the overall redefining of the technology-refresh strategy. This is logical given the previously stated position that obsolescence is redefined, too. Many businesses have well-defined and articulated technology-refresh cycles, which become dynamic in definition when the potential funding organization decides to retain the devices beyond the time specified in the governance model.

Cost is always relative. Does support of a device cost more if your department does not fund the support? Few would argue that older devices have a higher cost, and so the question relates to the capital or expense budgets, followed by the question of whose budget is impacted. Maintenance is a lifecycle element that requires a strong business case and quantified economics to optimize decision making.

SERVICE-DELIVERY STRATEGIES

Maintenance carries a significant cost if truly accounted for entirely. Many businesses want to remain in the maintenance business, however, because of its one-to-one relationship between the end user and IT. This is defined as a high "touch" environment. The strategy brings with it a level of goodwill and intrinsic value that is hard to quantify, but many businesses consider this important.

Other businesses have out-tasked or outsourced the maintenance (and warranty) to a third party, or third parties. These businesses are driven by service levels.

When maintenance is provided externally, there are two fundamental service strategies: per device or per event.

Per-device service strategy represents a retainer of sorts, entitling the end user access to a service provider with an agreed upon service level. Generally, the monthly maintenance cost is expressed in a per-seat, per-month figure over a period of time. This strategy permits the service provider to anticipate the call volume and define inventory for servicing a business. Per-event service strategy is self-explanatory.

Another service-delivery strategy for maintenance is referred to as time and material (T&M). T&M usually has an hourly rate associated with the work to be performed and a minimum number of hours associated with an event. T&M presents challenges in reporting for both parties: for instance, the time card submission and reporting for support staff; and for the business, the ability to audit and verify times charged.

T&M requirements should be fully understood before entering into an agreement.

The Business Case for Density

Depending on the geographic distribution of the client devices, maintenance is going to be easy or more challenging. The more centralized and dense the installed base, the more economy of scale may encourage maintenance and the use of depots. When the logistics and shipping are less of a concern, resources become easier to plan and the predictability becomes more viable.

Just as in other lifecycle-management functions, remote or less-dense sites will present a challenge because of the implications from downtime. Logistics are an important factor in the ability to provide maintenance services to remote locations.

THE HELP DESK

In maintenance scenarios, it is important that the help desk be intimately engaged. From generating the request for service, to the closure of the ticket, the information regarding a maintenance event is critical in managing a PC fleet effectively. When a business decides to maintain older devices, it is equally important for the help desk to identify root causes and track the history of the events.

Trending is an important awareness. If there are enterprisewide, installed base issues on maintained devices, a proactive approach needs to be developed quickly. Having the help desk track older-device activity is invaluable in the effort.

Despite this, the statistics are often not tracked or require considerable manual reconciliation.

Certainly, serial numbers are tracked, if provided, and can relate to the age of a device. If a manual effort is required, however, where is the reconciliation performed, and where does the responsibility lie in the performance of that work?

Due diligence is crucial to address the help desk and costing requirements for maintenance of an out-of-warranty installed base. One could argue that the warranty rigor should be similar.

ENTER/EXIT THE WARRANTY AND MAINTENANCE OPERATIONS

For maintenance and warranty decisions, entrance costs and infrastructures are often compartmentalized, and so the magnitude of the implications is not readily obvious or necessarily understood. Moreover, the potential implications are not necessarily of impact to the organizations making the decisions. In recent times, more and more exposure to the implications has become highlighted.

For some inexplicable reason, maintenance is an emotionally charged issue, regardless of who performs the work. Perhaps it is the politics, or perhaps it is the defending of the initial decisions. Whatever the cause, maintenance and related decisions are indeed a flashpoint for many businesses.

Organizations and enterprises need to remember that there are no right or wrong answers, only conscious business decisions. (This book will continue to repeat this as required to emphasize its importance.)

Maintenance and warranty require skill sets to deliver the service, and these skill sets are changing as more reliance is placed on remote DBD and more-modular, field-replaceable devices. With reliability improving, too, businesses should periodically (annually) review their support strategy to ensure that the initial decisions remain optimal.

In all businesses, resources, expenses, and capital are a finite resource (and often scarce). Businesses needs to constantly decide where to invest and where to reassess. In maintenance and warranty, the business decision is not where the cost is necessarily the least, it is where to invest dollars and resources to ensure the greatest return. Investing in areas of lifecycle that are driven by an industry-standard definition or an achievable service level may, or may not, be the best use of capital.

SUMMARY

Many businesses do not consciously explore alternatives in warranty and maintenance and frequently discover that the costs associated with this aspect of lifecycle support are more significant than initially believed.

The alternatives and costs vary significantly in warranty and maintenance solutions. Scaling has a significant impact on the overall cost for these lifecycle elements.

The warranty and maintenance strategy needs to be aligned with the formal technology-refresh plan; a lack of such a plan will increase the costs for warranty and maintenance. As the pace of technology evolution quickens from a hardware, software, and toolset perspective, it is likely that the warranty and maintenance strategies will become more variable.

When the warranty and maintenance plans do not address end-user requirements, the business units will generally address this situation by investing in Stealth IT spares and resources.

Because of increasingly enhanced DBD capabilities, desk-side support requirements will be redefined, and the skill sets required will become less of an issue for IT.

9

Asset Management

INTRODUCTION

Asset management is perhaps the most misunderstood of all the lifecycle elements. Historically, many businesses were not overly concerned about asset management. There was a belief that asset management simply could not be driven by a set of financial justifications and that asset management is a drain of costs. Asset management was difficult to cost justify in the past.

Many businesses have tried on multiple occasions to implement asset management. These experiences often are exasperating and usually quite costly. It was in vogue to point to a software packages, or packages, as part of the rationale of the failed implementation or as a part of the rationale to avoid further investments.

Asset management is misunderstood for a reason: The definition has never been thoroughly defined in a manner that lends itself to implementation. Closed loop lifecycle planning defines *asset management* as the tracking of assets throughout the various stages of lifecycle.

Businesses have used the following terms interchangeably with the term asset management:

- Asset tracking
- Inventory control
- Inventory management

To understand asset management, it might be useful to have definitions for the related terms. In closed loop lifecycle planning, all these terms have specific definitions and are not necessarily interchangeable. The following sections define these terms in context. The individual definitions, as you will see, are not the same.

ASSET MANAGEMENT

Asset management is the tracking of assets throughout the lifecycle. The management aspect assumes a level of integration into other business practices. Asset management is a more sophisticated approach and can identify assets at any point in the lifecycle: value, configuration, and user. Asset management is very dynamic, not passive.

The design object in asset management is to capture each "touch" that occurs with the access device and report the activity.

ASSET TRACKING

Asset tracking is not as dynamic as asset management, but asset tracking is a lower practice level. There is less integration with other lifecycle practices. Asset tacking is based on locating assets at particular moments in the lifecycle, and is not a focus on day-to-day movements.

INVENTORY CONTROL

Inventory control is a fundamental identification of a more static environment. Typically, inventory control is the rigor used in warehousing, staging in advance of demand, spares, work in process (staging), and other predeployment activities. Inventory control often functions from a philosophy of minimum and maximum reorder point, and is a part of the front-end and back-end lifecycle practices of acquisition and decommissioning. Another context is the addressing of inventory control as the finished goods and work-in-process approach. Inventory control deals with finished goods, works in process, and raw materials. Inventory control is more of a manufacturing term in its origin.

Inventory control is often operationally outside of day-to-day asset management or asset tracking, which focus on the installed base. Inventory control is often viewed as a standalone process.

INVENTORY MANAGEMENT

Inventory management means much the same as inventory control, but like asset management, inventory management requires a higher level of integration. It should be assumed that inventory management is not standalone and is an input into the asset-management systems and process.

Inventory management derives from the distribution environment.

WHAT DO THE DEFINITIONS COVER?

Whatever term is used—asset tracking, asset management, inventory tracking, or inventory management—the closed loop lifecycle planning approach covers both the hardware and the software elements of lifecycle.

Both hardware and software represent different types of costs, risks, and challenges associated with optimizing the lifecycle elements.

Again, historically, asset management was thought to be separate for hardware and for software. Often, even still, different teams are involved. Enterprises must, however, consider both as critical elements to manage.

NOTE: Many businesses use the terms *asset management, asset tracking, inventory management,* and *inventory control* interchangeably. Closed loop lifecycle planning suggests that the rigor and practice levels in each of these represent a unique definition and a different set of problems that the approach tends to solve.

IS ASSET MANAGEMENT A TOOL?

Simply stated, asset management is not a tool, but a series of processes captured by a tool or set of tools. No matter how comprehensive a software management tool is for asset management, it is implementation that will lead to success or failure, not necessarily the tool itself.

It is convenient to assign "blame" to a tool. It is usually more difficult to look internally and ask why the processes that provided the input into the asset management tool were not followed or governed. Processes work when there is a reasonable governance or policy that can be measured and reported. Without this level of commitment, you have less chance for success.

For any asset-management tool to be successful, the "touch points" should be captured and reported. This is all included in the matter of defining the processes.

Because each lifecycle function impacts the hardware and software, it might be useful to think of the touch points as cycle counts. In the closed loop lifecycle planning model, every element of the bill of material can provide input into the asset-management process and repository. For example, during acquisition, the following could be inputs into the asset-management process:

- Serial number
- Warranty/date of birth
- Location
- End user
- Make and model
- Software build
- Configuration
- Asset tag
- Relevant shipping information (bill to/ship to/sold to)

The key point is that in every step of the process and in every task, decisions can be made that relate to the type and nature of the information that could be captured.

Many businesses find it useful is to consider all contacts, such as a help desk call or a desk-side support call, a cycle count in terms of reporting inventory. If each end user has a monthly contact with the help desk, for example, asset-management updating could occur with each incident. This approach makes the asset repository much more accurate (a by-product of work already being performed).

THE COST JUSTIFICATION FOR ASSET MANAGEMENT JUST BECAME EASIER!

In the past, the financial justification for asset management was a challenge. The question was always raised whether the benefits represented a hard-cost impact or a soft-cost impact, with soft costs likely identified as the key motivation for implementation and investments. The investment levels were not small, so there was a fair level of scrutiny on the topic of asset management. The perceived business case benefits were also viewed as IT benefits, not considered a business unit or enterprise risk, cost, or exposure.

This scenario is no longer the case. With current regulations, personal privacy laws, and with the specter of new and growing regulations, asset management is no longer an option; it is a requirement to be comfortable in delivering the compliance sought by regulators and stakeholders. Businesses need to be accountable for information contained, accessed, and retained on client devices.

During the writing of this book, it seems that not a day has gone by when information was not somehow compromised in the circumstances surrounding access devices. The first fundamental of controlling and managing information is to have an appropriate level of control over the installed base. Security is addressed throughout this book, but as a building block in asset management, security is one of the key reasons to ensure that the enterprise has a high asset-management practice level.

It is important to know which access devices are in the installed base and where these devices are located at various times. This understanding relates to the physical aspects of asset management. Risk and penalties are clearly associated with this basic function.

No longer should businesses agonize over the financial justification when the loss of one laptop can result in millions of dollars of real costs. Not only is the financial and business case now easy to define, it is now a relatively simple process to calculate the entry costs, too. Aside from the risks and penalties, certain behaviors are expected in the day-to-day management and conduct of IT (and enterprisewide).

A business' *customers* fully expect a business to protect assets upon which their personal information resides. The day is soon to come when the ability to guarantee this will be a key differentiator between companies. Customers defer to those businesses that can validate and prove their security. For consumers, therefore, asset management is a given.

A business' *employees* fully expect the company to invest in and protect their personal information and data. Personnel files should never be vulnerable. Employees reasonably expect such protection and that their employer will exercise due diligence.

Employees also anticipate and expect that employers will not, through the conduct of its businesses practices, expose them to personal risk. This expectation might become one of the drivers for change in that employees will attempt to mitigate their exposure. This is an entirely reasonable perspective to have when dealing with the ever-changing world of access devices, and it is one other reason that businesses need to invest heavily in this discipline.

A company's board and senior leadership teams are expected to be fully accountable for the protection of the information that resides on access devices. The company's *stockholders* fully expect this level of commitment. If exposure occurs, or if a practice level results in exposure because the requisite investment was not made, stockholders should be made aware of the implications of that exposure (and the decisions that led to it, consistent with the overall lifecycle understanding that the implications of decisions, not necessarily the decisions themselves, are critical).

Finally, and equally important, *regulators* and *agencies* fully expect compliance with the intent and spirit of the laws (local, national, and global) that apply. To successfully operate in the global community, information needs to be protected.

Given the potential impact on all the constituencies identified, it is difficult to envision any reasonable scenario in which asset management is not a fundamental building block for these requirements and assurances. A business cannot protect information if it cannot locate and account for the assets on which the information resides or can be accessed. IT is typically the organization accountable for this going forward, even more so because the dynamics of the decisions are better understood by everyone impacted.

For the business case to be successful and timely, a critical success factor is executive support. Asset management should not be viewed solely as an IT initiative. Asset management is a business priority and represents such a key decision that the executives should (*and must*) support the investment and governance model. Ineffective asset management will be a career-limiting move. Senior management is responsible and accountable; there is no longer a tedious, political-cost justification process. The only real business question is the practice level and how much risk a business is willing to accept.

NOTE: Asset management is a requirement today to be compliant with regulations, privacy laws, and existing governance.

HARDWARE ASSET MANAGEMENT

A host of issues and disciplines particularly relate to the hardware aspect of asset management. These are relevant topics in closed loop lifecycle planning and are impacted by many of the lifecycle elements. This list includes the following:

- Shrink rates
- Patch management
- Linkage into inventory control
- Detail level
- Centralization
- Proactive level

SHRINK RATES

Regardless of the diligence, some shrinkage will always occur. Shrink rate represents the physical assets that at any particular moment in time cannot be specifically located. The shrink rate is relative to the size and scope of a business and its installed base. If a shrink rate is 1 percent to 3 percent of a small installed base, one might not be as concerned as a business with more than 20,000 devices might be. In the latter case, 200 devices is likely a cause of concern. As important as the percentage of the shrink rate, it is as important to remember that all it takes is one device to be missing to be a major breach. Therefore, percentages and hard quantities are all relative. The importance is that businesses do all they can at the practice level to avoid any breach in the first place.

During asset-management due diligence, businesses can attempt to locate any asset on its network. With client agents and various software "sniffers" that can look at online configurations, this is becoming a simpler task than ever before. Once it is not online, asset control may be lost. It is often a difficult to validate whether a device is the same device as on the network. This scenario makes the overall task of integrating the online and offline aspects of asset management more complex.

Shrink rate as a percentage is generally a good indicator of the asset-management discipline. Reconciliation is a requirement and should be proactive and a recurring part of the business-as-usual environment.

PATCH MANAGEMENT

Patch management suggests that all PCs are on the network, or will be on the network, and can be polled and accessed for upgrades, fixes, and so on. All devices on the network can be remotely administered to ensure compliance to configuration-management standards. The question is this: Can businesses have a solid patch-management practice without a solid asset-management practice level?

If patch management is scoped solely for the networked devices and application packaging, the task of patch management can be completed. However, it should not be concluded that by having a solid patch-management practice all the assets are indeed covered. Patch management and asset management should be reconciled, with the objective to ascertain which access currently has the appropriate patches.

Many businesses assume that when the patch-management function is working well, the asset-management function is working well, too. Unfortunately, that is not the case. For instance, a high proficiency at patch management when the devices are on the network and can be identified and remediated does not suggest that all assets are accounted for in this manner; neither does it guarantee that the same assets will appear on the network every day. The level at which patch management or asset management is practiced does not suggest that the other function is at a related level.

Therefore, the asset-management and patch-management teams are often separate. One team focuses on staging and integration (and on interoperability and prototyping [patch management]), whereas the other team focuses on the overall business issues associated with the installed base (asset management). In many cases, if not most cases, the tools are part of an overall suite of compatible management tools. However, there is the silo impact of each tower working independently and, in some cases, with little synergy.

In closed loop lifecycle planning, one fundamental best practice is to leverage every "touch"; patch management represents one of those scenarios in which the "touch" can be captured.

LINKAGE INTO INVENTORY CONTROL

The full installed base should be represented when discussing asset management. Just as a manufacturer would identify raw materials, work in process, and finished goods as the representation of its financial position, so should businesses reflect all the inventories in the various points of lifecycle management. Staging, deployment, decommissioning, and so on all are required to represent the full asset-management position.

The objective is not to make the reporting more complex, but to make the reporting more comprehensive as a representation of the true installed base. To develop a true understanding of the installed base, the full scope of the inventories is included into the scope of asset management, not separated by any artificial or organizational towers.

In many situations, asset management varies; and in the inventory area, local spreadsheets are often used to perform the inventory function. These spreadsheets should be withdrawn over time. With more standardization in the process, businesses can adopt standard toolsets for inventory and asset management.

DETAIL LEVEL

One of the initial decisions that must be made in asset management is at what level of detail assets or related components and peripherals should be tracked.

This is a key to the planning process. To a high degree, this should be reviewed frequently. Because the nature of access devices is changing—desktops, laptops, tablets, handhelds, and so on—the decisions regarding what should be tracked is ever changing. This represents yet another implication from other lifecycle decisions.

What to track as an asset is a matter of policy and governance (and just plain common sense). Closed loop lifecycle planning has a single set of criteria that may prove useful in its application. Given existing regulations (and anticipated future regulations), any device that could contain sensitive corporate information or personal privacy information should be tracked.

One challenge businesses face today is the optimal manner in which to address wireless and handheld devices. Although at the very early stage today, this need must be addressed. The exposure is potentially the same as for nonwireless devices, but security is made more difficult because wireless devices enable remote access.

Another criterion that some businesses use is a dollar threshold. Assets over a certain dollar amount get tracked, others do not. Although this criterion is perhaps acceptable for some financial asset management, it probably is not acceptable for lifecycle. Many businesses expense access devices, but the business requirements remain because it is the information that is relevant, not only the cost.

Related peripherals (for example, keyboards, mouse devices, and monitors) might not be tracked. Because accessories are expense items, these are not critical to the information retained about the access devices.

As a general rule, a device that retains corporate or personal information is an asset that needs to be accounted for regardless of the pricing or costs. Therefore, new approaches need to be developed as wireless and mobility begin to expand exponentially.

USB ports present a somewhat unique scenario because they permit access via thumb drives (also referred to as "flash drives" and "memory sticks"). These small, inexpensive and widely available devices present a significant challenge because information can be downloaded to the thumb drive (or uploaded from the thumb drive). Managing this level of sophistication will be a challenge. Businesses need to clearly define asset-management (and security) standards for these devices. Some businesses have actually taken steps to restrict access via these devices by governance and by "locking" the USB port.

It is easy to avoid the thoughtful decisions about what to track and simply conclude to track as much as possible. This is probably not a solid practice; therefore, track only what is relevant. Asset management is operational in nature, not to be included in a framework. Asset management is a deliverable.

CENTRALIZATION

Asset management is best provided at the enterprise level. In closed loop lifecycle planning, two lifecycle elements (asset management and help desk, covered in the next chapter) are best when scaled across the enterprise consistently. Having multiple processes, tools, and owners is clearly not optimal. Centralizing the asset-management function is critical for compliance with regulations and for overall lifecycle management.

Historically, asset management was quite informal, lacking a strategic direction. Having the ability to scale across the enterprise permits the correct investment in resources. Also, there is a point to be made about accountability. The CIO and other senior executives are accountable for the information relating to an asset or if the asset is inappropriately decommissioned or disposed of. Therefore, with accountability goes the responsibility to drive an appropriate governance model.

THE PROACTIVE LEVELS

When asked about asset-management proactive levels, many businesses generally concede that the function could be performed better. Asset management is quite complicated and should be scoped based on the potential impact of *not* doing it well. Many businesses still believe in silos: hardware and software. These businesses run the risk of missing the mark; it is the full combination of the two elements that represent risk.

If the objective is to account for all devices and the information they contain, asset management should be established so that the hardware and software compliance responsibilities reside in a single, enterprisewide organization. Risk cannot be spread by having multiple organizations share responsibilities that overlap.

Proactive asset management is the discipline of examining all the potential elements of lifecycle and determining the steps required for information capture. The flow of the work is important to manage from an access, information, software, and hardware perspective.

The impact of asset management is felt in all the lifecycle elements, so it must be performed well. As the other areas of lifecycle are explored, asset-management requirements should be identified. This is the optimal level of integration. Lifecycle-management elements can be optimized in many cases just by having more accurate information about the assets themselves.

Lifecycle management will likely become more complex as market dynamics change. As part of overall lifecycle management, asset-management rigor will therefore need to adapt, too. We are likely already seeing this today with the adoption rate of mobility. When businesses adopt devices today, they must determine how the new devices will be tracked and what tools and processes will be used. Reacting after the fact will prove costly.

SOFTWARE ASSET MANAGEMENT

Software asset management, although often linked to hardware asset management, has its own set of business implications and costs. As described in Chapter 4, "Acquiring Software," software represents the intellectual property to address business problems. Software is either assigned to an enterprise, a device, a site, or an individual. Sometimes the right to use the software applies to combination of these items. Businesses are offered, for a fee, a right under contractual terms and conditions, the right to use (license) the software.

The definition of software is important because it identifies the expectations that surround the usage of that license. These expectations include how and by whom software can be used. Software manufacturers generate their revenue and margins by expanding the use of their software and aggressively protect their intellectual property.

Enterprises that use the software also need to aggressively protect the software manufacturer's intellectual property as a basic tenant of the relationship. Closed loop lifecycle planning has a very fundamental assumption: that enterprises understand and are committed to use intellectual property appropriately and will take all necessary steps to protect their privilege to use the software. This is true for operating systems and for other business applications.

Software asset management is defined in closed loop lifecycle planning as the process used by an enterprise to appropriately control software licensing and related factors including costs. Because software is not a physical asset like hardware, and although the rigor is similar, the differences are more than subtle between software asset management and hardware asset management. The manner in which the software cost is incurred represents a much more definable cost than hardware.

Software asset management applies to all hardware devices (not only desktops and laptops) and is not restricted. Because software is a contractual license to use intellectual property, users assume a level of accountability by using the software.

NOTE: All software manufacturers reasonably expect businesses to apply asset management. A business should be aware of its software asset compliance as a part of intellectual property protection and should understand the cost implications and exposure that the lifecycle element represents.

HIGH-WATER MARKS

The *high-water mark* is a frequently used term in software asset management. It is not unusual for software license charges to be based on the number of client devices (seats). The basis for the calculation is set by the highest level of that metric during the course of a year. This highest level is identified as the high-water mark and represents the maximum number of users running the software product. This provides the software manufacturer license coverage for the greatest number of potential users of the software during the course of the year.

In some scenarios, software licenses are tied to a more static number as defined, for example, in the annual report, an agreed upon inventory, or employee levels. Usually there is a trigger, or tolerance, level that, if exceeded, calls for an incremental action. Software licenses could be decremented, but the high-water mark could mitigate that exposure contractually.

During acquisitions, divestitures, downsizing, or during periods of growth, software asset management becomes even more crucial. Licensing can quickly become a relevant variable cost.

It is absolutely critical that businesses fully understand software license agreements and the commitments and framework in effect.

SOFTWARE TITLES AND SOFTWARE MANUFACTURERS

Businesses quite often are unaware of the total number of software titles and the number of software manufacturers in the installed base. Part of the issue is the overall challenge to mange the environment so that these volumes can be regularly and appropriately reported.

It is somewhat easy to envision how many titles enter into the installed base. It is not unusual for in excess of 10,000 or more software titles and representing 3,000 or more manufacturers to reside within an installed base of greater than 10,000 seats. The numbers do indeed scale as the size of a business increases.

It is not enough just to process software asset-management reports. Resources must be applied and assigned the responsibility of reconciling the software titles and software manufacturers. Reports by themselves, without an action plan behind them, often serve no purpose. Although the reports might provide some comfort level, results could be misleading if the reports are not reconciled.

A number of software-metering and software-management tools and techniques are available for enterprises to use.

INVENTORY OFF-NETWORK

Work-in-process inventory and finished-goods inventory (which relate to staging and warehousing for client computing) generally count toward the software asset-management count. Often, these are overlooked because they are a part of the inventory control function that is not in the dynamic, networked asset-management process.

Another scenario is the population of standalone (un-networked) devices, such as training rooms or conference rooms (which might not be online). The key decision is whether those scenarios increment the asset count. The best guidance that can be provided in the inclusion/exclusion deliberation is to just ask yourself a question: If you were the software manufacturer, would these assets count? This question seems to be an easy one to answer.

OPERATING SYSTEMS

Operating systems represent the core of the software. From a costing, risk, and service-level perspective, retaining a single operating system is optimal for most businesses. Operating systems should be considered the building block or DNA of the core set of applications within an enterprise.

Other layered applications depend on the operating system for their software to function. Consistency within an operating system provides the best framework to build the lifecycle plan.

To asset manage the operating system, the asset records between hardware and software must be reconciled. This is one of the fundamentals of optimizing the installed base because all access devices are shipped with operating systems. This is the key linkage between hardware and software asset management.

ANTIVIRUS AND RELATED SYSTEM SOFTWARE

Similar to operating system software, antivirus and system software packages are generally, but not always, shipped with the hardware product. Usually antivirus and system software are parts of the core image. Because this is also part of the single common denominator, managing the hardware and the software asset-management records relate to the reconciliation of both domains.

ENTITLEMENTS

Software agreements address not only the basic licensing of the software, but also how the authority to use the software is conveyed. Software agreements also include a variety of entitlements that are either part of the licensing itself or available for an incremental fee. Eligibility for these capabilities is usually governed by volume, accounting, and reporting stipulations.

Whether a business is entitled to copy software, share documentation, or has rights to new versions and upgrades is not only a function of the contract, but also based on the business' ability to manage such distribution rights.

Agreements generally assume that businesses will comply with the terms and conditions and have the asset-management discipline to control what has been contractually committed. Although the intent might be there, the ability to comply is necessary, too. Just as with hardware asset management, software asset management is not optional.

Software rights are conveyed under strict trademark, patent, and copyright laws. Protection of intellectual property suggests that software rights need to be aggressively protected. Businesses that agree to use a software package agree to do this as part of the usage. Without effective software asset management, it is not clear how this commitment can be met.

THE AUDIT AND "TRUE UP"

Periodically, compliance audits are conducted by software manufacturers (and by both internal and external auditors). The objective of the audits is to confirm compliance with software agreements. Audits usually require documentation that the software has been acquired and is being managed as defined in the terms and conditions of the agreements. Audits test the high-water marks and usage parameters. An audit is always a compelling event and most always results in a "true up" (or formal reconciliation and payment).

"True up" is often an annual event, generally defined within an agreement. Audits, or the authority to conduct an audit, are generally conferred in that same agreement.

Software asset management is required to validate the number of licenses, versions, maintenance documentation, and overall entitlements. Without software asset management, the manual effort required to gather the source documentation on a timely basis would be extraordinarily onerous. Process, governance, and tools are required.

When hardware asset management is not at a high practice level, neither is software asset management. "True up" costs and penalties apply for not managing software in an enterprise. In the extreme case, violation of copyright and patent laws carries very strict penalties. Capabilities and requirements are (or should be) all known and understood up front. Therefore, software asset management is an enterprisewide requirement.

CASCADING

Cascading was discussed in detail in Chapter 7, "Moves, Adds, and Changes (MACs)." One of the challenges created by cascading is the tracking of licensing and related aspects of entitlements as systems are redeployed from end user to end user. Software asset management must be at a high practice level for cascading to be effective.

Many businesses view cascading from the hardware perspective only. The useful life of a PC is based on the ability to run the suite of software applications at certain speed, compliance, and standard levels. Included in this consideration is the ability to leverage existing licensing and entitlements. Although cascaded devices might not represent net new devices, they might not necessarily represent the same software product suite. Therefore, cascading places a burden on both hardware asset management and software assert management.

DATA MIGRATION

During cascading or during a net new installation, data is migrated from one access device to another. Early in this book, the question was raised whether access devices are exclusively for business or personal use, or whether these devices now represent a combination of the two usage models. Software asset management should have the capability to differentiate between business and personal applications.

As a general rule, if the device is in the installed base, paid for by the business, the business owns the responsibility for device compliance. If personal applications reside on or are otherwise used on the business owned computers, by default the business owns the compliance and cost aspects.

Note that having a governance model that prohibits personal applications from residing on a business-owned device does not mean that the enterprise is not accountable. Governance needs to be reported upon and enforceable to be effective.

During an access device migration, what is being moved from one device to another is known. Software supported by the enterprise and part of the software asset-management portfolio should be the only software migrated until the reconciliation occurs. Software assets outside of this scope should be identified and reported as exceptions and excluded.

HARVESTING LICENSES

As access devices are decommissioned and eventually retired, software licenses should be recaptured as a part of the "harvesting" process. Licenses that reside on the devices should be accounted for and included in the decrementing of the asset count. This decrementing should include not only the licenses but also all the entitlements attributed to the user. The "harvesting" addresses whether the business has the privilege of reuse of the licenses and privileges.

Because some businesses are not operating at a high practice level for end-of-life access activities, there is a tendency to believe automatically that the business is overlicensed. Without a closed loop lifecycle planning methodology in place, this assumption may, or may not, be valid.

Recordkeeping for disposition is an important element for lifecycle management. (It is important enough to be mentioned throughout this book.) Licenses can be "harvested" only if the records to back up the reconciliation are known and available. Software asset management is the methodology that enables the recapture of the software license. For businesses that refresh the desktops and laptops at 20 percent to 30 percent (or more) annually, "harvesting" is not an option; it is a requirement to ensure that the high-water mark is not excessive and that the net new devices, cascades, retirements, and static inventories are reflected in the software asset-management workflow.

SAME PURPOSE, DIFFERENT SOFTWARE

Many businesses find themselves in a position in which they have several software packages that perform similar functions. In many of these cases, the installed base contains multiple versions of the same software packages. The costs for these decisions (very likely not consciously made) can be quite high. The logical question to ask is this: What occurred to create this set of circumstances? In most cases, it is just a question of resources.

As stated many times in this book, it is not enough just to generate reports. Resources must be allocated to analyze the output. This analysis includes reviewing new software titles to ascertain whether existing packages in the installed base perform a similar function. The software-acquisition process presents an opportune time to examine the request. When the software title is already in the installed base, the consideration should be to reconcile titles so that the sheer number of titles can be optimized.

There will always be times when end-user choice or business-unit choice determines that software titles be acquired. The point here is that these need to be conscious decisions. The objective is not to necessarily decrease titles, but to ensure that the titles are appropriate and that a duplication of work is not being performed. More titles do necessarily imply more costs and complexity.

Because a majority of the costs are borne by IT in delivering service levels to end users, the impact overall of licensing, maintenance, version control, multiple packages, different terms, and patches may not seem to be important to the businesses outside of IT. However, at the enterprise level, service levels can be significantly impacted if these titles expand to a point of concern and cost.

NOTE: Many businesses do not have a process to determine the optimization of the software titles and manufacturers in its installed base. As a result, many businesses now have identified software rationalization as a major program to address the software asset-management issues.

MANAGEMENT TOOLS

Software asset-management tools have significantly matured and are now at price points that reflect higher adoption rates. Affordability is less of an issue than ever before. Tools are quite robust and are likely part of an overall modular suite of client management for enterprises. If not, most of the software asset-management tools can be integrated into other databases and toolsets.

Historically, one of the rationales for not having a compelling business case for software asset management was the actual cost of the software itself. The financial justification for the business case was more a function of perceived "soft" dollar impact and not balance sheet or income statement impact. Therefore, software asset management was low on the priority list, and many businesses simply deferred to manual processes or spreadsheets.

Business units outside of the centralized enterprise developed their own processes and tools that then became part of the political structure, and silos were created. Business units developed their own solutions to address compliance issues.

Still other businesses, observing at a particular moment that the functionality of the available software and the price points were not at a point that allowed the business to embrace the software, developed their own software (and hardware) management tools. Thus began an era in client lifecycle management of custom toolsets.

At that time, addressing the requirements by creating the software solutions in-house was perhaps the only way that businesses could be compliant and appropriately manage the PC and application fleet. At that time, it was also not fully clear when the market itself would catch up to the demands of the requirements being defined in the industry. Although a lot of tools were available, businesses believed that there was a wide range of requirements that only they could understand. For many years, this was the perspective.

In the 1990s, however, a peculiar set of circumstances occurred. The adoption of access devices became pervasive, the numbers of users increased, and the PC became ubiquitous. New access devices, more frequent refreshes, and more-sophisticated users resulted. But yet, there was another key dynamic: Software became as important (and some would say even more important) than the hardware it resided on.

New regulations were passed requiring higher levels of integrity in personal information, licensing, and governance. In a rather short period of time, software asset management, and the related toolsets for patch management and security, matured.

Software research and development paid off in new and comprehensive software, modular in design and architecture, and the affordability model was made easier by the tone and implications of the laws and regulations.

Given the fundamental change in market dynamics, even those large investments in custom applications that were made historically now needed to be integrated into a standard framework so that financial, operational, and compliance reporting could be optimized. The traditional perspective of "buy versus make" changed when the rules and regulations changed, but also when the number and nature of access devices changed.

This is now the environment that we find ourselves in today. Software asset-management tools have become so pervasive that the cost of change perceived to exist when migrating from a custom tool to a standard tool may be mitigated. Politics and culture aside, the fundamental business case has changed. Businesses are finding that retaining custom software to perform repetitive and compliant functions may, or may not be, the optimal solution that it was only a few years ago.

For businesses that reorganize, grow, divest, or acquire, migrating custom asset-management tools may add more complexity. No one had a crystal ball and could have seen the quantum improvements in software and how quickly these changes would occur. This does not mean that a bad decision was made; remember, there is no right or wrong in lifecycle—only conscious and unconscious decisions.

SUMMARY

Businesses are recognizing that asset management is one of the building blocks of lifecycle management. Without asset management at a reasonably mature practice level, the benefits of overall lifecycle management might not be achievable.

The quantification or business case for asset management has been simplified by understanding that exposure and risks are frequently the result of not knowing where an access device is or who has control over that access device. As accounts in the media about security breaches and business accountability become almost daily occurrences, the requirement for asset management will be more easily understood.

The quality of asset management does have a direct impact on other lifecycle functions and operations. Optimization will be difficult to attain if the investment in asset management is not made by a business.

Asset management is enabled today by the maturity of management tools (and the affordability of those tools) and the enhancements in the hardware products, which can and will have embedded characteristics for asset management. Asset management is likely in its most dynamic state ever, giving businesses the potential for greater control over their installed base.

10

The Help Desk

INTRODUCTION

The help desk can and should be the lifecycle element that is the first line of contact with the IT infrastructure for problem support and resolution. The help desk is a remote set of resources accessed by a number of means (but usually by phone) that are available to end users during certain hours of availability to answer and respond to IT questions that may arise.

The help desk is one of the fundamental aspects of lifecycle management and is a function in which the competency level needs to be high to satisfy the requirements of the installed base of end users. The help desk hours are variable from business to business, and can range from 24x7 to a weekly window excluding weekends.

The help desk is also important because to many end users and managers, it represents the initial contact with IT, and opinions are formed relating to the quality and services that IT can provide. An on-site help desk is a help desk where the resources are located on the business' premise. On-site may refer to both an insourced, out-tasked, or out-sourced help desk. An in-house help desk generally is defined as an insourced model.

The help desk has gone through many changes in recent times and is now enabled through comprehensive suites of software that make the delivery of end-user support more seamless than ever before. Despite this impact, just as with many of the lifecycle elements, there is a wide range of practice levels, service-delivery alternatives, and enabling software that makes the help desk unique in its construct.

It is in the help desk environment where the implications of other lifecycle elements are felt. Having more software packages, for example, results in the help desk requirement to be competent on more packages than ever before. Older client devices require experience in older operating systems and software applications. With the access device portfolio changing and the number and types of access devices varying, the help desk needs to have expertise in more than just desktops and laptops and the applications that reside on those devices.

The profile of the calls has changed, as has the level of competency of those individuals initiating the help desk call itself. The help desk is a true representation of how well certain other lifecycle elements are being managed and is a fundamental indicator of the overall lifecycle experience a business may have. The help desk is exclusively focused on the end user and the experience.

In all the closed loop lifecycle planning engagements I've been involved in (well over 200 at the time of this writing), the help desk remains one of the best indicators to assess overall lifecycle management.

HOW MANY HELP DESKS SHOULD AN ENTERPRISE HAVE?

Although the question of how many help desks a business retains might seem like almost a superficial question, the responses are often surprising. Help desks, like all other infrastructures, sometimes are created to immediately respond to particular business problems. Business units, often not wanting to await an IT assessment or a "lengthy" process, sometimes elect to address the problems themselves.

Partially as a result of this behavior, and as a result of the ability to pay or fund such a decision, in many scenarios there are clearly more help desks than one would expect.

User segmentation does play a role in the creation of help desks. Certain segments that have different applications than other end users or maybe a different service level may have created solutions as designed for their segment's access. It is not unusual for the sales force, executives, expert users, and others to have a unique help desk, or at least a higher/different service level within the help desk.

One of the important cost considerations regarding the help desk, however, is the ability to amortize all the start-up costs to the cost per call of the help desk. Therefore, a help desk consolidation effort is now occurring in most businesses, recognizing that help desks can now (through software and other rigor) support multiple user profiles; this might not have been the case before.

An overview of the help desk is not complete without a discussion about how the help desk applies to the executive segment. Typically, executives call a *remote* help desk for support. Therefore, the "help desk" for the executives often takes the form of dedicated desk-side support teams that are available to the executives to focus on this segment's needs. This is neither good nor bad, just another conscious business decision.

The implication of this decision is that the executive level might not know, appreciate, or understand the dynamics of the help desk as it applies to other end users. In this scenario, the perceptions of others that are communicated to executives reflect on IT and the help desk with no direct validation.

In some businesses, the executive profile might extend to quite a number of managers, so it is important to understand the importance of expectations and the variance in perceptions.

KEY METRICS FROM THE HELP DESK CAN BE A WINDOW INTO THE CURRENT STATE OF THE INSTALLED BASE

The help desk software generates a solid amount of data and reporting back to the management team that can be used for a wide variety of purposes. This information is important in setting future planning and to improve the end-user experience and for IT to better understand what dynamics are occurring in the installed base. Most help desk software packages in use today have these types of statistics available for consideration.

For comparative purposes, it is often useful to look at the statistics year to year to get a sense of what drivers might have changed over the past 12 months. The same set of statistics can then be reviewed for the past 90 days to observe trends that might be occurring in the installed base. The types of calls being received may reflect new systems being implemented, changes in reporting requirements for systems, or other normal business changes. The statistics gathered should be used to improve help desk resources, provide end-user training, or other actions, all of which should be viewed positively.

Just as with asset management, statistics generated but not reconciled or studied do not really add value. Resources need to review the information and ascertain whether any actionable strategies can be developed. It might also prove useful to have various stakeholders beyond the help desk personnel review the output so that the information can be directly related to the business operations that they are closest to in the field.

Too often, reviewers are the generators of the statistics, and it is believed that there is a goodness or badness associated with the information. Therefore, the information begins to have interpretations that might not be relevant to the end users or businesses.

It is important for businesses to define all metrics that are tracked and reported. Statistics should not have multiple interpretations.

NUMBER OF CALLS

The number of help desk calls is a solid indicator of the stability of the installed base. The number of calls from end users can be anticipated, and generally approach one per end user per month. If the number is higher or lower substantially from this premise, research can be performed to understand what dynamic is occurring.

The number of help desk calls is also important for a variety of other reasons. The cost per call, for example, reflects the number of calls that the infrastructure and overhead can handle. The number of help desk calls can also indicate other decisions, such as multiple applications, a program problem, or an older PC fleet inventory. The root cause definitions are actionable items that should improve help desk and end-user productivity, one key benefit of the help desk.

FIRST-CALL RESOLUTION

The *first-call resolution rate* is defined as solving the event that triggered the actual call itself. Resolution implies that the issue is solved and not escalated. It is important for businesses to have solid definitions for the terms included in all the metrics.

First-call resolution means that the ticket that opened the call is fully resolved; no follow-up is required. The ticket is closed, and another is opened if there is a follow-up issue to address. All issues relating to a ticket should be considered an integral part of the event and reflected in the ticket.

Another consideration when assessing the resolution rate is reconciling items. The reporting of first-call resolution rates should be self-evident; there should not be any requirement for anything except for the definition. If there are reconciling items, such as follow-on tickets or other action created by addressing the initial ticket, this should not qualify for first-call resolution.

Credibility is lost when resolution rates have reconciling items. This scenario should be avoided at all cost because it immediately impacts the credibility of all the other statistics presented. To ensure the credibility of the process, first-call resolution claims should be agreed upon by the caller.

Diagnose-before-Dispatch (DBD) Tools

DBD tools play an important part of the help desk's ability to close calls. For first-call resolution, DBD provides the basic questions that need to be asked to address the event that triggered the call. For escalations, it is the DBD that ensures that, if a desk-side support call is required, the engineer or desk-side support resource understands the skills set, parts, and other items needed to resolve an event.

For hardware calls, all manufacturers have mature and quite sophisticated DBD tools. This is indeed one of the key differentiators and is covered in detail in Chapter 8, "Warranty and Maintenance."

For software and other items, DBD often takes the form of a series of questions or stable-state discussions that serve to define the problem in enough detail that it can be passed on to another level with sufficient detail that another call is not required to ask fundamental questions. Asset-management information is crucial to a successful DBD process.

DBD tools today are advancing to the point that knowledge-based tools can provide immediate access for recurring problems or take the help desk personnel and escalation teams through the series of questions that assist in the framing of the resolution. This area is a growth area of the help desk technologies, and will most likely be fully represented in the next generation of help desks.

TOP TEN CALLS

When reviewing the help desk, it is always an excellent idea to ask for the top ten calls that they have received. One of the reasons for asking for call statistics year to year is to ascertain whether the call mix has changed. This can also ensure that the skill sets and tools are adequate to address issues as they arise.

It is interesting that the top ten calls, as follows (in no priority order), are generally consistent between businesses:

- Password reset (number one in almost every business)
- Printer locked
- Computer locked
- Shrink-wrapped software, "how to" questions
- Warranty/maintenance questions
- Provisioning
- Custom application questions
- Status questions
- Networking issues/connectivity
- Configuration issue

If the top ten changes, the profile of the call and support will likely change, too. Implementing changes to address the top ten calls will improve everyone's productivity within the enterprise.

ABANDON RATE

The abandon rate is the number of calls that do not get answered by the help desk. While the telephone is still ringing, the end user hangs up. All incoming calls into the help desk can be tracked in this manner. An abandon rate (to a certain extent) is normal; end users might get impatient, there might be a distraction while the phone is ringing, or there might be other valid reasons why the call itself was not completed.

In some cases, the ringing just goes on too long, or the calls are not answered for some reason, and the end user just terminates the call by conscious choice. The number of rings before pick up is another typical help desk metric that clearly impacts abandon rate.

When considering abandon rates, businesses must consider all these previously described scenarios. End-users expectation is an important factor.

Whether an abandonment rate is acceptable can be monitored. The industry ranges from 3 percent to 7 percent typically. It is important to remember who the end users are and what the statistics represent. If a mission-critical user abandons the call, there are generally implications from the event.

Just as other statistics, it is important that abandon rates be viewed over time. Although the weighted average might be in the acceptable range, there may very well be periods of time when the abandon rate is excessive, but the average does not trigger an analysis.

At times, such as a major deployment, the abandon rate is impacted. Peak times might occur, too. To the end users, those are IT issues, and the level of empathy might not be as high as anticipated.

It is also important to understand the impact of the abandon rate on other help desk metrics. Let's suppose that the first-call resolution rate is 80 percent. Let's further assume that the abandon rate is 7 percent. What this really means is that of the 93 percent of the calls that were completed, the first-call resolution rate is less than 80 percent.

Sometimes it proves useful to look at absolute numbers to gain an appreciation of the dynamics. Percentages are fine, but percentages often supply only a part of the story. In this hypothetical scenario, let's further assume that the call volume is 20,000 calls. The business case now looks like this:

Call volume = 20,000

First-call resolution rate = 80 percent

Abandon rate = 7 percent

In this scenario, the number of calls that did not get to the help desk, which is included in the 20,000 call volume number, totals 1,400 calls. Therefore, calls that could possibly be resolved on the first call are not 20,000 calls, but 18,600 calls.

The difference in the number of actual calls resolved is not 16,000 calls, but rather 14,880 calls. The difference is 1,120 calls resolved.

This brief example points out the importance of what is included in the statistics provided and the impact of interpretation of the information. Also, when you look at the absolute numbers, although 7 percent might not seem like much, perhaps 1,400 contacts could represent significance.

Remember that the help desk is the first impression many end users have of IT. The person whose call is abandoned does not care about the statistics.

DURATION OF CALLS

After the help desk picks up a call, the question becomes this: How long is the call. It is difficult to extrapolate on this point because some help desk calls can be quite lengthy and skew the overall averages reported.

If we assume that the duration of the help desk call is from five minutes to seven minutes, it is likely that most calls will fall into this range. With these types of metrics in place, improvements can be much more easily tracked than with more subjective approaches.

The goal should be to have the help desk call be as short as possible with the highest resolution rates. The availability of asset-management information, user profiles, and other mainstream techniques makes the help desk experience much more positive and shorter.

ESCALATIONS

Calls that are not first-call resolution are escalated. It is important to understand the nature and category of the call to know where to route the call for resolution. This is one of the areas where knowledge-based toolsets are favorably impacting the ability of the help desk to escalate faster and with much more accuracy.

The second- and third-level escalations for hardware and software should be predefined and the workflow architected so that calls can be tracked. Higher escalations can also represent more severity. Severity codes are a system that permits the assigning of impact to the end user and the installed base predicated upon a set of criteria. This denotes the maturity that the help desk discipline has now reached.

In all enterprises, regardless of size, automated help desk tools and alternative service-delivery strategies are available. Just as with asset management, pricing no longer represents an obstacle for entry.

REPORTING

Help desks should prepare a standard reporting schedule (weekly, monthly, quarterly, and year to year, for example). The reporting should be repetitive and not require a significant amount of effort to generate or customize if additional information is required to make business decisions. The package should be readily and easily available for all interested constituencies, including IT, business units, divisions, and end users.

Various reporting software packages are available, all with robust reporting capabilities. Businesses need to internalize that the help desk objectives include not only resolving issues and events as they occur, but also a decision to support software that facilitates improvement in the environment. Reports should be shared with managers outside of IT to ensure that there is no disconnect between the numbers and the perception of service.

COST PER CALL

Each help desk call costs something. Many businesses report the cost per call, but fail to include what cost elements are included in the cost build-up. Like any bill of material, it is important to understand what is included and what is excluded.

In the industry, the desire is to have a fully loaded cost per call. Specifically, that implies that all related costs—including individual contributors, managers, supervisors, contactors, software, networking, telecommunications, facilities, and all infrastructure costs—are included. The objective is not to have exclusions that then become reconciling items to the cost per call.

When senior and middle management look at the cost figures, generally the exceptions (that is, what is excluded) are not presented. Therefore, it is assumed that the cost per call reflects the complete loading of the costs. This may, or may not, be a fair assumption, so there needs to be a clear definition from the beginning setting forth the inclusions.

The cost per call can frequently be a bit challenging to calculate. Certain incremental costs—networking, software, telecommunications, and such—are often amortized over a period of time. When the cost per call is then compared to an industry-standard figure, the question that arises is this: Which components are being compared, and if estimated, what assumptions build the cost model?

NOTE: Businesses need to exercise caution when estimating the cost per call, first to ensure that all cost elements are captured, and second to understand what those costs are being compared to.

END-USER SATISFACTION

A fundamental aspect of the help desk is always an end-user satisfaction metric. End-user satisfaction is critical to manage and influences end users' perception of IT. To ensure that expectations are properly set on both sides, end users must know what the help desk goals are.

Measuring end-user satisfaction is a challenge. There are many ways to assess end-user satisfaction. The most common way to assess end-user satisfaction is via an end-user survey. These surveys are sent out after the help desk call has been completed. The survey might be a mailing to all those within the installed base who have contacted the help desk or to a subset of that population.

A series of questions are asked, and a rating scale (1 to 5) is often used to rate the service provided.

Another technique is the balanced scorecard. The balanced scorecard takes into consideration the customer-satisfaction scores, but also includes many of the defined metrics that the help desk is to be measured on. For example, should the population of abandoned calls be surveyed regarding their satisfaction? How the calls are selected—first-, second-, and third-level escalations—could be a predictor of how those end users will rate the service provided.

There is always a population of end users who will not respond to surveys, good input or bad. However, someone who has had a poor experience is more likely to want to talk about that experience (human nature being what it is).

The point to be made is that there is not one answer to the metrics and measurement of customer satisfaction. Generally, a number of factors go into the overall satisfaction metric.

NUMBER OF RINGS BEFORE PICK UP

The inclusion of this point in the discussion of help desk topics is to demonstrate that sometimes it is indeed the less-obvious items that can impact the most.

The number of times a help desk telephone rings before the call is picked up is a key decision, even though it seems minor. Often, it is not the help desk agent who picks up the phone but an automated responder, defining the wait time and thanking the end user for the call.

Even though this is an automated function, the less the wait time, the faster the caller can decide to remain on the line or have expectations set as to when the agent will speak to the caller. Callers appreciate the insight and believe that by setting expectations, there is a definite plan behind the coverage model.

Availability of the Help Desk

At one time, the general assumption was that help desks were available 24x7. The reason behind establishing these help desk parameters was that if there was a "chance" that end users might require support, the support would be in place.

As reporting became more available, and costs became associated with help desk support, businesses began to examine help desk usage more closely. Many businesses concluded that the coverage was not optimal and that the coverage parameters were too robust. (This is not true for all businesses, of course.)

From a business standpoint, it was clear that there were simply fewer help desk events on the weekends. The infrastructure costs to retain full staffing for the help desk became prohibitive, given the usage model. This conclusion demonstrates the benefits of having reports generated.

Support parameters for after-hours and weekend coverage can now be based on historical usage. The 24x7 model, although still an option for many businesses, is an elective support model and is charged at a premium cost to end users.

As other service-delivery alternatives have become more mainstream, such as self-help, the requirement for 24x7 and weekend coverage models has been redefined.

DOWNTIME

For a long period of time, downtime was considered a "soft" cost and not a cost that could be quantified and measured. Although this is just not true today, downtime was historically a difficult factor on which to base investments.

Downtime represents the inability to use the client assets assigned to the end users. It is not productivity, a separate topic and impact; downtime is more often an event that triggers the inability to perform work itself. In that respect, downtime differs from productivity (which concerns incremental gains in work).

User segmentation has resulted in some of the ability to quantify downtime, simply by profiling the obvious groups impacted and assessing the results of their work. The results have been translated to the overall installed base as a group. Although downtime costs vary among the installed base users, it is a common denominator.

Downtime is important to the help desk in assessing the impact of the help desk call on the end user and the installed base.

Consider this example. Let's assume that the end user is a sales professional. If the sales professional cannot generate quotes and proposals, the ability to close business and generate revenue for the company is immediately impacted. The longer downtime lasts, the less revenue-generating activities can occur.

Suppose the sales professional is to generate $1,000,000 in revenue per year. Divide that by 365 days (not necessarily business days), and you understand that downtime can be represented as $2,739 for each day. When weekends are adjusted and then actual workdays, the impact becomes more obvious.

Another example will further illustrate the potential cost of downtime. In the financial industry segment, an agent needs to be online for research, events, contact, and the actual order placement. In many cases, the orders can be for both buying and selling. Any downtime will impact one of the activities that a trader may perform. In the case of a transaction, even a slight delay could translate into millions of dollars.

If a stock is trading at $20 per share on a basis of 30,000 shares (or $600,000), and the transaction is delayed because of downtime and the stock loses 50 cents, the financial impact is $15,000. Although this example is quite basic, it highlights the point that downtime is not a "soft" cost.

Where the help desk fits into this equation is that the resolution time is a key metric. Escalation and severity policies seek to minimize downtime for all end users, but in particular those end users for whom downtime is mission critical and no downtime is reasonable. Although there will be other service-delivery and service-level considerations, the help desk's fundamental role remains the reporting and mitigating of the events.

NOTE: In closed loop lifecycle planning, downtime is *not* a "soft" cost. Downtime can be quantified, tracked, and measured. Businesses should consider making downtime a fundamental lifecycle metric.

STEALTH IT

The help desk is one of the factors in the formation of Stealth IT; end users do not call into the help desk because local resources are available to answer questions and provide local support.

Stealth IT can develop its own localized IT solutions that to a significant degree compete with the enterprisewide IT organization. The investment can be as nominal as best-effort support as required for the establishment of business unit databases or as specific as resources that scale within the business unit.

Some level of Stealth IT will always exist. It is when Stealth IT becomes considerable in scope and issues are blocked from root cause analysis that Stealth IT should be a concern. For issues that may develop across the entire installed base, Stealth IT is an issue.

One of the questions regarding Stealth IT is this: To whom do the resources that assist report? If these resources are trained and an extension of the IT functions, that is one scenario; if these are truly power or knowledge workers, however, the question is how they are investing their time.

Having the help desk be the focal point for all events is not a political issue; such a decision is made so that there is a record and history of events. Under a Stealth IT situation, it is not possible to perform root cause analysis because the events are unreported.

POLITICS AND ORGANIZATIONAL BEHAVIOR

The help desk seems to be one of the most politically charged elements of the life-cycle. Help desks are often managed by a team outside of the overall IT team, and perhaps that is a source of the dilemma. Help desk statistics often reflect what is and is not working effectively in IT, and perhaps that is an issue.

Another potential source of the politics is that the help desk "touches" an event and often delegates to other IT resources, and perhaps that too is another reason for the politics: the competition between the teams.

Whatever the reason, the maturity of the organizations is without doubt weighed down by the politics between the teams. Even when the team reports fully to IT, there is often an edge to the relationship.

When considering why this dynamic exists, you have only to understand that the relationship is based more on who performs certain work, in contrast to the service levels that all resources are committed to provide. Many times, there are separate metrics rather than an overall set of common metrics. If the help desk scores well and the desk-side support team does not, a clear win-lose relationship and competition develop (with regard to end-user satisfaction).

If the metrics are shared metrics based on an IT satisfaction level, however, to some degree the competition is lessened.

The first step is recognizing that elements of politics and organizational behavior exist. The second is to consciously decide to let the dynamics flow or proactively attempt to manage the impact. Many businesses see the relationship as complementary; others consider the politics as something to avoid. At the end of the day, IT as a discipline does not present the single face to the end user, and that is the critical impact of the politics.

END-USER SELF-HELP

One of the most significant advances in the near term for help desks will be more adoption of end-user self-help. The tools required for this are increasingly becoming mainstream. In previous chapters, you've read about the "death" of the casual user. The new end users come to their jobs with more PC literacy than ever before and a consumer experience that often rivals the enterprise infrastructure.

End-user adoption of self-help tools have often lagged. Why use a self-help tool if a resource is available for an end user to ask for help. Response times were reasonable, and the cost was transparent to the end user.

Today, certain end users prefer to perform at least some self-diagnosis. Frequently asked questions (FAQs) are often posted to intranet sites so that end users can attain quick and reliable answers.

In addition, access to help desk personnel requires a certain wait period (even if the phones are promptly answered), and the end user could already be "surfing" for the answer.

As the adoption rates improve and the quality of the software increases (and the costs decline), more end users will be comfortable with the self-help model. Most businesses would be pleased if in certain categories the self-help model becomes the desired way to address issues and events.

In the past, self-help tools were applied to a wide variety of problems, instead of a single issue. Perhaps this is one of the reasons that adoption as the standard was not as fast as IT would have hoped for. This evolving solution will be a factor moving forward.

NOTE: With end users becoming more comfortable with access technologies, it is likely that adoption of self-help tools will dramatically increase in the near term. The determining factor could be IT's desire to relinquish a level of control to the end users, not the end user's willingness to embrace self-help. This represents a significant change in perspective.

SERVICE-DELIVERY STRATEGIES

In the past, the help desk was often seen as one of the elements to retain in-house. After all, why wouldn't a business want to have the initial contact with its end users? As the industry and businesses matured, there was more focus on the service level than on the relationship. At this point, alternative service-delivery strategies became viable.

In the help desk environment, there are fundamentally three service-delivery strategies, each with its own advantages and disadvantages. The fourth alternative always exists: a hybrid of the available strategies.

Businesses need to decide consciously which strategy is the most viable to deliver end-user support. Unlike other decisions, the decision to enter or exit the help desk operation for client computing is a strategic decision, not tactical. The entrance and exit costs are significant and usually imply a larger set of changes than the delivery alternative.

The three service delivery strategies are as follows:

- Insource
- Out-task
- Outsource

The following sections discuss these three alternatives in more detail.

INSOURCE

Insourcing refers to retaining the lifecycle element (in this case, the help desk) internally. The labor, management, supervisors, and tools are retained by the enterprise. All the content and service levels are provided internally by IT, and the ownership resides with IT management.

OUT-TASK

Out-tasking is the shorter-term (typically three years) horizon that a business will use to implement lifecycle practices and determine at a later time whether to extend the term of the relationship, or bring the practice in-house. Another alternative after out-tasking is to decide to exit the business in the longer term (outsourcing).

Out-tasking has become a popular model because it can be more of an interim approach, deferring decisions while acquiring the practice levels. Sometimes the help desk calls can be separated so that the repetitive calls—usually for shrink-wrapped applications and break/fix calls—can be handled for less cost.

Other businesses decide to exit the level 1 call. Specifically, this means that the flexibility can exist to handle the variations in call volume by agreeing to a service level delivered remotely. This model is becoming increasingly popular because this is where the timeliness of the response and the predictability of the service level can most easily be secured.

OUTSOURCE

Some businesses decide that the help desk business is not a core competency and decide to exit that business completely. The term is typically a five- to seven-year (or greater) duration. In this scenario, the business is completely handed over to an outsourcing company that fully performs all the help desk functions (and usu-ally more of the lifecycle functions, too).

Outsourcing works well in those environments where the business decides it is time to exit. If there is a hesitation, the outsourcing is usually not fully successful.

NOTE: Many businesses are considering or have implemented "offshore" outsourcing as a part of the IT delivery plan. The costs implications are well known and frequently dramatic. It is worthwhile for all businesses to explore this alternative in the context of overall lifecycle management.

AUTOMATED CALL DISTRIBUTION (ACD)

ACDs can be viewed as either a terrific innovation or an obstacle depending on the point of view. ACDs are the automated voice responses that all of us as consumers and as internal help desk users interface with daily.

The IT perspective is that ACDs can immediately answer the phone call, set expectations on when help desk agents will be available, assist with authentication that the end user is entitled to contact the help desk, and ask preliminary ques-tions (answered by voice or by number) to identify the type of problem. ACDs can also advise callers of websites where FAQs or self-help may be available. Finally, if there is a system outage or a known issue, the ACD can acknowledge the issue.

All these ACD functions just described are positive and result in the least-cost alternative in advising and managing the help desk, but there is a downside. By leveraging more automation, it might be possible to reduce help desk headcount, which perhaps translates into longer wait times. This could then result in a longer time to resolution and the related end-user satisfaction issues that may arise.

The biggest impact might be a bit more subtle. When an event prompts an end user to call for support, it is logical to assume there is a bit of energy, anxiety, or at least some level of tension. If instead of talking to an individual, there is what seems to be an endless stream of dialogues with a computer (which must be responded to before the user can chat with a help desk agent), frustration could easily set in.

This is somewhat of the backlash to the technology. If there is to be a set of prompts, the architects need to balance the need of the end user to achieve some level of support with the need of IT to delay the support until there is availability.

DEPENDENCY ON ASSET MANAGEMENT

The help desk depends significantly on asset management, both for hardware and software. The first part of all help desk calls, to understand what the stable state of the system is, is to ascertain the source of the call. Having the user profile and asset-management information available to the help desk agent initially will save time and decrease the number of questions that the agent needs to ask.

The first minute or so of a help desk call could easily be reduced via asset-management reporting that enables data gathering and availability of that information to the agent. The more information that the agent receives up front, the more precise the discussion can be regarding the actual problem that initiated the call.

In the help desk scenario, the time to solution and the duration of the call are key metrics. An asset-management practice level that is high reduces the duration of the call.

This dependency is one of the reasons that when the decision is reached by a business to outsource the help desk, asset management outsourcing is often suggested by the service providers. Having this lifecycle element as a part of the portfolio will improve the ability of the help desk and enhance the overall service experience. Accurate caller profiles improve call resolution and give end-users more confidence in the system.

SERVICE LEVELS

The help desk, as all lifecycle elements, is driven by service levels and defined metrics. Frequently, end users and field organizations are unaware of the service levels. The service levels include abandon rate, call pick up, DBD rates, first-call resolution rates, escalations, and so forth.

When end users are not aware of the service levels, it is virtually impossible to exceed expectations because there are no expectations initially set. This implies that, at best, a help desk experience will meet the requirement. In most cases, it is likely that some aspect could be performed better or faster if the end user has no other expectations.

Service levels must be communicated to the population being supported for the service levels to be relevant to the end users. This might explain why a balanced scorecard is needed when assessing end-user satisfaction. Consciously or not, end users compare their experiences with help desks within their IT department with their experiences as consumers.

The help desk is one of the few lifecycle elements that truly needs to be promoted. A communications plan and market feedback are important elements of success.

CONTINUOUS PROCESS IMPROVEMENT

Closed loop lifecycle planning has a specific definition for continuous process improvement (CPI). Continuous process improvement refers to the plans of record to reduce costs, avoid costs, improve quality, and improve service levels (in this case, the help desk).

In help desk operations, the key is to identify how to reduce costs by leveraging different service alternatives, such as self-help, knowledge base, and service-delivery strategies (such as the handling of shrink-wrapped "how to" questions). The key to the CPI plan, however, is to best understand how to stop the event from being a help desk call in the first place.

As self-help becomes adopted more widely and the hardware continues to be more modular and reliable, these help desk calls will be avoided. In the near term, as the DBD and knowledge base becomes mainstream, the help desk will clearly be favorably impacted.

Perhaps the most significant impact will be derived from the maturity of management tools that enable self-healing remotely. In a short period of time, as technology becomes more modular, users become even more sophisticated, and software tools become yet more comprehensive, IT support as it is known today will change.

When remote software was developed that permitted the help desk to secure control of an end user's desktop or laptop to perform diagnostics and repair, this was seen as revolutionary. It was actually evolutionary.

The evolution of the help desk, and IT support in general, has mirrored the developments of the consumer market to a significant degree.

THE EVOLUTION CONTINUES

As one thinks about the future of IT services and the help desk in particular, it becomes clear that in the near term, more self-help and remote services will become the norm. With the advent of self-healing and remote sessions, potentially with video, there will clearly be a new generation of lifecycle-management practices.

The remote-control sessions and the advances in software have already changed the help desk operations in the basics of how the help desk responds. It is highly likely that the support model will advance more to a delivery model that embraces more of the deliverables defined by the maturity of networking and management tools.

From a business viewpoint, the terms *help desk, service desk,* and *call center* will all merge. As the traditional internal help desk secures more capacity because of improvements in technology, process, and tools, the impact will allow the resources to expand the types of support offered.

There will be a more expansive service portfolio and a commingling of customers and end users. This suggests that there will be technology and business drivers that will frame the evolution of the help desk.

A trend has been identified in businesses requesting access and integration into the manufacturers' level 2 and level 3 support resources. This trend strengthens the business case for selecting manufacturers that have a global, robust infrastructure. This strategy will further improve resolution rates and create a much tighter linkage among a business' supplier base.

Many businesses have different definitions of what precisely level 2 and level 3 help desk support and escalation represents. If an issue cannot be resolved by the incoming help desk agent, it is escalated to a defined level 2 resource. Depending on the organizational structure, size, and other considerations, the second and third level can be various individuals or even third parties. The second-level help desk is considered dispatch for hardware-related issues. For software-related issues, the second level could be software developers, application owners, or in-house resources.

Level 3 resources are the experts in the particular area of escalation. For example, if the issue appears to be a particular software application and the in-house experts cannot address the root cause, it might be that level-three resources are the software manufacturer. If the escalation is in reference to a custom application, the software developer who wrote the code itself might be part of the escalation.

SUMMARY

The help desk will emerge as one of the keys in reducing the costs to deliver life-cycle-management services. Businesses have recognized that the more resolution that can occur remotely, the less the cost to deliver the services. Desk-side support will become more of an exception (in contrast to being the standard manner of delivering support).

To continue in the progression, more self-healing, self-help, and diagnostics will be required; this is occurring at the time of this writing.

Simultaneously, the cost to deliver the service itself is declining as a result of various service-delivery alternatives and a higher scaling and level of core competency of service providers.

The help desk statistics give businesses an excellent picture of the state of the installed base, which can be an actionable set of reporting.

As the help desk evolves, the capabilities will become more accessible to the end users in more of a self-help catalog of services. Because of the help desk advances combined with user segmentation (as discussed later in this book), the enterprise will be able to manage its support portfolio more as a variable cost than today.

11

Program Management

INTRODUCTION

Program management is the "glue" that holds the lifecycle-management solution together. One of the conclusions from the closed loop lifecycle planning research is that lifecycle management is a program. Lifecycle management delivers the best set of economics and services to the end-user segments based on the scope of the solution. However, to deliver the solution, program management is required.

Program management represents the high-level coordination and integration of the disparate lifecycle operations into a single solution set. Program management is the single point of contact and accountability for the lifecycle-management solution. In the research performed, I noted that businesses that did not make this investment or embrace this concept had substantial problems in the achievement of their goals.

Delivery of the lifecycle solution is complex. The complexity comes from not only the size and scope of the engagements, but also from the fundamental integration of the bill of material, which, without a plan, simply does not come together. The program manager, among other responsibilities, owns the plan.

The skill set of the program manager is widely varied but includes the following characteristics:

- Experience
- Training
- Communications
- Knowledge
- Flexibility
- Maturity

These represent the characteristics that must be present in the makeup of the program manger for lifecycle management to succeed.

PREREQUISITE EXPERIENCE TO BE SUCCESSFUL

The program manager must have extensive experience. The experience is not only driving lifecycle management to completion at other venues, but also experience is driving change throughout an organization.

The program manager should be experienced not only in program management, but also in the various lifecycle elements under the program that are required to be managed. The program manager needs to have at a minimum an operational understanding and experience in lifecycle.

Generic program management skills are transferable, but the lifecycle experience is unique and specific in the construct.

TRAINING CREDENTIALS

A program manager should have a number of formal training credentials to validate the leadership role he or she needs to play. Being credentialed as a program manager is important because most, if not all, of the team that is a part of the program will have a similar number of year's experience. The program manger needs to demonstrate that time and effort went into differentiation of his or her skill sets.

COMMUNICATIONS

Although a program manager needs to be a solid communicator (a given in the role), the program manager also must be able to create or manage the creation of a marketing and communication plan. Many lifecycle initiatives are not fully successful because at various levels throughout the enterprise, the end users, managers, supervisors, and even senior executives may not understand the value proposition or why certain activities and decisions are being made.

INDUSTRY AND BUSINESS KNOWLEDGE REQUIRED

A program manager needs to have solid knowledge about best practices, industry direction, and specifics in what the business itself is considering. Knowing what other companies are doing in lifecycle management is an important point of reference. The program manager also must be an expert in the stable state of the business. All levels of employees are counting on the program manager to have the correct perspective regarding lifecycle.

Although similar knowledge in the same industry is valuable, it is equally important to understand what others outside of the industry of a business are doing. This knowledge might result in adoption of leadership practices. Lifecycle is defined already for the program manager; the task is to create a strategy that permits the custom implementation in a business that yields the benefits of cost reductions, cost avoidance, improved service levels, and compliance. This is not a first-time position.

FLEXIBILITY TO ADAPT

No program ever runs smoothly and without changes during the execution. One of the key traits for the program manager is to be flexible. Flexibility is a requirement because there will constantly be changes and alternatives to consider. As policy, process, and procedures are defined, there must be an accompanying openness to consider a wide variety of input.

In lifecycle, it is often difficult to be flexible because there are operational definitions to consider and governance to develop. This is one of the traits that the program manager must possess.

MATURITY IN DECISION MAKING

Because there is no definitive right or wrong decisions in lifecycle, the program manager must be cautious about managing conflict and a wide array of differing perspectives and personalities. Maturity is a trait that will assist the program manager to ensure that organizationally there are no "winner" or "loser" categories in decisions that are cast.

Maturity will balance the decisions and scope the discussions so that emotions are removed from consideration. When thinking about the various constituencies impacted by the lifecycle decisions, it is clear that there will be conflict, but the maturity level should ensure that the conflict does not become emotional.

PROGRAM MANAGEMENT VS. PROJECT MANAGEMENT

Closed loop lifecycle planning differentiates program management from project management. Although many use these terms interchangeably, these represent different skills sets. Both program management and project management are important to the success of lifecycle management.

Program management reflects the total scope of the lifecycle engagement. Project management represents the specific lifecycle elements. A program will have only one program manager; there will be multiple project managers.

In a closed loop lifecycle planning engagement, there will be only one program manager, only one owner of the overall delivery. The project team and project managers will have deliverables layered as a part of the program.

When the bill of materials identifying each of the lifecycle elements is presented, each may have its own project team, or a combination of teams underneath the overall program of lifecycle. The program itself is only as strong as the deliverables under each element (or project); because you have read throughout this book, all lifecycle elements are interdependent.

IS THE PROGRAM MANAGER THE CHANGE AGENT?

The question is often asked whether the program manager is the agent of change within a given business. The simple answer is that the program manager is *not* the agent of change. Certainly, the program manager represents and is a part of the dynamics, but is not the change agent per se. The program manager has the actual deliverables to consider and may not be the individual to socialize change within an enterprise.

As mentioned in Chapter 1, "Closed Loop Lifecycle Planning Methodology," the sponsoring executive, the CIO, is likely the agent, and the CIO will identify someone on staff or management to precipitate change. More often than not, this individual is not the program manager.

The interaction between the program manager and the change agent is quite frequent. There should be no confusion, however, between the agenda of making change and the program manager who executes changes. The roles are quite different, and although the individuals need to be on the same page in terms of direction, the roles should not be confused.

THE PROGRAM MANAGEMENT OFFICE (PMO)

The program manager effectively runs the program management office, or PMO. The PMO is the organization under the direction of the program manager. The PMO will have a number of project managers for various lifecycle elements, and also other resources.

The PMO will likely have some of the project mangers reporting directly to the program manager. Perhaps this is on a full-time or part-time basis. In many scenarios, the project personnel report to the PMO on an interim basis while the deliverables are defined. There are many ways to construct the PMO.

A number of other "staff"-type functions operate under the PMO, including the following:

- Administrators
- Billing coordinators
- Logistics coordinators
- Tool management
- Documentation

These represent just a few of the staff functions. Some positions may be temporary positions while work is being developed, whereas others may be permanent, just reporting to the PMO in the interim.

One of the initial decisions that a business must make is the duration of the PMO structure. Is the PMO a one-time-only transitional office or a permanent infrastructure? This is one of the fundamental decisions that must be made.

THE COST OF THE PMO

Most would concur that the PMO and the program manager are critical success factors in lifecycle management. And, generally, the program manager requires a difficult skill set to acquire and source. Program managers that meet and exceed the characteristics defined earlier in this chapter are hard to find.

Despite the general agreement on the importance of the program manager and PMO, the program management and the PMO are often the most scrutinized of all lifecycle costs. One reason for this is what businesses are willing to pay for such resources. Typically, however, it is because of the lack of a defined value trade-off. The expenses and cost of failure, or the cost to repeat the processes, are what the comparison should be, not the actual cost of the program manager or the PMO itself.

Many businesses are on the third iteration of asset-management implementation. If the program-management resources and commitments had been included up front and an implementation plan defined with empowerment, it is likely that the processes would have been more successful. The costs to redo the implementation are the higher cost than the cost of driving a successful program.

The PMO costs stand out after the cost of the program management itself. Businesses need to select a lifecycle strategy that they are comfortable with as a team. In many cases, lifecycle does indeed get reduced to a "who do you trust" proposition. If there is concern that the program-management functions, project managers, and the PMO are too robust and costly, immediately discuss this topic thoroughly.

Increasingly more businesses, regardless of their scope, are finding that both internal and external leaders may not embrace an engagement unless the full PMO parameters are agreed upon.

TRANSITIONAL VS. BUSINESS AS USUAL

Programs have many phases. Aside from the rigor of preparation, one of the key elements is the transition from today's stable state, or current state, to the new future state. For many senior program managers, the true challenge of a program is the transitional phase, when all the dynamics (cultural, political, operational, and organizational) are in motion.

The transition phase has a level of excitement that makes it unique. Many program managers have developed specific expertise around transitional phases and excel at this type of execution. During this phase, it helps to have the program manager and the change agent working very closely.

These same program managers often are not interested in running or engaging in a program after the transition phase has been completed and the business-as-usual phase commences. As a matter of fact, these particular program managers may become "bored" by the business-as-usual (BAU) mentality of the program.

The skill sets required in the ongoing BAU phase are not the same as in the transitional phase. Therefore, turnover may occur, and in truth, may be desirable. The same skill set required in the transition is very likely different from that required in the BAU stage. In the transitional phase, developmental, educational, and operations expertise is required (diminishing after the scenario for change has been defined). The skill set includes the overall organizational execution, working closely with the executive sponsors and the change agents.

In the BAU environment, the skill set required is for the ongoing support and development of the continuous process improvement plan. The BAU program focus is not the planning and design, but the ongoing maintenance and enhancement.

In many scenarios, there is even a transition engagement document that defines the role during transition and another engagement document that defines the ongoing maintenance of the deliverables. The skill set required for ongoing support is operational excellence in delivery of lifecycle management. The objective in this phase is more of a delivery focus on defined metrics and reporting against those metrics.

NOTE: The skills sets and mission of a program suggest that the transition program manager is likely to be a different person than the BAU program manager. Transition program managers are change agents that have the skill set to introduce and implement challenging changes, whereas BAU program managers excel at continuous process improvements.

PROGRAM MANAGEMENT: INTERNAL OR EXTERNAL

One basic topic to address is whether the program manager should be a member of the internal infrastructure (or should the program manager be one of the functions for which an outside resource would prove advantageous). A business case can be made for the resource outside. Without concern for the political and organizational ramifications, the overall program might be more successful. Certainly, this would be more neutral in terms of impact.

External program mangers, if they are under a specific engagement, could bring outside experience to the program. This experience should translate into a shorter time to implement.

The internal program manager brings the knowledge to the table of the existing infrastructure and would likely need less "ramp-up" time. The advantage of an internal program manager could be more adoption of recommendations if the resource is accepted internally. This acceptance is a key success factor.

The point is, a business case can be made for either internal or external, but the decision needs to be specific to the program under consideration.

NOTE: Part of the business case for external program management is that the outside program manager is less likely to participate in internal politics or organizational issues. The expectations for an outside program manager are more easily scoped, through a contracted statement of work, than they are for internal resources.

MARKETING AND COMMUNICATIONS

Marketing and communications is a key role often overlooked in complex programs. There should be a proactive marketing campaign to position the initiative with the end users, business units, and potentially impacted personnel.

Not only should the initiative be discussed in a communication plan, the initiative should also have a formal communication vehicle. The communications often take the form of a newsletter, web update, or intranet mailer. Presentations to employee forums and management meeting are also common.

As a part of the PMO, there would be a dedicated marketing and communications team to drive the messaging to the business.

If lifecycle management presents a change or paradigm shift, the requirement for more marketing and communications becomes greater. The messages presented should position potential changes, solicit feedback, and access adjusting plans as feedback is received.

The help desk is a valuable resource to be integrated as a part of the marketing and communications plan. When calls are made to the help desk, the help desk could advise of future potential changes (or as part of a follow-up to the call, advise about the initiative). It is not unusual as a part of the end-user satisfaction process to advise end users of changes that could potentially improve or impact their environment.

Most end users would want to know (in contrast to not being advised or hearing about potential change informally). When change is communicated informally, it might not be the appropriate context that the program would prefer.

Many businesses overcommunicate to avoid any confusion or any misconceptions regarding the process.

NOTE: In closed loop lifecycle planning, the marketing and communications resources are generally internal resources. The mission statement should fully communicate the lifecycle strategy and program status to the end users and to the business community at large.

MANAGEMENT TOOLS

A discussion regarding the PMO would not be complete without a brief reference to the toolsets. There is, of course, a set of tools that the program office and the various project teams use to report the progress against goals. Preferably, all the program and project teams use the same tools, so that milestone charts, metrics, and critical path items can be identified. The greater the number of tools used, the greater the lack of coordination. One of the roles of the program manager is to select the reporting and management tools to be used as a part of the PMO.

Most third parties (if the decision is made to secure the resource externally) will come to an engagement with a preferred set of tools.

Aside from the program tools, many lifecycle engagements have required the assessment of management tools for consideration. The PMO could identify the tools available to a selection process as a part of a bidding rigor. Each program manager will come to the program with experience and potentially a preference.

The key distinction is whether the experience and preference represents a bias. It is important when discussing the management toolset to understand and agree between the PMO and the business on the correct set of guidelines to follow. In one respect, the business wants the experience; in another respect, it is seeking unbiased opinions. These ground rules should be defined as a part of the engagement up front.

Management tools will play an ever-increasing role in how lifecycle management is delivered. The discipline exercised by the PMO will be critical to the architecture, design, and selection.

Chapter 23, "Management Tools" (online) discusses management tools in more detail. With regard to the program office, the point here is that management tools are mandatory for the execution of a lifecycle-management program.

GLOBAL COMPLEXITIES

Lifecycle management is already quite complex without the added impact of a global solution. Lifecycles that include a worldwide focus have an added dimension: How can a program be consistently implemented when the different countries have unique laws, regulations, and relationships that govern how business is to be conducted?

Global lifecycle requires a strong PMO and another skill set. Global lifecycle should not be a first-time event for a program manager to begin learning. The experience factor in this area is important. Assumption levels and milestone charts must rely on local customs/nuances to determine how work will be accomplished. It is not feasible to envision a PMO delivering global lifecycle for the first time. If a business does not have someone with this experience in-house, I strongly suggest that this is an excellent skill set to hire or to contract for delivery purposes.

Global lifecycle is not a "one size fits all" proposition; it is custom. Although there are certain functions and service levels that may be mirrored, how the service levels are achieved and whether those expectations are appropriate must be assessed.

A PMO must know that the lead times, for example, for acquisition may vary from country to country. Given that difference, the service level may be different or an inventory position may be required to achieve the service levels required. Only an experienced, global program manager would know where these issues may occur.

An alternative approach is to learn as the program progresses, which likely mean either failure or, at least, a painful lifecycle experience.

It is important as a business to clearly separate the marketing from the delivery capabilities of internal and external providers. Although well intentioned as a general rule (after all, no one would mislead), it is not unusual for providers to think that a successful lifecycle engagement is equivalent to any other engagement. However, global becomes the "tie-breaker" in terms of the complexity factor.

GLOBAL EXPERIENCE

The experience in program managing global lifecycle is clearly one of the differentiators between personnel, manufacturers, and service providers. Global program management represents a level of complexity that pales in comparison to a single geographic program. Global program management is not an area for training; it requires a reasonably high competency level in all the skills discussed in this chapter. The global program office is not an area to avoid investment.

Experience globally suggests that each region and country within region presents unique challenges and requirements. Managing such diversity is challenging in many respects; but most important, an enterprise cannot afford the risk of not anticipating requirements that are part of the global equation.

Drawing on their collective experiences, a global program manager and the respective project managers will likely have a unique approach or strategy based on what has succeeded in the past or based on recently learned experience in the industry.

A solid program manager, just as in all disciplines, is well read and studies the environment in which the program office is expected to deliver. Aside from the contractual statement of work, the quality of that work is impacted by the global experience level.

SUMMARY

The PMO and the program manager in particular represent the "face" of a program to a business. Whether internal or external, the PMO must concentrate on solution delivery, with a constant focus on the quality and communication of the program.

The cost of the PMO is almost always a point of contention, regardless of whether it is internally or externally staffed. Regardless of the cost (not price), the key is in understanding that the strength of the PMO is likely the single critical and identifiable success factor in implementing lifecycle management.

Ensuring that a strong communication plan is in place as a part of the PMO (marketing and communications) will go a long way toward increasing end-user and business-unit adoption of lifecycle management principles and strategies.

If the program is global, a PMO is a necessity for success, not an option.

12

Disposing of Client Devices at the End of Life

INTRODUCTION

In closed loop lifecycle planning, *disposition* refers to the processes required to decommission client devices. Interestingly, a growing number of lifecycle-management solutions start with end-of-life strategies. One of the reasons for this is that the rules and regulations are now very clear about business responsibilities. In addition, business units and end users are less concerned about the politics associated with end-of-life responsibilities, and in most cases are relieved not to have that accountability.

In this chapter, the entire range of end-of-life strategies is explored. There are many dependencies in the disposition lifecycle element. The processes include the following:

- Physically de-install, migrate data, and back up
- Move to secure areas
- Update asset-management records
- Cleanse information (protect data)
- Cascade or dispose?

PHYSICALLY DE-INSTALL, MIGRATE DATA, AND BACK UP

When a new client system is installed, the existing device is de-installed. In closed loop lifecycle planning, *net new* refers to an incremental device added to a PC fleet, not a replacement device. Although this might seem simplistic, it is not surprising that businesses overlook the de-installation process, assuming that it is included in the installation process. The actual de-installation is a straightforward labor operation. There are, however, dependencies on many of the other lifecycle operations, including backup and data migration. It is assumed that when the net new system is available, the setup is complete, and so the de-installation is facilitated.

Before the system is de-installed, the new system should be fully ready to be installed. The readiness includes personal settings, data migration, and backup. Personal settings are typically completed as a part of the staging and integration effort, or if custom, during the installation script. Data migrations can occur in a number of ways.

Data migration, given the maturity of management tools, can often be completed remotely. In other cases, data migration can occur on-site during the installation itself. The rigor in data migration differs between desktops and laptops. Data migration is generally an IT function; however, with the maturity of end users, many businesses are considering self-migration of data. End users are typically directed where information is to be stored or archived. (By the way, most end users do not correctly follow this direction.) In this way, the process can be scaled and replicated. It is often most expedient to have end users back up to a known local drive or to the server. Closed loop lifecycle planning notes that self-service will become more prevalent in the near term.

NOTE: Today, most data migration is addressed at the end-user site, not remotely. The trend in management tools is to provide for the capability to perform remote, after-hours access, which could include data migration. With laptops, you can use an event such as an annual sales forum, for example, to scale the data migration through the use of a management tool. Self migration is becoming mainstream quickly.

The importance of data migration is to ensure that the business continues without end users being impacted by the loss of information. This is a serious business implication; and with current regulations, if you're dealing with sensitive information, it is the enterprise, not only the end user, where the exposure may reside. End users reasonably expect that there will be continuity in the refresh to a new device. In many cases, data migration is associated more with the installation process than with the de-installation process. In either scenario, it is importance that ownership of the operations be established.

Quite often, multiple resources are engaged. Facilities will handle the physical movement of the devices, and IT will perform the install, de-install, and migration. Each of these lifecycle activities need to be understood in detail.

MOVE TO SECURE AREAS

After a device is de-installed, it is often moved to a corner of an office or cubicle, where it stays for a time before a resource (usually facilities) picks it up and moves it to a secured, locked area. The period of time that the device sits in this interim inventory position may vary from business to business.

It is during this period when a level of vulnerability exists. In many instances, if not picked up on a timely basis, devices could be used for spares, cascaded, cannibalized, or otherwise "disappear." During this transition phase, asset records might not be fully updated, so there is exposure in several different areas.

In many cases, the secure area might not be fully "secure." In this informal environment, the rigor of lifecycle-management is reduced, and the risk becomes great.

NOTE: Businesses need to determine the level of enforcement that is desired in empowering the lifecycle-management team. Establishing a policy or governance model that permits net new access devices to be deployed by end users without the required return should be immediately flagged as a deviation and reported. The results should be actionable. Without this level of adoption, the governance is easily unenforceable. Accountability based on the regulations for intellectual property, data protection, and overall security (including personal privacy) should be part of the enforcement rationale. It is compelling.

UPDATE ASSET-MANAGEMENT RECORDS

As assets move from being part of the installed base, to off the network, to a transition inventory, and ultimately to disposition, the asset records need to track the progression through the cycle. This is not an easy process, particularly if resources outside of IT, including Stealth IT, do not feel compelled to maintain up-to-date recording. The assets that are in the transition phase may be difficult to size. This is a similar reporting process as work-in-process mode for a manufacturer.

Having up-to-date asset-management reporting will always present a challenge. However, it is important to remember that under current rules, laws, and regulations, if an asset is missing that may have sensitive data on it, it likely needs to be reported. This is indeed a high standard. The transition phase likely needs to have a stronger governance policy than most businesses have today.

CLEANSE INFORMATION (PROTECT DATA)

One question to be asked after the de-installation process is when the data is to be cleansed. It is not unusual for the de-installation script not to include the cleansing of data. This suggests that, as the devices are moved to a location (an office or a cubicle), the devices are not cleansed and could have proprietary information. This information might, in fact, be at risk of exposure.

In some industry segments, such as banking, insurance, and pharmaceutical, devices are retained consciously in the "as is" state due to industry requirements, business practices, or regulatory requirements. These requirements could also stem from legal requirements. In many cases, there should be a secured retention strategy in place supported by detailed asset recordkeeping.

NOTE: Many highly regulated businesses, or businesses that have sensitive information on devices, quarantine the devices or the disk drives for a period of time before disposition occurs.

In other cases, the workflow is more informal than formal. Security needs to be a more significant role in the overall movement of assets. If the devices are not cleansed while in transit from the office or cubicle to the secure area, when and where is the device actually cleansed?

Many businesses ship devices to a disposition agent to perform the cleansing and disposal itself. Often, the devices are not cleansed in transit to the disposition agent. Businesses might want to reconsider this scenario, particularly in light of current security events.

Manufacturers are introducing and including levels of encryption on devices, and the cleansing could become part of the product attribution in the near future. In upcoming technology refreshes, businesses might have the opportunity to fundamentally change some of the lifecycle elements as a part of the initial acquisition phase.

The counterposition could be made that there will at least be one cleansing of the disk at the time of disposal, so the cost may not be justified if incremental. This conclusion, however, does not reflect the reality. Businesses need to invest in the protection of the data on their access devices; most likely, these costs will be incremental.

CASCADE OR DISPOSE?

Chapter 7, "Moves, Adds, and Changes (MACs)" discusses cascading as one of several alternatives available to a business. *Cascading* is the repurposing of an access device for reuse internally by another end user.

In general, cascading is a business practice that works when the maturity levels are high in asset management. Cascading is often a result of which organization owns the PC budget, and their belief in the benefits of expense and indirect dollars compared to a capital expense dollars. This section focuses on the actual disposal of the access device itself.

NOTE: Under closed loop lifecycle planning, cascading is optimal when an access device is within an 18- to 24-month window (when warranty is available). Beyond that period, the useful life of the access device is typically not extended beyond 12 to 18 months and will go outside of the warranty window.

Cascading has a critical dependency on the maturity of the asset-management practice and should not be seen as avoiding the capital expense of the trade-in, because the trade-in value would exceed the residual value in many cases.

One of the trends in closed loop lifecycle planning is the centralization of the enterprise PC spending with IT. Part of the rationale behind this trend is the improvement in practice levels and controls that can be implemented in disposal, asset management, and the reduction of cascading devices. This trend reduces risks and costs in the overall lifecycle-management of access devices.

In the disposal of devices, the actual disposition is generally performed by a disposition agent. The disposition agent coordinates the packing and shipment of the devices to a facility where the devices are re-inventoried and reconciled with the shipping documents. In the disposition agent's facility, the devices are cleansed.

When the hard drive is intended to be reused or destroyed, it is standard for the hard drive to have its data cleansed or wiped by randomly writing data across the entire disk. Standard in the industry is the "three-pass" wipe, the Department of Defense (DoD) standard. This practice effectively wipes the devices for ultimate disposal.

Businesses and their disposition agents need to mutually define several disposition strategies as viable. From that decision, the appropriate terms and conditions can be established. The alternative disposition strategies include the following:

- Remarketing
- Demanufacturing for sparing
- Demanufacturing for disposal
- Hybrid

NOTE: The business should consciously decide the optimal manner to dispose of access devices. In closed loop lifecycle planning, fewer alternatives and strategies are preferable to multiple strategies. More flexibility does not equate to tighter control.

REMARKETING

The disposition agent might determine that there is remaining value in the decommissioned assets. After the devices have been cleansed, the disposition agent might know of secondary markets for the devices. Assuming the terms and conditions permit, and the devices are properly cleansed, the devices could be resold.

There are a few important considerations to ensure that the initial businesses decision is a solid one. The first is that the business will receive documentation that the devices have been cleansed. This is generally conveyed through a legal document listing the assets and the actions taken. The second consideration is that the legal title to the devices passes to the disposition agent so that the devices can be resold. The appropriate laws, regulations, and sales taxes are then the responsibility of the disposition agent as a part of the cost of sales.

Many remarketers of used equipment have programs that share proceeds from remarketing efforts when the fixed costs, including the three-pass wipe, are exceeded. Although not a significant sum typically, this strategy does provide an offset to some of the disposal costs.

Often, none of the remarketing sharing reverts back to IT in terms of their budget. More often, the dollars are retained at the corporate level and not applied to IT. Therefore, when IT is asked to reduce costs and improve service levels, the funding could be reallocated back to IT to reflect where the savings have actually occurred. It bears all the expenses and might not be able to participate in the benefits of their planning. In fact, this penalizes (to a degree) IT for implementing the best practice.

DEMANUFACTURING FOR SPARING

In some scenarios, it is not the client devices themselves that have value, but the components. The devices could be demanufactured, and the components harvested. In these cases, components and peripherals are usually sold to service providers, where there is demand for these parts.

One of the advantages that the PC manufacturers bring to the table up front is either their own service infrastructure or that of partners who provide a more ready market for spares inventory. One of the considerations of the business is to determine where the best set of economics resides.

The remainder of the device itself is addressed through the processes described below.

NOTE: Demanufacturing and sparing will likely be different for laptops and desktops. In closed loop lifecycle planning, the optimal useful life for a laptop is less than 3 years (30 months), whereas desktops can be truly useful 4 years (and beyond if the user profile is correct, although the operating system and performance of business applications would make a 5-year business case weak [not even considering maintenance and support issues]). The acquisition price of the net new devices (not to mention the speeds and features) and the trade-in value would undoubtedly be the best economics.

DEMANUFACTURING FOR DISPOSAL

When there is no remaining residual value, or if the terms and considerations do not permit harvesting, and after the three-pass wiping and cleansing is completed, the devices are ready for destruction. Both national and international environmental regulations restrict how assets can be disposed of, and so reporting is essential to ensure compliance.

Businesses should ensure that a "certificate of destruction" is received as a part of the process. This certification denotes that the disposition agent has complied with all relevant regulations.

Toxic material might need to be identified and encapsulated or packaged according to defined specifications. Any precious metals may be recovered. Plastic chassis may be demanufactured into pellets. These represent typical considerations in the demanufacturing process.

HYBRID

It is not unusual for a business to have multiple alternatives available and to have all viable within a business operation. The key for security and compliance is to ensure that the service-level requirements are documented in such a way that there is no confusion regarding the required work to be performed and the risks associated with each decision. Historically, many businesses have donated older desktops and laptops. The rigor in cleansing and protecting information and licensing is the same in the donation category.

PARTNERING AND SCALE

There are a number of local, regional, national, and global disposition agents. Just as in every other lifecycle element, understanding the work to be performed is key. Due diligence is required when selecting a disposition agent.

Although liability can be transferred contractually, some violations might result in shared liability. Even if shared liability isn't a risk, negative publicity surrounding a regulatory/legal violation could affect a business both in dollar terms and in goodwill.

Selecting a disposition agent is another conscious decision to be made. Scale, local relationships, and core competencies are criteria to consider. When the scale becomes national or global, the issues involved become much more complex. This level of complexity requires consistency. Moreover, density can play an important role. When the scale becomes significant, the number of disposition agents diminishes in number with the desired core competencies.

To whom a business provides its products and services may also impact the criteria. Part of the rigor is not only to comply with all the laws and regulations, but also to mitigate any potential exposure. Simply put, larger partners tend to mitigate the risk more because as a business their assets are greater. (This is not to suggest excluding one category of company from another, but instead is a reminder of the decisions that must be consciously made.)

After the governance has been defined, many businesses believe they have reached the end of the liability or responsibility chain. Although creating and advising through the governance model is a step forward, it might not be enough. The governance model must be audited for compliance and tested aggressively. In many businesses, the governance model is not enforceable or cannot be tracked effectively. This lack of discipline makes the governance model weaker. Disposition is one of the more immediate steps requiring action in lifecycle today, which is why there is increasing emphasis on this aspect from the market.

If disposition occurs in multiple locations, multiple countries, and includes multiple devices and is completed through multiple partners, the challenges to manage governance is significant.

NOTE: Size matters! The larger the enterprise (particularly if it's global), the more important a disposition partner whose size and scope substantially mitigates risk. For this reason, many manufacturers have aggressively entered the disposition market.

It is reasonable to consider a sole disposition agent as a vendor that addresses multiple platforms and third-party devices and components, including non-IT assets (such as copiers, printers, and fax machines).

INDUSTRY SPECIFICS

Because certain industries are more regulated than others, retention and disposition are major factors to consider. Part of the governance model is defined by the industry or regulators themselves. Recent litigation highlights some of the requirements. Often, the standards are set higher in these industries. As discussed in the Bonus Section of this book, "User Segmentation: A Complement to Closed Loop Lifecycle Planning," certain user segments might require a higher practice level, too. Note, however, that the standards have already been raised for all businesses.

INTERNAL DISPOSITION STRATEGIES

A number of businesses have consciously (or perhaps unconsciously) decided to enter the disposition operation. Entry into the disposal business suggests a rather robust infrastructure with an agent at the end of the environmental conclusion. These businesses also fit the operational profile of those businesses that cascade access devices. As in all other areas of closed loop lifecycle planning, best practices are a must.

DISPOSITION IS NOT AN EMPLOYEE PURCHASE PROGRAM

Disposition is not, and should not be, either a formal or informal employee purchase program. There is a solid rationale behind this assertion. After all, business computers are *not* personal computers. The configurations, components, software, and so on are not intended for or packaged as a consumer/personal device.

At the time of disposition, most devices will be out of warranty. Therefore, the purchaser (the employee) needs to understand the true cost. There is also the need to ensure that the employee understands that the internal business infrastructure is not to be used for this device.

Licensing is generally not transferable from a business license to a home personal-use license. Licensing issuers could prohibit the employee purchase scenario.

The employee purchase might lead to the inclusion of proprietary business information access.

Finally, when employees do require support on these devices, local resources are likely to be involved, at least on occasion. This could include the help desk and other IT resources.

Historically, disposition to employees was considered an entitlement or informal benefit. From the business perspective, selling used PCs to employees requires the collection and reporting of sales taxes and other transference accounting. When businesses fully explore leveraging the disposition as an employee purchase program, does this then become a reportable benefit? Often, the risks and costs can quickly become prohibitive. It is important to remember that the employee also needs to sign off on the agreement to dispose of the device in accordance with environmental regulations, because now the business is acting as a reseller of used equipment.

ENTRY INTO DISPOSITION REQUIRES INVESTMENT

If a business decides to enter the disposition business itself, investment must be made in inventory management and logistics, and the practice levels must be high. In essence, the infrastructure needs to be responsive to all reseller regulations. Even human resources should be engaged to ensure that any previous end users are not liable for the asset or information.

Scaling and governance enforcement are important because of the additional "touches" required to support the disposition operation.

Some businesses accumulate access devices and then auction off used equipment. Although revenue is generated, this revenue should be offset by the costs and investments required to support the effort. A conscious business decision can then be made.

One of the fundamental questions is not whether the operation can be handled more effectively internally at a lesser cost, the true question is whether this is where a business wants to invest it resources.

WHAT IF THE MARKET CHANGES?

A critical criterion for entry to and exit from of all lifecycle functions is how the infrastructure could adapt if fundamental changes occur in the product mix. The shifts between desktop and laptop, the preponderance of PDAs, the new technologies of tablets and convergent devices—all these suggest that entering into the disposition business requires keen insight into the residual/secondary market.

This requires analysis and resources to study the markets.

Another market consideration is declining prices. Perhaps the prices decline to the point that residual and remarketing becomes a negligible aspect of the operation's contribution.

This question is vital, too: If the decision is made to exit this operation, what is the cost of change? The conclusion to be reached is that this is one area where entrance and exit costs are impacted directly by the market and easily changed in a short period of time.

CRTS

Of particular interest in closed loop lifecycle planning are cathode ray tubes (CRTs). Today, flat-panel monitors are replacing CRTs. However, there remain large fleets of CRTs in businesses today, and of course, businesses can still acquire net new CRTs. The CRT is somewhat unique because often these devices are not necessarily replaced with the access devices; these are retained until they are simply no longer operational. This could be in the four- to five-year (or more) range, depending on the business.

Environmental regulations for CRTs have become considerable. Annually, the disposal costs of the CRTs will increase significantly. State and local regulations are already in varying stages of approvals.

For those businesses with substantial CRT fleets, there may be a date in the short term when the price of flat-panel monitors, less the cost of disposing of the CRTs, becomes compelling, or at least neutral in its guidance.

It is important to note that there will also be a point in time when the cost of disposition of the CRTs will suggest more of a planned refresh strategy to avoid costs that are likely to become quite high.

Also note that although CRTs are still available, they are less available than in the past. As CRTs become less of major manufacturers' portfolios, they will become obsolete in a short time (and have a small after-market).

Driving this end of life are end-user demand and the better cost economics. Although the acquisition price remains different (which will normalize), the cost picture in terms of energy, footprint, economics, and other considerations is compelling today.

Because of the environmental implications, disposing of CRTs will become a cost issue for many businesses whose monitor fleets today are CRT based.

NOTE: CRTs are doomed, both because tier-one manufacturers are phasing them out and because of the increasing cost to dispose of them. The asset weight and shipping costs will become a cost driver in the future as the disposal costs begin to bridge the gap of the difference in acquisition pricing.

RESIDUAL VALUE

Disposition strategies often revolve around the discussion of residual value: what the access devices are worth at the end of their useful life for the business. Residual value needs to be viewed in the context of any expenses required to prepare the device for the disposal action.

In many instances, residual value is likened to a roller coaster ride. For businesses, it is desirable to dispose of an asst before the momentum of the "roller coaster" drives the residual value down. Also, continuing with this analogy, the speed of the loss of residual value is exponential.

There is a short time timeframe during which a device has a level of value and the time when it will cost a business to dispose of it.

TRADE IN OF OLDER ACCESS DEVICES

One alternative to disposition as a standalone lifecycle element is to consider aggregating residual value and netting the value as an offset to the acquisition price of a net new PC. One of the challenges in doing this is, as described earlier, the enterprise holds the offset dollars at a corporate level. IT bears the burden of the expense, but enjoys none of the benefits from a well-constructed disposition plan. This is one of reason that makes the trade-in alternative attractive, because it aligns expenses and revenues with the organizational reporting.

Perhaps the most compelling point to be made about the trade in is that it does not necessarily align with the residual value alone. Of course, trade ins will include the residual, but manufacturers, partners, and resellers could combine market share and upgrade objectives regarding trade ins, with trade ins becoming more of an allowance than a pure residual strategy. This clearly suggests that a trade in could exceed the residual value.

A trade-in approach also has the benefit of reducing at least one extra step in the overall disposition process. Just as in maintenance perspectives presented in this book, trade in will become a mainstream strategy very quickly.

It may help to think of a trade-in approach as a packaging strategy, not a residual or disposition alternative.

END OF LIFE

When the help desk determines that it can no longer support either a certain configuration, platform, or operating system (or business application), the access device is effectively at its end of life within the enterprise. To categorize an installed access device as obsolete (at its end of life), businesses must consider many things. Under a closed loop lifecycle planning model, businesses must establish and document criteria that results in an enforceable and manageable end-of-life strategy. The criteria could include the following:

- Minimal residual value.
- No support or billable support for older units and operating systems.
- No available maintenance support for break/fix (no sparing).
- Unacceptable configuration to support antivirus or security applications.
- The cost to upgrade exceeds the remaining book or residual value.

Any one criterion in the preceding list, and especially any combination of them, should result in a decision to dispose of an access device.

PAYMENT IN ADVANCE

The consumer market provides validation for the concept of payment in advance for disposal. In many states, when you buy a consumer PC, part of the price goes to cover a portion of the anticipated disposal cost of the device. More and more states will likely be adopting this type of legislation.

This will become a cost consideration in the bundling of the technology-refresh strategies as businesses deal with new legislation.

DOES LEASING MITIGATE END-OF-LIFE RISKS?

In a lease, the ownership of the asset generally resides with the leasing company. Therefore, after the business' data and information has been cleansed, the asset disposition becomes the responsibility of the leasing company.

So, the simple answer to the question in this section heading is "yes." The answer "yes" does not mean that the costs are not passed on to the enterprise, or are not included as a cost of doing the leasing business, it just means that the risk of disposal is effectively mitigated.

Leasing as a service-delivery strategy is covered in depth in Chapter 14, "Service-Delivery Strategies." Disposition is a key finding in lifecycle-management research.

WHAT ABOUT OTHER DEVICES?

Disposition is at a reasonable maturity practice level in the industry. Many companies can perform the work quite well. For desktops, laptops, CRTs, and traditional devices, the rigor is quite well known and understood. However, mobility devices, such as PDAs, smart phones, and other handheld devices, present a disposition challenge. In these newer technologies, it is not unusual to find that the end users are not aware of any disposition strategy, and therefore the replaced device may be placed unused, but with data residing on it, in a drawer or other easily accessed area. These devices are pervasive.

Although many of these devices are server based for connectivity purposes, these devices can still retain information, such as electronic mail and contact lists. Closed loop lifecycle planning suggests that these strategies be defined, governance documented, and follow-up determined.

For example, are company-owned assets required to be returned to the business upon transfer or termination? If so, what does the business do with these devices after they have been returned? Many businesses do not have a handheld disposal plan. In some cases, employees have stated that they simply do not even know what to do with the assets.

The support, accounting, tracking, and disposing of the other nondesktop and nonlaptop devices may well exceed or be equivalent to the cost of PC disposal.

When non-PC devices are determined to be an important part of assisting employees to perform their jobs, the full cost of the asset needs to be identified so that the cost, risk, and service levels can be determined. At the time of this writing, the market is now beginning to identify this as a major gap in lifecycle planning.

SUMMARY

Disposition has taken on more and more importance because of increased regulations (related to both physical disposal and protection of sensitive information).

Local, regional, national, and global partners are engaged in the lifecycle element of disposition of client devices. The entry cost into the business is not significant, and many businesses can provide such a service. However, businesses do need to be concerned about the size and scope of the disposition agent and the practices that the agent can effectively deliver.

Businesses must be able to rely on the core competency of the work being performed because that work (and its documentation) represents a risk-mitigation proposition for the enterprise.

The disposition process begins with an enterprisewide strategy agreed by all the business units that becomes an enforceable governance model. It is not enough merely to publish guidelines; there needs to be accountability, reporting, and tracking.

Scaling of the partners and a statement of work clearly defining the work to be performed, supplemented by periodic audits that the statement of work is being complied with, are other steps in the process.

Disposition has gained in importance because the exposure is very real and requires notification to the impacted population when it is not performed correctly.

13

Technology Refresh

INTRODUCTION

Closed loop lifecycle planning defines *technology refresh* as the planned replacement of client devices. Businesses, as a part of their governance model, need to have a proactive strategy for client computing, including expectations regarding the optimal timeframe to manage the PC fleet. In the industry, there are quite a number of opinions and positions regarding the timing of technology refresh. It is surprising how variable those opinions and positions have become.

Technology refresh can often be a cause of debate internally within a business. The perspective of the technology refresh is based on the position one has within a business. To end users, the issue is stability and flexibility; to IT, the issue is resources and service level; and to management, the issue is risk and cost. Often, these issues are in contradiction to the other issues. Business performance may cause management to delay a refresh because of its cost and or potential disruption. The existence of a good plan can help make this decision less emotional.

The technology-refresh strategy does not necessarily equally apply to all user segments, nor does the technology refresh apply to all net new acquisitions of access devices. According to research performed in closed loop lifecycle planning, there are only four key drivers of a technology refresh, as follows:

- Price
- Price/performance
- Business applications
- End-user demand

PRICE OF AN ACCESS DEVICE

Every business wants to be in a position to take advantage of any major or significant adjustment in the industry regarding the price of an access device. Pricing for access devices is volatile and responds to several stimuli, including demand and innovation. This is not to suggest that a technology refresh is influenced solely by pricing; it is not. However, pricing may initiate a desire to reassess the refresh cycle.

Businesses need to be mindful that price doe not equal cost, and that what may seem to be a solid pricing decision may have cost implications. In short, technology refresh should not be driven by price, but price is always a consideration in any decision regarding access devices.

At the same time, PC manufacturers and distributors are dealing with declining margins and a quickened innovation cycle.

PRICE/PERFORMANCE

Price and price performance relate not only to processor speed or chipset, in closed loop lifecycle planning performance includes other features that improve the overall value proposition of the device itself. These features could include manageability, security, and serviceability. Performance usually relates to application processing speeds, but at the access device level, improvements may not be discernable at the end-user level, so the features become part of the overall performance criteria.

An end user, for example, will measure performance by the time it takes to "boot" the devices and the time that the "hourglass" appears on the screen. When an acceptable level is achieved, changes will be noted if it is less; however, speeds at some level, may not be noticed or considered material. In Chapter 20, "Interoperability and Prototyping" (online), it was noted that the software and usage of the access device has an impact on the configuration and the ultimate speed of the access device.

At some point, price itself becomes less of the differentiator because all suppliers are within a quite narrow bandwidth. Features that improve the performance will likely drive fundamental changes in access devices, with performance being defined as the ability of the end user to continuously use the access device. New form factors, multiple devices, and innovations are changing some of the fundamentals regarding how performance may be defined in the future.

NOTE: As manufactures provide more and more capability for the same or lower price than prior hardware products, businesses need to determine whether it is less costly to manage one or two configurations instead of trying to configure a single system to meet functional end-user requirements.

A technology-refresh plan needs in its basic construct the ability to adapt and embrace changes in the market.

BUSINESS AND SOFTWARE APPLICATIONS

By far, most technology-refresh plans will be triggered by business application requirements. The scopes of the business applications include shrink-wrapped applications, operating systems, custom applications, security applications, business-unit-specific applications, and even future potential applications contemplated.

When access devices are due to be refreshed, businesses should look at the planning horizon commensurate to the useful life of the device. If the application requirements may change, a business needs to consciously decide what the optimal configuration is. The objective is not to go back to the device and upgrade it during the useful life. To that end, many businesses overconfigure certain aspects of access devices to accommodate for these circumstances.

The scenario to avoid is investing in a technology-refresh cycle and plan only to upgrade disk, memory, graphics, or other configuration consideration and incur incremental costs. However, many businesses prefer to invest in the lowest common denominator of cost in the hope of avoiding costs. This again needs to be a very conscious trade-off made in the light of all available information.

New regulatory requirements and reporting needs may also serve to expand the business applications required. It is clear that new laws and regulations will require businesses to be even more accountable for the information and manageability of the access devices.

END-USER DEMAND

There will always be certain end users that, either because of their position within the business or the job responsibilities that they perform, will have requirements (perceived or real) outside of the scope of the technology refresh. The access devices and the cycle to refresh may very well be unique. Depending on their role within the organization, the requirements may very well be appropriate. Certain functions such as development and engineering, for example, may benefit greatly from price/performance features that are available, but the timing to take advantage is more immediate than for other end users.

Still others, such as sales and executives, as another example, rely on the access devices as a part of the impression that they present to their customers, colleagues, and competitors. Again, this is likely appropriate in the organization. These represent the types of conscious decisions that need to be made in the context of the overall technology-refresh plan.

Another category of end users engage in a different technology-refresh strategy just because they can. In these cases, it is not unusual to discover that a funding organization simply approves of the strategy.

There will always within all organizations be end users who will want to be outside of the technology-refresh cycle. There will be those who will provide the "99 reasons" why they or their team is the exception. The challenge for businesses is to determine the balance between governance and flexibility.

The key in technology-refresh planning is to have enough scope that a majority of the installed base is covered under the project. The more exceptions, the more "nervous" the plan becomes, and the more costly and complex the installed base becomes.

Business decisions will always impact the technology plan. A decision to implement a new system for competitive reasons, mergers, acquisitions, and divestitures may overrule an existing technology-refresh plan. A well thought-out technology-refresh plan will address and identify potential considerations that would impact the existing strategy.

The "exception" may often become contentious within a business because introducing more access device diversity will likely increase the related support costs outside of the price itself.

Y2K IMPACT

Now that the four drivers of technology refresh have been identified, it is important to explore the constituencies impacted in more detail. As a compelling event, many businesses' perspectives regarding technology refresh have been based upon the experiences of Y2K (in both a positive and negative perspective).

In Y2K remediation, with all the concerns regarding technologies, virtually every business addressed their installed base. The focus was on the stability of the platform, its vulnerability, and the readiness for Y2K. Applications were tested, and platforms either refreshed or upgraded.

Post-Y2K, all businesses took a "deep breath." Y2K was quite costly and resource intensive, but brought businesses much closer to their end users and installed base, many for the first time in such an important planning process. Part of the postmortem thinking clearly was "glad it is over, and can another such effort in the future be avoided?" Many businesses that had planned a technology-refresh strategy decided to extend the life of the installed base to lessen capital expenditures, but also to recoup some of the one-time-only expenses. It was at this timeframe that the thought processes regarding technology refresh were reformed to a very large degree.

Different constituencies had now formed definitive impressions regarding the requirements for a technology refresh, and how the refresh itself could be approached.

Executives viewed the refresh as a one-time-only cost, a significant but required cost. The objective would be to mitigate any further type of large-scale investments such as had occurred. It is about this time that it was believed that cost could be avoided by extending the life of the client devices beyond the planned refresh cycles.

End users viewed the PCs as a tool and finally believed that the tool had the attention of the enterprise. Businesses seemed to truly care about productivity and the speed of executives using the client devices. Expectations were more clearly defined about the importance of the PC.

IT viewed Y2K as a key compelling event that focused the enterprise on the environment that they were dealing with day to day. Persons and organizations, that up to that point expressed no real interest in the PC fleet, developed rather strong perceptions and became stakeholders.

Security learned from Y2K just how vulnerable the installed base could become. Although this could be an acknowledgment, Y2K served as a "wakeup" call of sorts in terms of recognition that viruses, hacking, and other events could become very serious, very quickly. As all the readers know today, this perception has become reality.

USEFUL LIFE

One of the basic definitions for lifecycle to be successful in a business is to determine the useful lifecycle of client devices. Once again, it is likely who is asked the question. For accounting and finance, useful life is easily understood. Client devices, desktops, and laptops are either fully expensed or depreciated. If expensed, decisions need to be determined about the timeframe that the devices are to remain in the fleet. Expense management becomes a key consideration for the technology-refresh cycle.

The accounting and finance rules are much clearer when client devices are depreciated. If a desktop or laptop is depreciated for three, four, or five years, that is the assumptive useful life of the asset. Quite often, however, after the depreciation period, it is assumed that the desktops and laptops are "free" or at no cost. Because price does not equal cost, and it is the acquisition price that is depreciated, the judgment of whether a device is "free" is based on depreciation of device pricing. This judgment can lead to incorrect, but conscious decisions.

Useful life should consider a variety of perspectives and viewpoints, not only one. A basic premise of closed loop lifecycle planning remains that it is not necessarily the initial decision that is important, but the implications of that decision. The dimensions that should be considered in total to determine a thoughtful technology refresh should include all facets to arrive at a conclusion, not only one dimension such as depreciation.

It is only when all the considerations are factored in that an optimal technology-refresh project can be defined. This is similar to the approach that management uses holistically to make business decisions in general. The "dashboard" should consider the following factors: cost, risk, and service levels. When these factors are uniquely defined, the criteria for the technology refresh can be defined.

USEFUL LIFE: WARRANTY OR MAINTENANCE

After the useful life has been determined, the warranty or maintenance strategy can be established. In Chapter 8, "Warranty and Maintenance," closed loop lifecycle planning was clear that warranty is generally preferable. Because manufacturers' warranties are typically three years, the logical conclusion is that the useful life may be three years.

When the actual cost of a service event is factored into the determination, the first service event outside of the warranty window is often greater than the benefit of retention beyond three years. Some businesses use this outside-of-warranty event as the trigger for a technology refresh. When a device requires a hardware service call, instead of a desk-side support call, the device is simply replaced. Many businesses operated with this strategy and deem it quite effective.

The opposing perspective is that this replacement strategy is an unplanned event that could exceed the levels of a planned refresh and, quite possibly, the budget. Because it is unplanned, the scenario could lead to spikes in service, support, and capital expenditures. Finally, this approach encourages more informal strategies, including Stealth IT.

If the "replace not repair" approach is leveraged, it is important that the help desk track the devices that are outside of warranty so that trends can be identified and the number of events actually measured. Many businesses do not track at this level, and the perspective becomes more subjective than definitive. If a piece of hardware or a component fails within an access device, the cost of repair may well exceed the cost of replacement.

DESKTOPS AND LAPTOPS DIFFER

It is important to note that in technology-refresh planning, one size does not fit all. Desktops, laptops, tablets, and other access devices have a different useful life, cost profile, and possibly end-user profile. This is quite logical because the devices are fundamentally unique. Technology-refresh strategies should differ based on the type of wear, usage, and end user. This is followed by the fundamental criteria of cost, risk, and service levels.

A level of due diligence is suggested before making decisions regarding the useful life of each technology. The issues should also include all aspects of the access suite and the social aspect of the decisions. The rigor and due diligence for the technology is discussed further in the Bonus Section of this book, "User Segmentation: A Complement to Closed Loop Lifecycle Planning."

As a general rule, the lifecycle for desktops is viewed from three to four years. The three-year lifecycle is generally viewed as optimal. For laptops, the lifecycle is typically viewed from two to three years. Although two years may be optimal, there are budgetary issues to address, making the likely refresh cycle in the range of two to three years. Of course, desktops and laptops can be retained beyond the ranges presented in this section. The suggestion, however, is for businesses to seriously assess the implications to cost, risk, and service levels.

Given that desktop and laptops are fundamentally targeted for different usage models, if the technology-refresh cycles are identical, that should at a minimum trigger a conversation regarding the strategy. Interestingly, the same strategy does not always generate the conversation of the technology-refresh strategies. This could be attributed to the financial constraints as contrasted to the business issues related to the two profiles.

Technology refresh has become even more complicated by the overall explosion in the suite of access devices in the industry. Various devices have different refresh cycles. The desktop and laptop refresh cycle may have an impact on when these devices are refreshed, too.

An example of this is an end user who has a desktop or laptop device and also a PDA. Does the PDA get refreshed at the same time as the desktop or laptop? Does the PDA get treated as a bundle with the refresh? Even more basic is whether the PDA is even tracked the same as a desktop or laptop. The answers of many of these questions may not be readily available to businesses, and in any cases the answers are "no"; the PDA is outside of the desktop and laptop refresh cycle and is not viewed the same way. The point is that the technology refresh should apply to all access devices and related to the overall portfolio.

As handhelds merge with cell phones, the discussion becomes more complex, although this reduces two devices to one. Knowing the cost of support for a device is essential to determine whether the merge is cost-effective.

NOTE: Because of the manner that some businesses measure and report costs, the access devices that an end user leverages to access business information may be spread across different cost centers and not reported in the aggregate. Closed loop lifecycle planning research has found that much of the access costs are understated because of this complexity.

PROJECTS THAT INCREMENT THE ACCESS DEVICE FLEET

From time to time, projects may require new access technologies as a part of the scope. Software development projects, business application projects, and security projects are examples. Projects will usually have their own budget and funding model and be outside of the budgeting of the planned technology refresh. This does not suggest that projects are outside of the technology-refresh project itself, just that the funding may be from a different source.

It also does not suggest that projects outside of the planned technology refresh are not subject to the standards or the refresh plan.

NOTE: Closed loop lifecycle planning determines that a planned technology-refresh cycle is the optimal approach for an enterprise to adopt.

Communication is the key to ensure that there is linkage between both the project and the technology-refresh plan. There is often an additional economy of scale because the technology refresh itself is a project, perhaps in the overall program management office (PMO). At a minimum, the timelines are aligned so that both projects are effectively planned.

Many businesses rely on separate project funding outside of the planned technology-refresh project itself to provide incremental funding. In some cases, the devices are not planned in the refresh cycle so that the funding can be derived from another source of capital. Each business must determine the correct funding vehicle for its enterprise. One of the key considerations for technology refresh is that it is a cycle that is repeated over time. Reliance on a one-time project to assist in funding could establish expectations in the future regarding the funds required for future refreshes.

The consideration is whether the other projects represent a funding source for technology refresh or should technology refresh as its own project be the sole funding consideration for access devices lifecycle. This is an issue that many businesses are addressing today.

NOTE: Many businesses that do not have defined technology-refresh plans and leverage projects to drive the refresh cycle exceed the percentage of refresh that would have been addressed under a plan. In essence, there is overspending that uses the project as the financial justification. This is referred to as the "effective technology refresh rate."

OUTSIDE OF THE CYCLE

Projects represent only one scenario that could and often does result in an out-of-cycle technology refresh. In all businesses, there could be numerous, and very appropriate, scenarios resulting in out-of-cycle activities. The cautionary note is when the number and volume of out-of-cycle requests become the norm. The technology-refresh plan begins to be less effective when it becomes exception driven.

Technology refresh can become quite political within a business when the number of exceptions suggests that the governance model is not applicable across the enterprise.

Given businesses experience in performing technology refreshes, there should be established a percentage that the refresh plan would logically cover; in most businesses, this is in a range from 85 percent to 95 percent. (Higher percentages occur in those businesses that have an enforceable governance model.)

Many businesses confuse the one-off demand for an exception in technology refresh, but these are different scenarios. Special requirements need to be addressed with flexibility, but once addressed, it is likely that the technology-refresh plan could apply.

UPGRADES

In some instances, the configuration requirements suggest that "only" incremental memory or disk (or other component) needs to be added to an installed device. It is not unusual to have funding limitations that may only support the incremental component costs. Depending on the age of the device, and the business circumstances, of course, the true set of economics may present conflicting perspectives.

Although components may be perceived to be inexpensive, the true costs would include not only the acquisition price, but also the identification of which devices require the upgrade, the labor to deploy, the potential downtime, the logistics, and the asset management. An upgrade may or may not require as much time as a net new device, but the effort, including the post-installation checking, may make it so.

Many businesses minimize the impact of an upgrade by suggesting that the time invested for a desk-side support visit is shorter than the installation call, and certainly the capital expenditure is less. From a closed loop lifecycle planning perspective, the question is whether the useful life of the client device is extended or whether the remaining value is enhanced. If the useful life is extended, does the business intend to extend the lifecycle another 12 to 18 months?

A simple rule of thumb is looking at the depreciation of the device and the annual depreciation expense. If the upgrade exceeds or approaches that cost, perhaps more scrutiny is warranted. Given the costs of the technologies, the threshold is quite low to approach an annual depreciation level. This dynamic may have changed for many businesses that viewed the pricing of the access devices as the threshold. It is now simple to see that an upgrade of $150 suggests that a business review its approach.

Another guideline relates to the age of the device itself. If the device is within the 18- to 24-month window, the question to be asked is not only about the required upgrade, but whether there is a problem in underconfiguring the net new device. Just as with cascading business practices, many businesses prefer a "no-upgrade" approach. If upgrades do extend the useful life, a revision to the technology-refresh plan of record should be addressed.

NOTE: Businesses will be challenged to make the upgrade argument for desktop technology fit into a solid business case after 12 to 18 months of the device being installed.

THE ROLE OF ASSET MANAGEMENT

To have an effective technology-refresh plan, there must be a reliance on asset-management information. Asset management provides the fundamental information to build the technology-refresh plan.

When asset-management reliance is considered, the data elements desired become evident. For a technology-refresh plan, asset management should provide the following:

- Make and model of the device
- Serial number of the device
- Overall hardware configuration
- Overall software residing on the device
- Components and peripherals, including docking stations
- Upgrades, if any, from initial configuration
- Location of device
- End user, if any identified
- Department, if any, identified
- Age of the device, date of birth
- Access devices' MAC addresses

In many cases, when the information is not available, manual effort is required. Reconciliation can be a time-consuming effort, but should be considered a fundamental role in the technology-refresh strategy.

The challenge of asset management is more significant with laptops than desktops. Most automated tools easily capture devices that are on the network, but laptops may be offline or otherwise unavailable at the time of the inquiry. Much planning is required to ensure the proper capture of the information.

LEASING

In Chapter 14, "Service-Delivery Strategies," leasing is addressed in detail. Many businesses lease desktops, laptops, and other access devices. For client computing, the term of a lease transaction can range from 24 months to 60 months depending on the business. This section explores leasing as it impacts the technology-refresh strategy only.

Because a lease is a financial vehicle, it is reasonable to assume that the term of the lease is representative of the useful life. The financial plan assumes a certain rate and residual over a period of time, resulting in a payment stream for the business. The duration of the lease itself is the de facto technology-refresh cycle.

Because leasing is a financial vehicle, there are obvious cost implications regarding extending a lease or retaining the device at the end of the lease term. From a technology-refresh perspective, if an enterprise is leasing, extensions and returns are critical issues to address, and fundamental to the economics.

Extension of a lease can occur for several reasons, many of which are quite valid and appropriate. Requirements, projects, or regulations may require extensions. Development on a particular device may be deemed necessary. However, in the majority of cases, leases tend to be extended in lieu of acquiring net new devices. It is quite similar to the business decision to retain a depreciated device beyond the depreciation term, except that the business does not own the device in a lease; the leasing company owns the assets.

In a lease, the impact of the decision to extend has a measurable impact financially. However, there is an impact beyond the leasing expenses, which are similar to the determination of costs when depreciating.

Extending a lease may suggest that the initial term was not correct, which again suggests a review of the technology-refresh plan. Extending a lease is tantamount to an unsecured loan because the initial term amortized the assets on the leasing company's books and was already factored into the payment stream. Extending the lease impacts the remaining value of the device.

Some businesses buy the assets at the end of the lease to hedge the impact somewhat. Although this is quite a common practice, it still suggests that the initial technology-refresh strategy may be somehow flawed.

Just as in owning and expensing or depreciating assets, leasing assets without a reasonable practice level of asset management weakens the technology-refresh plan. The significant difference is that there is a monetary cost, defined in the terms and conditions of the lease, to address the inability to locate and return the assets.

IS THE TECHNOLOGY REFRESH "LIKE FOR LIKE"

One of the key components of the technology-refresh strategy is whether there will be a "like for like" refresh. User segmentation and innovations in technology will have an immediate impact on the answer. The technology refresh is a plan that will trigger such a review of the replacement technology. Businesses should seize the opportunity to consider alternatives at the time of the refresh planning. Businesses that make the assumption of like for like might deny themselves the opportunity to adopt new and innovative technologies.

End users will typically assume a "like for like" technology-refresh cycle. The refresh becomes an entitlement. Replacing a laptop with a desktop, a desktop with a thin client device, and other alternative scenarios are usually viewed by end users (and their management) as relinquishing a level of control and status. Focus should remain on providing the optimal access devices for employees to perform their work; however, technology refresh is both a technology business driver and a cultural implication. It is often the cultural aspect that is ignored or not fully considered until it is raised by the politics of the infrastructure.

If access devices are viewed as a suite or bundle, with incrementing technologies such as smart phones or PDAs, technology refresh is no longer a "like for like" proposition.

The wide adoption of mobility will certainly change the profiles and technology alternatives available. The traditional boundary of technology refresh that was desktop and laptop oriented should be expanded to include all access devices. The annual technology-refresh strategy should examine the budgets for all devices, not only desktops and laptops. The annual budget should be compelling when it refocuses on all access devices and user requirements. It is the management of the overall portfolio that will determine ultimately the cost, risk, and service levels.

To illustrate this point regarding portfolio management, a review of the primary key metrics may be useful. Previously, one of the key ratios was the number of desktops and laptops an enterprise had per employee. Software license agreements, asset-management reporting, and IT staffing leveraged this ratio as a key operating metric; it is still valuable today. The optimal objective is typically to come as close to one device per employee as possible.

Today, perhaps it is more relevant to express the ratio as the number of access devices that an employee has that could access company information. PDAs, for example, have an acquisition price approaching desktops, with the support cost approaching a laptop. In many businesses, the costs scale to where the PDA and laptop are equivalent. Yet, PDAs are often not included in the scope of the technology refresh, nor are these devices considered to influence whether an employee requires a desktop or a laptop. The impact the PDA could have on the one-to-one desired end-state goal is that it could double the impact of the number of devices that an end user may retain. From a cost, risk, and service-level perspective, a false sense of confidence could occur if these devices are not included in the technology-refresh consideration.

All access devices should be included in the technology-refresh strategy. The plan should include all the planning for the acquisition and deployment of access devices. Lifecycle should be extended to all of these devices because the implications are quite similar. It is not clear how effective budgeting and security measures could be taken without this rigor in effect.

Chapter 12, "Disposing of Client Devices at the End of Life," clearly noted that many of the nondesktop and nonlaptop devices did not have a disposition strategy in place; the same is true for the technology-refresh strategy, too. The implications of this is that the device is acquired, but it is not clear how long it will remain in the fleet, nor is it understood what to do with the device when it is refreshed and no longer in use. When this fact is combined with the already complicated product mix, the variable of what is the replacement strategy becomes more concerning.

The challenge is greater because the newer features and enhancements occur at a very rapid pace, which always increments technology refreshes and to date does not decrement the refresh. To some degree, nondesktops and nonlaptops remain as discretionary items, not under the auspices of the overall technology-refresh plan; this dynamic is rapidly going to change.

"BIG BANG" OR PHASED TECHNOLOGY REFRESH

A significant amount has been written about, and there are a lot of opinions regarding, the "big bang" versus a phased approach for technology refresh. The "big bang" suggests that the best set of economics can be achieved by a one-time-only event (technology refresh) that would raise all end users to the same level of standardization. It is assumed that standardization across the board is the critical cost driver (refer to the Bonus Section of this book for more information).

From a purely academic perspective, having a homogeneous installed base, with the same image and support, could yield the best cost perspective. However, with such access device diversity and the advent of user segmentation, the best cost will be derived by managing the overall product mix within a given user segment.

For the "big bang" to work, the "perfect storm" is required. A detailed project plan, a robust project office, a readiness of the end-user population, a scaling of products, deployment teams, and a business model for minimal disruption. These are but a handful of the considerations.

There are clearly areas where there is the ability to aggregate demand and deploy, often to a common geography (a campus, a location, a building, a site). To perform a "big bang" across an enterprise is a momentous task. No doubt, some businesses do this; the scaling would likely be the critical success factor.

Despite what to many appears somewhat obvious, particularly today with such diversity, the "big bang" concept has continued. Many businesses now refer to any large-scale refresh to a site, building, or location as a "big bang."

The phased technology-refresh approach simply states that over a period of time, the installed base will be refreshed based on a defined plan and predefined criteria. Typically, one third to one fourth of the installed base would be refreshed. The rationale for the phased approach is that the scale and scope is less disruptive and easier to mange and execute. Under a phased approach, the one-time-only costs are mitigated. Another perspective is that a phased approach is more economically feasible. A phased approach avoids the considerable investment in hardware and infrastructure at one time.

When all the costs are weighed, including the tangible benefits of standardization (including the warehousing, resources, PMO, cost of capital, and so forth), it would seem that most businesses would be more comfortable in the phased approach. If risk is added into the equation as an element to consider, risk is certainly mitigated in the phased approach.

The determining factor really comes in at the end of the economic discussion: If the "big bang" did result in the best set of economics, can a business embrace it? Change by its very nature is unsettling. Change in the deployment of the technology refresh on a scale contemplated by the scope of an entire installed base may find obstacles in a business (such as being able to adopt culturally to all the required dynamics).

Given this backdrop of the "big bang" and the phased approach, just where did the "big bang" come from? Most likely, when businesses looked at Y2K and Y2K remediation, because of the implications, large enterprisewide installed bases were refreshed, upgraded, or otherwise addressed. In the postmortem of Y2K, the mentality was "thank goodness that is over and we do not have to go through that again." But, the results for the most part were favorable. Therefore, the "big bang" was validated as a strategy.

Also, at about the same time, more and more businesses embraced TCO (the total cost of ownership). In TCO, standardization plays a dominant role in the economics.

These two factors—Y2K and TCO standardization—led to the packaging of the "big bang" from a marketing perspective and a business perspective. The marketing message was facilitated because many businesses had the precise experience in both Y2K and TCO.

The "big bang" approach has validation in areas beyond access devices. Some businesses are exploring the "big bang" for CRT fleets or for printing fleets. A key element is the ability to scale with minimal disruption to the end user.

MERGERS AND ACQUISITIONS

When businesses acquire or divest, this is clearly a compelling event. In most (and likely all) scenarios, there will be a plethora of access devices, tools, software; and likely all related lifecycle elements will be somewhat different by the nature of two different companies. Of course, there would be synergies and commonality; after all, it was a buyer-seller relationship.

Determining the access device strategy is one of the basic first steps. The result is often an immediate intersecting of cultures, processes, and preferences. If it is assumed that each business has a mature lifecycle-management plan, selecting the optimal approach would not be straightforward. The scenario is more complicated when businesses are at varying levels in lifecycle practices.

Typically, a team is assigned to explore the current states, and chartered with identifying the best practices and consolidating the approach. However, more often as a result of expediency, the determination of which lifecycle practice is selected becomes how quickly one company can transition over to the new company's approach. As a point of reference, the acquiring company generally leads the practice discussion.

Culturally and organizationally, interesting behaviors develop that may, or may not, diminish over time. You might recall the phrase "the way we used to do this function at Company X before was...."

A clue to the maturity of the lifecycle practice is how quickly the lifecycle conversation proceeds before the legacy discussion or frame of reference occurs.

The relevance of this discussion with regard to the technology-refresh topic is that quite often a merger and acquisition triggers a technology refresh. It is important that the decision for the technology refresh be based on the strategies of standardization, image management, security, service level, and costs. User segmentation may play a role in this scenario. There will always be an inordinate level of politics internally regarding mergers and acquisitions, but it is not desirable to ignore the impact that the technology refresh could have on the culture. Often, there will be restructuring funding available on a one-time-only basis to align the businesses.

REQUESTS FOR PROPOSAL (RFPS) AND REQUEST FOR INFORMATION (RFIS)

One opinion holds that a technology refresh may be an ideal time to consider the generation of an RFP or RFI. Although RFPs usually occur with a timing of the refresh, if a business adheres to a phased approach, the technology-refresh strategy is truly a business-as-usual operation. Under this scenario, the technology refresh itself is not necessarily a compelling event.

If a business refreshes devices on a planned monthly basis, a technology refresh becomes a recurring part of the day-to-day rigor. When the business practices the "big bang," however, a business case for an RFP could be made.

A few points should be made regarding both RFPs and RFIs. RFPs and RFIs are not "free" to a business. A simple rule is that the RFI/RFP process can cost up to 1 percent of whatever it is that is being requested. In some cases, the percentages can be higher. The costs include the following:

- Bid generation
- Cost to review, full team
- Interoperability and prototyping
- Technical assessment and configuration
- Disposition
- Negotiation
- Legal review
- Image development
- Processes and workflow
- RFI questions and conversion to RFP
- Third parties, if required

The list of investment and cost is significant. The preceding list is only a partial sample, but sufficient to demonstrate that the technology-refresh timing may be challenged by the requirements and rigor of the full RFP process.

Most purchasing teams have a governance model and rigor based on timing and business conditions. There is becoming more widespread adoption of pricing models and methodologies that should result in similar output and results of RFPs.

NOTE: With all the investments made in the websites of the manufacturers and partners, the RFI may begin to be nothing more than accessing information from the web identifying the core competencies and establishing parameters.

TECHNOLOGY REFRESH: THE DISRUPTION FACTOR

Many businesses need to understand the level of disruption that the technology refresh could result in and address the disruption in terms of downtime. Downtime for many businesses is often quite difficult to quantify and measure.

Technology refresh sometimes takes on an identity of its own and results in a level of apprehension in the end users and the installed base. The "big bang" is particularly susceptible to these concerns.

It is important to remember that a prior bad experience by an end user is remembered far longer than the good experience. Because of this, the perception of IT by the end user can easily be formed and defined by the technology-refresh experience.

Just as lifecycle is a program, technology refresh is a project within the program. One of the key considerations of the project is obviously to minimize downtime. As user segmentation and the variety of access devices become more diverse, technology refresh will have even more impact on end users as more devices are required to be synchronized.

Desk-side support is the most costly of the service-delivery strategies. The increasing role of management tools, help desk, and remote support will minimize disruption in the future and create a new dynamic for technology refresh.

SUMMARY

Technology refresh is a critical part of an enterprise's continuous process-improvement plan. Planned technology-refresh cycles will almost always yield the best set of economics for a business. Yet, the budgeting process may drive behavior and realities that do not favorably align with the market and potentially create a noncompetitive situation for a business.

The technology-refresh cycle parallels a business' adoption of innovation, productivity, and security. The technology-refresh process should permit an enterprise to embrace innovation and benefits and not create a barrier to take advantage of improvements.

There should be a technology-refresh plan for all access technologies, not only the traditional desktops and laptops.

Many businesses still view the technology-refresh cycle as a budget "exercise" as contrasted to validating that value (quantified) that the features and speeds can provide.

Just as with asset management and help desk, technology refresh should be consolidated and addressed at the enterprise level. The economies of scale and financial advantages for standardization are greater, particularly if the scope of the technology is global.

As discussed in Chapter 11, "Program Management," technology refresh is a program and requires program management discipline to be successful.

14

Service-Delivery Strategies

INTRODUCTION

After the individual lifecycle elements have been addressed and defined, a business can turn its attention to the optimal service-delivery strategy. The service-delivery strategy is the approach taken to provide the service level to end users. Historically, the numbers of service-delivery alternatives were few for businesses to consider. Just as other lifecycle elements today, a growing number of alternatives are available today. Each of the service-delivery strategies has its own unique economics and considerations, including overall entrance and exit costs.

The traditional choices were related to buying or leasing as the financial vehicle and related to insourcing, outsourcing, or out-tasking as the service-fulfillment strategy. Each of these alternatives is discussed in detail in this chapter. To a high degree, many of the alternatives have become commingled in terms of how a business may opt to view these alternatives. Although many of the alternatives can be combined, the complexity increases as alternatives are customized further than the initial tender from the providers, including internal.

The business case for the service-delivery alternatives needs to begin with an appropriate baselining of the cost today of the current state. Despite the prevalence of the total cost of ownership, many businesses still do not know what the true costs are to deliver lifecycle management. Therefore, regardless of which service-delivery strategy is selected, there will always be a question about what the cost-reduction and cost-avoidance models were before the adoption of the approach.

When determining the service-delivery strategy, the cost of change is a factor to consider. The cost of change, under closed loop lifecycle planning, is the overall entrance and exits costs related to a lifecycle decision. Transition costs also represent a significant portion of the overall cost picture. Excessive transition costs may mitigate some of the financial benefits and extend the return on investment. Regardless of the scope, the transition timeframe, risk, and cost are key determining factors when selecting the service-delivery approach.

To begin, the alternatives must be specifically defined so that all the constituencies, including the decision makers, are all in accord regarding what is being discussed. Although this might seem basic, it is not. It is not unusual for the definitions themselves to be a point of contention, both within the teams and contractually when there is an agreement to proceed.

It is first important to establish the definitions for the following:

- Insourcing
- Out-tasking
- Outsourcing

INSOURCING

Insourcing is the service-delivery strategy that identifies the resources to provide the service levels as an employee of the business. In other words, it is the internal resource or headcount that delivers the service. A conscious decision is made that the labor to deliver the service level will be provided by the business itself. The key distinction is the headcount, which is a part of the business.

Using its own headcount to deliver service can be a solid strategy if the business requires service levels beyond those contractually or operationally committed, or desires a higher "touch" because of the relationship between IT and the end users or IT and the business units. For example, many firms in the financial sector, because of the time-sensitive nature of their business, have a high "touch" environment to ensure that their traders of currencies, bonds, stocks, and so on have instant support.

Insourcing is quite common and of particular importance when the environment is particularly custom with applications that were internally developed. It is generally believed that although retaining its own headcount may be more costly in the long term, the service level might otherwise not be able to be delivered.

There is also a case for the insourced approach when a business simply does not believe that it can rely on any third party for support. For these businesses, it is a level of confidence or trust.

Some businesses (for example, self-maintainers or self-warranty providers) may opt to remain in a lifecycle operation because of the investment to date, which is perceived to be a "sunk" cost. The cost of change is thought to be too high to precipitate a change in strategy.

Insourcing also has the advantage of protecting an otherwise exposed workforce. It cannot always be assumed that if the work to be performed were performed by another, that the worker could be transitioned to another position within the enterprise.

It is not unusual for a gray area to appear in the insourcing model when subcontractors are used rather than a business' own headcount. When this occurs, it becomes a bit difficult to assume that the service delivery is insourced; this represents more of a vendor-managed or out-tasked model.

One of the keys to insourcing is that the business in essence declares that the services being delivered are core competencies, and a conscious decision is made to remain in that "business." When third-party labor is used, the position becomes less compelling. Sometimes the term *staff augmentation* is used to describe this approach. At the end of the day, it is using third parties to deliver service, and the business is managing the labor force. This vendor-management approach is not true insourcing, but has the characteristics that base the business case on retaining control of the operation internally.

OUT-TASKING

Out-tasking is different from outsourcing. Out-tasking is the service-delivery strategy that permits a third party to deliver a scope of lifecycle-management services. Out-tasking is usually accomplished through a service-level agreement, also referred to as the statement of work.

The terms and conditions are usually more flexible than outsourcing, and there is generally not a transition of personnel, assets, or tools. Out-tasking is generally covered by a multiyear agreement umbrella (typically three years). There are annual milestones for renewal, with terms and conditions for cancellation or termination, and sometimes termination with or without cause.

Out-tasking is designed to be a flexible approach for businesses that understand the need to get to best practice levels but may lack the key personnel, skills, or tools to achieve this objective. The approach is to contract, for a defined period of time, a service level that once achieved can be documented and then transitioned in-house, or out-tasked again, or perhaps then outsourced if the gap seems too significant to accommodate.

The key to out-tasking is that the flexibility is derived by the driving of the service levels and the cost to deliver the service itself. Out-tasking scopes vary, and there is a rigor in change orders. Both the supplier and the business should be concerned about "scope creep," services provided beyond the contracted levels. This has cost implications and affects end-user expectations with regard to the potential transitions of services.

Out-tasking is quite popular and has a viable strategy for some time, so it is a mature lifecycle-delivery alternative.

The quality of the service delivery often depends on the two basic themes identified in closed loop lifecycle planning: the help desk and asset management. These functions must be provided in a quality manner so that the supporting operations can be performed optimally. Otherwise, there will be quality issues. Most of the out-tasking agreements will highlight this as a critical dependency.

Today, the out-tasking model is referred to within the industry as "shared services." Although this represents a level of due diligence in definition, the shared-service model remains the out-tasking service-delivery alternative.

OUTSOURCING

Outsourcing represents a decision to formally exit a lifecycle operation. Unlike out-tasking, outsourcing generally assumes a transfer of assets, personnel, and potentially toolsets (licenses). An outsourcing relationship covers a longer term than out-tasking (five to seven years or longer, in contrast to three years).

The outsourcing terms and conditions are much more rigorous than out-tasking because personnel and asset buy-out are involved. The scope is generally much more comprehensive and usually includes the outsourcing of the help desk and asset management.

Outsourcing is not for all businesses, only those with the maturity to exit a business operation and be comfortable with the choice. Outsourcing is a service-delivery strategy that permits the transition of staff from one business to another. Headcount is transferred.

Outsourcing agreements are defined service levels in detail and are replete with contractual language for performance and penalties. Outsourcing usually occurs in two phases; the first phase being transition, and the next being transformation of the people and processes to meet the service levels that the company could not achieve on its own.

In an outsourcing agreement, the outsourced third party becomes the IT department to fulfill demand requests. Outsourcing generally has a robust scope and can scale globally.

TACTICAL SERVICE-DELIVERY APPROACHES

Based on closed loop lifecycle planning, there are six service-delivery approaches for a business to consider. Each of these alternative approaches can fit into the model of insource, out-task, or outsource.

These alternatives are as follows:

- Buying à la carte
- Bundling
- Leasing
- Utility
- Virtualization
- Hybrid

BUYING À LA CARTE

À la carte buying suggests a traditional approach where each element of the lifecycle is procured separately as if there were no relationship among the elements. The economics and pricing of each element is standalone and may be linked (or may not be) with other lifecycle elements. The objective in this purchasing lead approach is to secure the best standalone price on the lifecycle element under consideration.

The à la carte approach is often seen when the electronic auction is the vehicle for pricing. The definition for bidding is quite narrow, and the focus is exclusively on the pricing of a particular lifecycle element. Many businesses rely on this mechanism as the vehicle for pricing, and it works well in those environments where the focus is on the pricing.

À la carte is not intended to be solution oriented, nor is it designed to be more than the pricing vehicle solely. A fair amount of experience drives the behaviors in this area, and it is not unusual for businesses to rely on this approach for a wide variety of products.

Value add is not a substantial part of this approach because it tends to add cost or increase pricing. One of the concerns raised in this approach is that the trend in the market is for more to be embedded into the access devices. Based on this, the à la carte approach might require manufacturers to avoid having the business embrace those items that could reduce costs.

NOTE: The à la carte approach will rarely lead to service levels acceptable to end users. The à la carte approach frequently is the least-optimized alternative.

BUNDLING

Bundling is the inclusion of certain elements into the product as a product attribute. For some time, warranty and extended warranty levels were among the few product attributes that could be included at the time of the point of sale.

Today, there is a host of factory-oriented services, and the list is expanding. These services that are delivered as a part of the manufacturing process can be a part of the product build and therefore included in the overall price of the product itself. The key is that the service needs to be determined at the point of sale to become a defined part of the product itself.

Of course, these services can be quoted separately and under a separate à la carte approach. The problem in doing this is that the timing when the service is most likely to be delivered is at the time of manufacturing. Examples range from imaging to asset tagging.

Bundling can offer other economic alternatives for businesses. It is possible that if the accounting and finance teams of the business concur, the costs of the factory-provided services performed at the point of sale may be amortized along with the product if the determination is made internally by the business. This amortization permits the smoothing on the one-time-only spike that might be created by the inclusion of the ancillary services.

In many cases, the bundling is provided without a breakdown of what each of the elements costs. The rationale is that some elements may be more margin oriented than others, and the manufactures may provide a "turnkey" solution. In these cases, the bundling is firm and likely cannot be fairly separated. The overall service level is defined, but the pricing for the individual services is not provided, hence the bundling concept.

LEASING

Leasing is an alternative approach that has been available for quite some time. Recently, there have been some changes to leases that are worthwhile to address.

There are fundamentally in client computing two types of leases: capital and operating leases. The main difference is that one is on balance sheet (capital leases) and one is off balance sheet (operating leases).

The FASB (Financial Accounting Standards Board) has established rules that businesses need to understand before determining whether a transaction is a capital or operating lease. Specifically, FASB 13 addresses the criteria and interpretation. It is required that the business make this determination; a supplier cannot.

Depending on the metrics that a business desires to drive, the decision whether client computing will be a capital or operating expense will be pursued.

Regardless of the type of lease selected, several fundamental changes in leasing are noteworthy, including the following:

- Like-for-like conversion
- Assumptions for loss
- Captive leasing partners
- Forgiveness for condition
- Overall structures
- "Buying down" the rate factor
- Financial asset management

Like-for-Like Conversion

In the past, many businesses have had challenging experiences with leasing and as result struggle with leasing as an alternative. One of the reasons is that leases would require that a specific asset, identified by a specific serial number, be returned to the leasing company as a part of the end-of-life conversion. However, it should be noted that leasing has significantly changed over the years and is much more flexible than ever before.

Many businesses lacked the overall asset management to be able to address the specific device by serial number due to a variety of reasons, among them cascading, repair and replace (laptops), lost assets, and other situations. Part of the reason for this is that asset management as a discipline has had many definitions and priorities over time.

Sometimes the leasing companies enforced the clause that requires specific asset return, but sometimes not. When they did, a penalty or premium would be paid. From the contractual perspective, this was covered and addressed by the terms and conditions, so it was a term considered up front.

However, this end-of-life return has convinced many businesses that leasing is not viable. As mentioned several times in this book, leasing when there is poor asset management is not likely a solid plan, but that point is different from the behavior that accompanies the end-of-life resolution.

Today, leasing companies provide for like-for-like conversion (assets that are similar in configuration to that which is on the leasing schedule itself). This flexibility is designed to provide for the scenarios where the asset is not lost (in general) but where it was replaced under warranty or otherwise cascaded.

This added flexibility permits a business to manage its PC fleet a bit differently if the dynamics are such that the service-delivery strategy may inhibit the return of the actual serial number but the overall population is similarly configured and the asset management practice is acceptable. This concept has made leasing viable again for businesses that otherwise might not have embraced the option.

NOTE: It is unfortunate when a poor asset-management process precludes a company from using leasing as a business strategy.

Assumptions for Loss

At the beginning of the relationship, there might be some security considerations about why a percentage of devices may not be returned at the end of the lease term (due to replacement, loss, cascading).

It is now possible to establish a set of assumptions that would permit the creation of a leasing structure that would assume a certain level of loss. These assumptions could allow for a percentage of components or peripherals to be retained, too.

By addressing this assumption, the businesses and the leasing partner have a set of expectations up front, and the rate and residuals can be established accordingly. It is when the losses are unplanned that the stress is placed on both business and leasing company to work through these issues. Precedent is important, so there may be little flexibility that could be provided. This is the reason why understanding the installed base lifecycle practices is important as a key criterion in determining whether leasing is viable.

Types of (Captive) Leasing Partners

Three types of leasing partners can be a part of the client computing solution, as follows:

- Partnered leasing
- Third-party leasing
- Captive leasing

Partnered Leasing

Partnered leasing is the relationship that a leasing company has with a manufacturer. This is generally marketing or a "go to market" relationship. Both leasing company and manufacturer are independent but have an overall marketing or otherwise defined relationship.

The relationship with the business is between the leasing company and the business itself, with the manufacturer available to assist in "brokering" the relationship.

There are many solid relationships as described in this category. These relationships are driven by the confidence that the three parties informally share. Contractually, only the leasing company and the business are parties to the lease.

Third-Party Leasing

True third-party leasing is an independent leasing category. A third-party leasing company competes based on rate, residual, and the credit worthiness of the business. The companies tend to be aggressive and quite often may, or may not, retain the leasing paper internally to their company.

The business case for the third-party leasing company is much the same as the à la carte approach in buying product: It is procurement driven, not based on relationship or value add, but driven by pricing (which in this case is rate and residual). The terms of the leases in third-party leasing are important because the sole relationship is the finance relationship. There may or may not be additional flexibilities available.

NOTE: The key for this category is where the desire is purely based on the rate and residual of the tender.

Captive Leasing

The captive leasing approach is not new; it has been available in one form or another for quite some time. The captive leasing relationship suggests a tight contractual and business alignment between the leasing company and the manufacturers. In many cases, this could mean there is a sole-supplier relationship or exclusivity, or it could mean that the leasing company is a part of the manufacturer itself.

The importance of the captive leasing model is of interest. In a leasing relationship, if the manufacturer becomes a stakeholder in either the lease itself (if the leasing company is a part of the manufacturer) or if the manufacturer is a party to the relationship contractually as an exclusive party, the dynamics of the leasing relationship are fundamentally changed.

Although there remains a set of terms and conditions, and although these are enforceable, the manufacturers have become a stakeholder in ensuring that the financial relationship and the incumbent relationship are managed to the satisfaction of all parties. Sometimes this means that the manufacturers may intercede to assist in resolving issues as they arise during the relationship.

This account-management function is the value add of the relationship. This may or may not make the captive leasing company the least cost, but it certainly could be the least-risk alternative.

Forgiveness for Condition

One of the changes in leasing today is more flexibility in the definitions of the condition of the returned devices. Particularly in the partnered or captive leasing relationships, this is an area where the leasing company, the business, and the manufacturers can add value beyond the rate and residual. Although this certainly does not preclude any third party from making the same business decisions, it does not provide the leverage of ready and contractually enabled partners to assist in the resolution.

Condition of the returned devices is quite subjective, and the ebb and flow of these discussions are quite literally dependent on what is at stake in the relationship. If the leasing is subject to the request for price (RFP) process, frequently the trade-off by the leasing companies is the enforcement of the contract terms as contrasted to the potential to secure a further financial footprint. In other words, a company can use the next leasing cycle to impact the end of the current leasing cycle.

Overall Structures

Leasing structures have also fundamentally changed from previous practices. In the past, leases were assigned a specific start and stop date, and the timing and expenses were prorated. Today, it is possible to have leases that are co-terminus and have a common start or end date (if desired). In addition, lease structures can be made so that there is a quarterly sweep. This suggests that leasing payments will always be a month in arrears.

These developments in the overall structures of leasing provide businesses a more flexible and customized approach. From a lifecycle perspective, many of the features permit the capture of information and timing, which can then be reconciled with the lifecycle approach.

"Buying Down" the Rate Factors

One thing that makes leasing a different scenario than before is the ability of the manufacturers to "buy down" the lease rate factor. This is performed by an allowance in the hardware pricing that the leasing company secures. In a captive or partnered leasing approach, this can permit more aggressive rates to address the rate and residual strategy that is often a part of the process. Suppliers use the rate buy down to commingle both residual value and additional product discounts.

Financial Asset Management

All the information on leasing schedules (Schedule A) can be made available as a database for the business. This permits a business to have another feed into the asset-management repository and improve the level of detail recorded and tracked.

Although not a substitute for asset management, it certainly can provide another way to capture substantial detail.

NOTE: One of the potential key benefits of leasing that is frequently overlooked is the ability to load all the leasing schedule information into the asset-management repository. This enables businesses to proactively manage the due dates and improve accuracy and strength of financial reporting.

UTILITY

The utility concept is not new. The utility strategy is defined as a cost per seat, per month. This cost per seat includes the product and services. Stated another way, a utility represents the cost per seat, per month for a defined service level that includes the access device itself.

As a service-delivery strategy, this was a common approach in the early 1990s. As a service-delivery strategy, the utility was often equated with the outsourcing of the client infrastructure. However, the utility is in the mid-point between full client outsourcing and the out-tasking service-delivery model.

Under closed loop lifecycle planning, utility refers to a cost per seat, per month for a defined service level. A utility is a service agreement, not a lease. Within the utility concept, there are two models, too. The first includes the product, but the second does not.

The utility works the best when the product is included as a part of the cost per seat, per month because the overall approach is not a lease but a service agreement. A fundamental difference exists between a lease and a utility. In a lease, the relationship is between a leasing company and the business. In a utility approach, the relationship is between the service provider and the business.

The service-only approach, in which the product is excluded, is more of a managed client arrangement and should not be confused with the utility. The utility is a turnkey approach. Technology refresh, product decommissioning, and related lifecycle elements are all included. The concept of the utility is similar in its construct to a telephone service. If you are an end user, your expectation is that all you need to operate and use the phone is available. This would be true in a utility-based service.

The utility can be highly flexible and include the services that are mutually defined and agreed upon in a statement of work. The contract is generally in line with the out-tasking model of three years.

An interesting dynamic in a utility is that the various lifecycle elements are not priced out independently to a business. For some businesses, this creates a level of discomfort because they want to know all the empirical pricing. A lot of time is spent in requesting the à la carte pricing so that the overall approach can be reviewed by a business. There are several problems when a business requires this level of detail.

The first challenge is that from a service-delivery strategy, the utility must provide a cost per seat, per month. As a part of this, there will be the hardware associated with the delivery. The product and services defined are embedded. For a utility to be a service tender, there must be the integrity of the per-seat cost. By breaking out the bill of material, the utility might not pass the accounting rigor as a service agreement.

The second challenge is that the bill of material will have certain elements all at unique price points and margin levels by the service provider. The utility permits the service providers to "blend" the profitable and less-profitable aspects of the solution into a competitive tender. By breaking down the bill of material into the elements, the service provider is limited in the overall packaging of the per-seat arrangement.

The third challenge is likely the most significant to overcome. If the business requires the elemental pricing of the lifecycle functions, perhaps the utility model is not the optimal solution for the business. A more traditional shared-services model might be more appropriate for the business.

As mentioned earlier, it is important that the current state costs be fully understood so that the service-delivery alternatives can be considered in the appropriate context. The utility approach requires that the change between the current and future state be well defined.

VIRTUALIZATION

Virtualization is increasingly being adopted in the industry as more attention is paid to the information lifecycle and control of office users. *Virtualization* is defined as the ability to access information remotely through the access device whose infrastructure is remote and likely in the data center. The availability of network bandwidth has made virtualization possible for a wide range of end users.

It is widely conceded that a locked-down desktop environment can deliver the least-cost alternative on that platform. If the actual device is only the access input, and no local data is stored, the essence of virtualization is captured.

Server-based computing or thin client computing is the initial technology alternative that presented these types of alternatives to the market. The utility basis for timesharing and the "consumption" models have taken the industry to new levels of virtualization.

In a virtual environment, the end user has full access to the authorized applications and is assigned privileges, but does not have the ability to locally possess information. The information lifecycle management is provided generally through the data center.

The next (or even present) generation of virtualization will go well beyond traditional thin client computing. Blades on servers and PCs are becoming widely available as alternative solutions. Blade technology for servers, workstations, and PCs represents the technology where all the components are stored on a board (blade) that resides in the data center, not at the end user.

The progression of the market has evolved from centralized computing to the decentralized computing mode, and now the pendulum has swung back to a more centralized model. The market will determine just how far the pendulum will swing, but regulations, privacy laws, and governance will likely play a role that was not a factor before.

HYBRID: A COMBINATION OF SERVICE-DELIVERY ALTERNATIVES

In service-delivery strategies, it is quite possible that a business will take the features of various service-delivery alternatives and create a hybrid model that is most comfortable to the business. One could argue that even in a fully outsourced environment, a business still retains certain decision and lifecycle functions in its operations.

Recognizing that each relationship will have some unique characteristics is important because lifecycle management is unique to each business.

The hybrid model will permit businesses to adopt the level of service delivery that is most comfortable to the enterprise. Businesses should resist the temptation to totally fit into templates and packaged approaches that may not represent at least an 80 percent fulfillment of the requirements. In many instances, the 80 percent solution is more than adequate to address certain areas.

Standard service offerings fall into this category. Predefined service levels and common deliverables are a solid initial step into a more comprehensive approach to lifecycle service-delivery strategies. Businesses should focus more on the service level first, and then the service-delivery strategy. One of the fundamental considerations in closed loop lifecycle planning is that the bill of material defines the service levels, and the "who delivers" that service level is what this part of service delivery is all about.

OTHER SERVICE-DELIVERY CONSIDERATIONS

Determining the service-delivery strategy is more than accessing what organization will deliver the service: insource, out-task, or outsource. The key to success may well be all the considerations outside of the service-delivery alternative except for the implications of that decision.

In this section, the following topics are explored:

- Role of procurement
- Vendor management
- Service-level management
- Platform: In or out?
- Pride of ownership
- Multivendor or sole supplier
- Remaining infrastructure personnel
- Lifecycle-management: Whom do you trust?
- Declaring core competencies
- Tools: Owning them and selection
- Mergers, acquisitions, and divestitures

ROLE OF PROCUREMENT

The role of procurement in the out-task, outsource, or hybrid service-delivery strategy will change. Businesses need to be prepared for the impact of those changes and as a part of the decision criteria determine whether the implication is desirable.

Procurement, if the business has acquired lifecycle through an à la carte approach, will find that the role has been altered to be more of a vendor-management role collaborating with IT than the more traditional role. Pricing becomes less of an issue after the agreements have been approved and signed, when the focus shifts to delivery and investment.

NOTE: It is essential that procurement understand the required service levels to ensure that they do not trade service level for product price.

With this as a prime area, many businesses find themselves in a position where purchasing aligns with IT to provide the continuous process-improvement plans as a part of the assignment.

VENDOR MANAGEMENT

Vendor management is different from managing a traditional buyer-seller relationship. Vendor management suggests that at some level decisions have been made regarding the supplier base, and there is a high level of collaboration.

The skill set in vendor management is unique and often requires more interpersonal and management skills. Some businesses view the vendor management as akin to a program or project manager in terms of the skill set requirements. Many businesses fail to recognize the fundamental differences, and the relationship does not fully develop as it could.

Some of the warning signals include the perception by the teams that there is "constant" negotiation or renegotiation, a concern about "scope creep," or a general concern about the services delivered. In any case, the importance is that communications be open and candid, including the point whether the actual relationship is robust enough to solve business issues or become an obstacle in solving them.

Vendor management is not a discipline that is easily adopted. Recently, there have been more formal classroom and industry perspectives on this discipline. The relationship assumes well-defined processes understood and agreed to by both parties.

SERVICE-LEVEL MANAGEMENT

Service-level management differs still from vendor management and procurement management. Service-level management requires that there be an established formal set of metrics that can be measured and reported for the service delivery of the program or project. It is critical that the metrics be concise, clear, and well communicated.

Service-level management is a developing discipline that has as its basis the management dashboard as an example of how to operate in the environment. The dashboard reflects those key metrics by which the project or program is classified as exceeding objectives, meeting objectives, or not meeting objectives.

Over and above this level of reporting is the quality of the services provided. Many businesses use a color-coded system to report on the status.

The key driver in service management is that members of the team are rewarded and penalized when the objectives are reported.

The service-management function is delivered through the joint program management office (PMO), as described elsewhere in this book. Common metrics do make a lot of the issues that occur day to day easier to resolve. Each lifecycle element will have its own service-management metrics that will then roll up to the overall dashboard metrics.

Quality metrics are typically measured in terms of end-user satisfaction and completion of the assigned work under the service-level agreements.

Whether insourced, out-tasked, or outsourced, the service-management metrics are applicable. If insourced, the internal infrastructure team needs to operate as if they were a service provider, so that the service becomes the focus and the quality. It should be noted that the cost is not an issue in the service-level management discussion because it is assumed that this decision was already determined and the focus is now the deliverable.

PLATFORM: IN OR OUT?

When businesses make a service-delivery decision, one of the questions to be specifically responded to is whether the scope of the decision extends to the platform itself. The inclusion of the platform is important for a variety of reasons. What role, if any, does the platform provider play in a service-delivery decision?

With the trend in the industry to have the manufacturers provide more of the portfolio of lifecycle services as a part of the product embedded, the manufacturer's role is not insignificant. Part of the lifecycle strategy may be delivered as a part of the product tender.

Another reason to ask this question outright is the impact that the service decision has on the incumbent suppliers and the competitors. If the service provider is aligned with a hardware or software manufacturer, it is reasonable to advise the competitors of the landscape and the scope of the decision. If the product is within the scope of the service agreement, does the service provider or the business determine who the platform provider will be?

This might seem fundamental, but experience in lifecycle suggests that when a decision is made, and there are outstanding and aligned relationships, at a minimum influence must occur that impacts the competitive landscape. In some cases, the business retains the privilege to select the products that the service providers will support. In other cases, the business is neutral and defers to the service provider. Service providers often have an alignment with manufacturers, so the service decision may lead to the platform decision, too.

Businesses need to ensure that the decisions are consciously made. Often, a de facto decision is made when the implications are not thoroughly considered.

PRIDE OF OWNERSHIP

It is important for the business to understand that certain service-delivery strategies may include the platform as an embedded attribute of the solution. Many businesses need to get through the emotions of such a relationship. Whether the client assets are on the balance sheet or on the income statement as an expense is important if there is a perceived "goodness or badness" associated with the decision.

Many businesses explore outsourcing and out-tasking and do not relinquish the assets on the balance sheet. Among the rationales is included the accounting treatment, but also the emotions of having its business' assets not owned by the business itself. The value of the assets on the books versus their street value may be an important consideration as to whether the assets are transferred. Assets below street value that are transferred will result in a higher service price.

Whose financial statement the assets appear on is less important than the emotions of why the objection would appear in the first place. Buyer's remorse, or the second-guessing of business decisions, is quite common and is a normal part of human nature. It is important, however, in the service-delivery decision that the emotions quickly be put aside so that the vendor-management and service-management focus can be acted upon.

In many businesses, the conversation continuing may equate to the belief that a service-delivery decision is not final. This may result in reducing the effectiveness of the strategy and impact the overall quality of the solution. At a minimum, this could impact the morale of those supporting the end users.

MULTIVENDOR OR SOLE SUPPLIER

The decision in selecting the service-delivery strategy may have the implication of the selection of a sole supplier. A solid business case can be made depending on the business and the requirements of either a sole-supplier or a multivendor environment. The advantages and disadvantages are well known and understood.

It is not that obvious sometimes that selecting the service-delivery strategy is a de facto setting of standards. Businesses need to be very clear about the decisions that are made and what decisions are not made. Addressing the direction is a key consideration in the effectiveness of lifecycle management.

Nothing is worse than having suppliers continue to compete for business that is not available to them to win. The opposite is also true; nothing is worse than a business needing competition to be established and have the competitors determine that there is not a clearly defined opportunity to compete. There is always the fine line between decisions made and decisions contemplated, but in the service-delivery lifecycle elements, the responsibility is on the business to communicate to the supplier base.

Although this may or may not be a comfortable scenario, it is important because of the implications relating to the various portfolios that suppliers bring to their customers. Service providers may routinely use third parties for certain events, and this should be understood and agreed to as part of the contract.

REMAINING INFRASTRUCTURE PERSONNEL

Whatever service-delivery strategy is selected of the three alternatives, there will be remaining personnel in a businesses infrastructure that will still align with the operational goals and objectives. The role of the personnel will vary from vendor and service management described in this section, to platform selection, interoperability, prototyping and testing, among others.

In out-tasking and outsourcing, these are obvious issues for a business to address. It is important to remember that the scope of lifecycle does not necessarily suggest the full scope of the lifecycle elements. Businesses may elect and often do elect to remain in certain core functions. Even in the insourcing model, if a more focused service-delivery strategy is selected, the job responsibilities and organization often change. The dynamics are not restricted to out-tasking and outsourcing.

The remaining infrastructure personnel must have clearly defined roles and responsibilities. When this is not provided, it is not unusual to view a competition of sorts between the internal teams and the external teams (or in the case of insourcing, one internal team against another). Such competition takes away from the end users and the mission of service and should be avoided.

This suggests that the infrastructure teams have a collaborative relationship with the business model and participate as stakeholders. When the "us versus them" culture begins, it is difficult to change without a fair amount of stress. It is common for transferred personnel to be required to remain on the account at least through the transition phase of outsourcing.

LIFECYCLE MANAGEMENT: WHOM DO YOU TRUST?

One of the conclusions drawn for closed loop lifecycle planning is that lifecycle management is often reduced to a simple proposition: Whom do you trust? During the investigation process, the core competencies of all the potential service-delivery partners will become evident. The gap between internal and external suppliers may be quite narrow.

Often, the determining factor is which of the alternatives appears the closest to the culture and values shared by the business. In many cases, this may seem to favor the insourcing approach, and it should. Insourcing as a solution may always have the advantage of the local relationships maintained. The key is the ability to scale and cost effectively sustain headcount in providing lifecycle.

During the investigation at the same time when the pricing, cost, and service levels are explored, the key determination, or the "tie breaker," could be the solution that addresses the end user and the business in the most appropriate fashion consistent with the business today.

In lifecycle, lowest price does not always win. As a matter of fact, pricing becomes less of a factor in lifecycle (assuming that the ranges are somewhat narrow) than other IT decisions because the impact on the end user and their perception of IT is at stake. Lowest pricing may suggest that the quality that is required to follow up, assess satisfaction, and mitigate risks is not as robust as it may otherwise be required.

The service-delivery strategy is a strategic decision made by multiple levels of management and cross-organizational boundaries.

NOTE: In closed loop lifecycle planning, trust and credibility play a tremendous role in the decision-making process for businesses selecting lifecycle partners.

DECLARING CORE COMPETENCIES

One of the frequently asked questions during the investigation of service-delivery strategies is this? What are your core competencies? This is an important question to ask, and businesses must be comfortable with the response. The proposition begins with the business itself in asking that very question.

What are the lifecycle operations that are considered core to the business and that the business desires to remain in going forward? Interestingly, many businesses take an opposite approach, suggesting that "everything" is on the table for discussion, knowing that there are pockets of core competency in which, if a choice were to be made, it would be desired to remain.

It is important when assessing the service-delivery alternatives that the various solutions have the perspective of what is working well within a business and whether that operation can be integrated into a solution or otherwise leveraged. Although this is often viewed as a bias, it does set expectations for the investigation so that the business can have the full advantage of the optimal manner to leverage internal expertise.

Likewise, there is the same question to ask the competitors: What is your strength? Interestingly, most of the service providers will respond that overall lifecycle management is a core competency, and this may very well be the case. A lot of the weight given to the response relates back to the scope of the lifecycle program under consideration. For example, if the scope is global, there simply will be fewer service providers that would have a global core competency.

Many, if not most, lifecycle service suppliers have partnerships with other businesses that could complete any "gaps" that their solution may not directly address. Businesses should not dismiss these. The ability to partner effectively to deliver lifecycle management is not something all companies can effectively perform.

When service suppliers respond that all the lifecycle is their core competency, this is likely a true belief. The key is the definition of lifecycle management and the requirements of the business itself. This is when the question "whom do you trust?" comes into play. The key in lifecycle management is having the team that effectively delivered the solution before transferring that experience to the business under consideration.

Meeting the PMO or program manager as well as the architects is a key step in ascertaining the core competency and frequency that the services are delivered. Although each lifecycle-management relationship is unique, there is typically a set of terms and conditions and a template statement of work that can form the basis of the knowledge up front. The willingness to appropriately share is an indicator of the trust.

TOOLS: OWNING THEM AND SELECTION

Management tools play a significant role in lifecycle management. One of the decisions that a business needs to reach as it explores service-delivery alternatives is whether the business or the service provider will be responsible for the tool and tool selection. The tool, in this context, is the actual management software and suite used to perform various lifecycle-management functions. It should be noted that along with all the deliverables with a toolset is the policy, process, and procedures that make that tool effective in an enterprise. The level of input, control, and ownership that the enterprise desires should be specifically defined in the service-delivery strategy.

The decision is not only what toolsets are to be used, but who actually owns the tool (the service provider or the business). Ownership is important because it represents a cost element in the lifecycle approach, but also it is important from the perspective of tool selection.

Most service providers have their own or a favored toolset that they use in lifecycle solutions. Similarly, most businesses have invested in toolsets that are installed today in their operation and current state. The discussion of whose tool is to be used is important as lifecycle is enhanced and tools are upgraded and sustained over time.

Many lifecycle engagements are said to be "vendor neutral." Although this might be true at some level, given that closed loop lifecycle planning suggests that lifecycle experience is a key determining factor to consider, businesses should be seeking to leverage the bias as strength. Also, it is important to recognize that although there may be a preference, it certainly does not preclude alternatives.

In those instances where the toolset is a part of the solution, businesses often reserve the rights contractually to the tool or the database as part of the program construct.

If toolsets are custom or proprietary to the service providers, the conscious decision needs to be made as to whether that is an appropriate solution to leverage for the lifecycle-management operation of the business.

A key lesson from early lifecycle experience is that the toolset is to be a key component of the decision. The rights to the tools and the information are paramount. If the tool is commercially available, are the tool rights transferable? These are the types of inquiries that need to be part of the overall due diligence in the software decision for service delivery.

A final point to be made is the cost impact and implications if the business retains the toolset and the service provider is required to interact and integrate with the business' tool. What are the support and cost implications?

NOTE: It is not a good idea to require service providers to use tools with which they do not have broad and deep experience.

MERGERS, ACQUISITIONS, AND DIVESTITURES

Mergers and acquisitions are a part of the fabric of business today. As businesses determine what the service-delivery strategies are to be, it is important to consider the impact that an acquisition or divestiture may bring about.

The service-delivery strategy must be able to scale if that is the decision; and if not, there needs to be a vehicle to disengage as required.

It is interesting to note that in many mergers and acquisitions there is a parallel period of time when the dual infrastructures are retained. Typically however, there is only to be one. If the service-delivery alternative is not selected, the transition, property rights, intellectual property, and databases are transferred as defined by the agreements. Provisions regarding this event should be a standard part of the planning process.

The divestiture of a division or group may impact the economics of an existing agreement and must be considered as part of that process.

REFERENCES

A standard part of every lifecycle program and every RFP that is issued is the request for references. The first point that should be noted is that there should *never* be a poor reference provided. To some degree, the request for a reference is a rhetorical question: Tell us where you have done this well? All alternatives—insourcing, out-tasking, and outsourcing—should be well prepared and ready for the inquiry (and they are).

Businesses have tried to hedge for this response by asking this: Where have you failed? Again, the responses suggest that these are well rehearsed (as they should be) or in essence a "no" response to that question would be appropriate. The rationale is that lifecycle does not care because of one reason: It is always more complicated than that. Typically, it is the readiness of all parties, not the core competencies, that is the critical element. In assisting businesses, this is a question that should likely be reframed to ask about the critical success factors and profile the gap between a successful program and a failed one.

The references question could also be framed by asking about the installed base that the service supplier supports and the profile of the stable state. Not business names, but rather what is the scope of the overall lifecycle operation that a service provider supports. This addresses more fully the real question of whether the lifecycle-management business is a core competency and whether the bill of material offered is reflected in the installed base supported.

KNOW THE BIAS

Remember that there is no such thing as an unbiased consultant or supplier. Experience suggests that all of us as individuals and professionals build our experience based on what was delivered. The process to get to that point was learning.

Learning results in understanding what works and does not work. The bias occurs when what works becomes translated into a belief that the experience is the *only* approach that works. The professional understands the difference, as do suppliers and a businesses; it is represented as the trust factor and confidence they place in its relationships.

Businesses want the experience; it is important to explain any bias or preference in services, tools, platforms, and so on. This permits a more open dialogue that a business can rely upon. When these preferences are not known, they become "hidden." One of the goals of lifecycle management is a lack of "hidden agendas."

Businesses also have their bias. Sometimes it is more difficult for the service providers to identify these because the business is driving the behavior. A business, for example, may indicate that the help desk is open for consideration for out-task or outsource, when in reality that decision could not be made. Service providers may spend countless hours preparing information that is used to revalidate the present direction. If the direction were known, the sharing of best practices might have been a better direction in which to proceed.

PLAN FOR THE BREAKUP

The discussion of the service-delivery strategy would not be complete if the disengagement plan were not addressed.

The planning for the end of the life of the service-delivery relationship is never a comfortable negotiation. Both parties desire to protect the best interests of their respective businesses. The issues become more complicated in the outsource model, where there is transference of assets and personnel. In some respects, these agreements are difficult to end in terms of the termination. It is difficult to reenter into the lifecycle operations in an outsourced scenario because the entrance costs are so high.

The out-tasking approach may be less costly in terms of the reentry costs, but there still remains a hurdle rate to be overcome.

Businesses would like to secure a cancellation-for-convenience clause. This basically states that if the business decides to move in another direction for whatever reason, the agreement would support a change. Although this may be negotiated, if there is a clause, it will likely have a penalty or walk-away penalty provision. This permits the service provider to recoup investment, margin, and a part of the lost revenues. These types of clauses are not often found in lifecycle-management agreements.

Included in the agreements are usually clauses that refer to the defined service levels and the remedies available to address the service if the metric is missed. These clauses are part of the terms and conditions, but also a part of the statement of work or the service-level agreement.

Finally, a clause defines the nonperformance or a consistent missing of the defined services. Again, the remedies are outlined in the core set of agreements.

In the negotiations, it is important to have purchasing/procurement/sourcing, legal, IT, and personnel from the program team involved in the negotiations, at a minimum. Beyond the terms and conditions and the accompanying statements of work, there are generally no other agreements.

Milestones and renewal periods need to be clearly defined and observed.

The volume of documentation required for a lifecycle engagement is not trivial and can be quite complicated. Because of this, the "out" clauses are as important as the actual service levels that the agreement is based on.

The mergers and acquisitions agreements also need to be clearly defined in the agreement. Aside from the termination consideration, the agreement should contain the provisions regarding how incremental business, such as a new company, would aggregate to the agreement. Not only is the pricing a consideration, but also the sizing and scoping of the deliverables. Does more volume, for example, suggest better pricing, or does it suggest increased costs to manage the volume? This is the type of discussion and set of decisions that should be prominently determined in the agreements.

Another example is the question of service-delivery pricing and costs if there is a change in the product mix supported or the profiles. Although this might seem simplistic, this could be a significant issues going forward with all the device diversity that the industry is experiencing.

Agreements can never address and anticipate all scenarios or circumstances, but the agreement should provide the decision framework and identify those situations that are common in the industry.

SUMMARY

The service-delivery strategy that a business determines to use to implement life-cycle management represents a critical decision point regarding cost, security, risk, service level, and of course, end-user satisfaction.

In many cases, determining the service-delivery strategy is not viewed holistically, but as a tactical response to specific requirements that are known at the time. To validate this point, one needs only to look at the number of requests in an RFP that ask for alternative solutions.

However, when requesting alternative solutions, most RFPs hold that these suggestions are not part of the criteria and may (or may not) be even considered.

The market is rapidly changing, and the portfolio and available service-delivery strategies are changing at the same time. An election of a service-delivery strategy needs to consider the variable of a changing market and a potentially new set of dynamics. For example, if closed loop lifecycle planning is correct in identifying future trends in management tools, services embedded in products, and self-help (for example), the service-delivery strategy today may well be different tomorrow.

In lifecycle-management, the service-delivery strategy is perhaps one of the most dynamic areas of innovation that impacts and includes all areas of lifecycle technologies discussed in this book to date.

15

Security and Risk

INTRODUCTION

Issues regarding security and risk are drivers for lifecycle management. Interestingly, while the practices and elements themselves become aligned, there is little attention focused on the implications of risk and security regarding the lifecycle decisions themselves.

It is as important to explore each of the lifecycle elements for risk and security issues as it is for optimization. Decisions need to be consciously made, and those implications understood. This chapter introduces yet another set of working guidelines for lifecycle management. Many of these topics have been discussed elsewhere in this book, but not in the context of a "risk cycle," which addresses the bill of material and determines risk associated with each element.

Many businesses believe that with password protection, firewall, a level of encryption, stewardship, and a governance model that the security and risk are mitigated. To a degree, that is correct, of course. There is also a set of additional decisions that are made that impact the environment that are potentially as important as those decisions.

In analyzing lifecycle management, it has become clear that lifecycle management is clearly a strategy that not only mitigates cost and improves service levels, but it is also a technique that can be invaluable in assessing risk. In research performed in closed loop lifecycle planning, the concept of the "risk cycle" was identified. The *risk cycle* is the process during which the risk associated with each of the lifecycle elements is assessed to determine the potential risk considerations that could be addressed.

In Chapter 24, "The Quantification of Benefits and Value of Closed Loop Lifecycle Planning" (online), risk was rated low, medium, or high. This chapter provides additional criteria that can be used by the practitioner to arrive at some of the decisions regarding the weighing of the factors.

Just as the lifecycle drill-down explored optimization, this chapter explores the security and risk implications of lifecycle management. For ease of review, this discussion is separated into the following topics so that they can be related back to the lifecycle elements presented earlier:

- Acquisition
- Software
- Staging and integration
- IMAC (installs, moves, adds, and changes)
- Warranty and maintenance
- Help desk
- Asset management
- Management tools
- Program management
- Disposition
- Inventory
- Technology refresh
- Home office
- Printing
- Personnel
- Stewardship
- Cascading
- Internet downloads
- Cameras and peripherals

ACQUISITION OF ACCESS DEVICES: WHO DECIDES?

The initial thought one may have regarding the security and risk aspect of acquisition is confusion over why the topic would be present in this element. The question is introduced as a function of who is authorized to receive which access devices or set of devices. Although this is addressed in detail in the Bonus Section of this book, "User Segmentation: A Complement to Closed Loop Lifecycle Planning," the importance to the security and risk discussion is that the decision over what device an end user will have often defines the level of risk associated with the information.

If left to their own discretion, of course, most end users would desire mobility, PDAs, and perhaps more options than required by the work to be performed. Risk cycle asks the question of what is the exposure in the end user having this device. It is not to ask whether the end user should have such a device; the risk cycle suggests that the risk is higher with the more mobility in the installed base.

From a lifecycle perspective, the rationale is to ensure that the measurement and risk are assessed so that the population can be best managed. The number of laptops and PDAs, for example, may suggest a set of tools and tracking software for these devices. As the scale increases, so does the need for more comprehensive management; otherwise, risk dramatically increases.

Pursuing the questioning from the risk perspective, not cost, provides the perspective of optimizing the overall risk in the installed base.

Businesses are now just beginning to understand, for example, the impact of PDAs on the security and risk of the business. In essence, a PDA is equivalent in many ways to a laptop computer, but the governance model is far less stringent than laptops (for the most part). Therefore, the industry is seeing exponential growth of PDAs and is trying to catch up on a governance model that explains why the access device was granted in the first place as a viable technology complementing the existing portfolio.

This does not imply that having a PDA is not correct for the end user; it is to suggest that one of the criteria besides the costs and ease of doing business is the associated risk in having a population of PDAs where the governance model is beginning to be defined and executed.

Entitlement is not a risk-mitigation plan. Often, the rationale for a certain device is management's approval. Sometimes this approval occurs not in the context of risk, but in the context of cost and position. Part of the findings of closed loop lifecycle planning is that management seeks the counsel of its lifecycle teams and will respond to the information. The point remains to identify all the elements and provide the basis for a sound, conscious decision.

It is important that the overall installed base be metered for risk. This suggests that the lifecycle team arrive at a conclusion regarding the assignment of risk and communicate that risk to the appropriate management. The risk associated with lifecycle management begins with the decision about the product mix and the acquisition of the devices.

The risk associated with devices will drive the tracking of the assets with remote-locating software and the level of encryption. All mobile devices should be password protected and the disks encrypted. Certain user segments should be tracked remotely. PDAs should also have the same levels of control and accountability.

SOFTWARE

When the focus was on the cost and practice levels, one of the keys was the metrics regarding the number of titles and manufactures of the software products. If the client devices are indeed business computers, the business is accountable for the software that resides on these devices. From a risk perspective, this suggests that compliance, maintenance, version control, and documentation are all requirements and the responsibility of the business, not the individual. This is a very important distinction.

The risk is not only the compliance with all the software copyright and cost regulations, but also the appropriateness of the titles in a business environment. Many businesses are surprised not only by how many titles there are, but also what the titles are. Although there are codes of conduct and various governance models applicable, this does not mitigate the risk if a business incurs a violation of intellectual property or copyright regulations.

The importance of the volumes of the software titles and authors is that it is a solid indicator of risk. For many years, businesses have weighed the benefits of a lock-down environment from the flexibility that the end users requested. One of the direct implications of the number of titles and software manufacturers in place in the installed base is the flexibility initially that resulted in the environment (which may or may not be acceptable).

Software rationalization is a key risk-mitigation program for many businesses. Addressed previously as a cost imitative, it also has the benefit of addressing the compliance with the intellectual property in the installed base.

Many businesses process reports by business unit, and then break the reports into categories to permit the business unit to determine the reconciliation. When the reconciliation occurs, the process can be effectively centralized and managed with a reasonable starting point.

STAGING AND INTEGRATION

The staging and integration provides an opportunity to explore where the work is performed and who performs the work.

When examining where the work is performed, it is important from a risk perspective that the area be secured to protect the inventory that is work in process. This suggests that real estate be assigned and that the access be limited to those requiring access to work on the devices in preparation. In many businesses, the staging and integration area is not secured, and the process is informal. Although this might permit the work to be performed, it does not raise the protection of the actual assets and could result in inventory shrink or the sharing of the image with unauthorized parties.

The business case for staging and integration is that the area be secured, and preferably certified, if possible. If internal, the access must be reviewed, and security processes adhered to for resources.

From a resource perspective, the persons performing the work should be fully authorized and cleared at the security level. If the persons performing the work are contractors, or temporary employees, the nondisclosures, indemnifications, and other legal requirements should be followed to reduce risk.

In many businesses, sign-out sheets are required to access secured areas, and the real estate is locked to provide for the retention of the assets.

Often, the data migration or setup of a device may occur in the staging area; therefore, there is a need to protect company information and intellectual property as well as personal privacy that may be contained on the access devices.

INSTALLS, MOVES, ADDS, AND CHANGES

It might help when considering security and risk regarding IMAC activities to think that you are providing access and entry to your "business" to the providers of this service. If the service is delivered by in-house resources, it is important that these teams be provided full access to all the information on the access devices as a part of the work being performed. Internally, there is often a level of security and approvals required to be in possession or to have access to such information.

In other scenarios, the work to be performed is out-tasked or outsourced. In these cases, access is permitted to resources outside of the business. The risks are greater because the legal requirements are defined. Businesses must ensure, for example, insurance, nondisclosure, background, and so on are a part of the rigor.

A standard part of any contracting agreement, whether out-tasked or outsourced, is the fundamental security and risk clauses. However, in many businesses, only parts of the lifecycle are contracted out. This places an extra burden on the business to understand the implications of the "handoffs" between service providers as a part of the risk cycle.

During the IMAC work, the use of thumb drives may be required for data migration or applications. Thumb drives represent a single point of risk. The newer computers have as a feature the ability to manage USB ports (which would include thumb drives). In addition, software is available that will provide similar functionality in management control to reduce risk.

WARRANTY AND MAINTENANCE

Similar to the IMAC providers, it is not unusual to find that the warranty and maintenance providers are third parties (excluding those businesses that are self-maintainers). These third parties need the same authorization and agreements as the IMAC providers. Although it is not designed that these providers have access to data and other information, it is not unique that the opportunity would not present itself. A business needs to assess risk in permitting the access.

When the laptops are the maintenance or maintenance devices, a different service delivery than on-site support may occur, such as mail-in support. Although fundamentally different from on-site support, the mail exchange presents a unique set of risks. If the laptop is not encrypted, the information contained on the device is in the mail system. This suggests that the service-delivery strategy may not be appropriate for all end-user segments.

Consideration should be given to how to protect data when the mail-in strategy for warranty and maintenance is provided.

HELP DESK

The help desk in many businesses is becoming more of a call center and service desk combination. Therefore, there is more and more information that could be available to the help desk about the end users. This has both a positive and negative potential.

As an end user, it is expected that the help desk will have access to employee information relevant and required for the resolution and support of an event. This is to be encouraged because this will reduce costs and improve the time to repair.

The risk comes in when too much information is provided, which may include personal information not required, but available. Many businesses have recognized this and now have strict governance models for access to information. However, what occurs when the help desk, service desk, and call center converge to handle both internal and external events?

If certain information were available to a call center where the employee was also a participant in a plan, there could be crossover information. Remember, the same resources may be used in certain scenarios to leverage costs.

The help desk also has profile information regarding a person's user segment, the configuration provided, and associated other devices. This information should be addressed confidentially, as required. As user segmentation becomes mainstream, more information will be collected and available to the help desk. From a risk perspective, the information should be that which is only required to resolve the event.

ASSET MANAGEMENT

Asset management itself does not present the risk; the risk is identified in the output reporting from the asset-management repository. It is not unusual to have asset-management reports that are quite voluminous in detail. The problem often arises where there are not resources assigned to review the output reports and assess risk. Asset-management reporting is only useful if it assists in decision making. Part of the decision making is risk assessment.

Asset-management reporting should have a specific number of defined reports that will assist IT in determining risk associated with hardware and software. Many of these elements have been reviewed from the cost perspective, but now need to be placed into the context of risk.

For hardware, the shrink-rate factor suggests risks. If the reports provide information on desktops and laptops, differentiating what is in the shrinkage can assist in defining the risk. The fundamental question is of the devices that are not accounted for; what are the laptop and desktop breakdowns?

For software, the scope of the software titles and manufacturers should provide insight into the compliance and copyright alignment. Also, reconciling the reports to procurement records and disposal records is a requirement to mitigate risk.

The asset-management reporting should specifically identify areas where risk or compliance is an issue and suggest the magnitude of the exposure. Otherwise, the reporting is of little use to the risk cycle.

MANAGEMENT TOOLS

Similar to the discussion of the asset management (which is just one of the management tools), there is a need for the management tools to report on issues that directly relate to risk and exposure. An example is in the patch-management area.

If older devices require significant software patches to be compliant to business standards, the report to management should include the identification of the size of that population (because it is not only that one patch that represents the problem, but the ongoing support and risk that those devices represent).

When the management reporting is viewed in its totality covering patch management, configuration, help desk, and asset management, it is not difficult to envision a set of management risk-oriented reports that would frame the exposure of a business. To be effective, reports need to be actionable. From a risk-mitigation perspective, the numbers presented in management reporting should frame the security levels of the business practices.

In most businesses today, different groups provide pieces of the management reporting. Hence, the full-risk picture may be difficult to comprehend. The reporting should be consolidated in such a manner that the reports do not require much interpretation. There is also a scenario in which the reporting is not fully integrated, either. In these situations, the message regarding risk can be obscured.

PROGRAM MANAGEMENT

One of the ways to mitigate risk is to have the program manager be the single point of contact for the consolidation and interpretation of the reporting and practice levels. The rationale in aligning this function is that the risk mitigation and security align well with the continuous process-improvement process.

Many businesses view the program manager and the program management office as a cost, and not in terms of the value that it can deliver. Part of the role of the program office is to mitigate known risks and anticipate those risks resultant from the lifecycle practice levels. An experienced program manager would know, for instance, the reporting that would permit the "painting of the risk picture" to senior management.

The follow-on would be the suggestions for improvement tying the risk to the cost and benefits.

DISPOSITION AND THE IMPACT ON SECURITY AND RISK

Disposition represents the obvious point of risk within a business. Despite this, many businesses do not invest the appropriate level of commitment to perform this lifecycle function at a high practice level. From a risk cycle perspective, disposal has environmental issues, data-integrity issues, personal privacy issues, and intellectual property issues, among others.

ENVIRONMENTAL

From an environmental risk perspective, there is the risk that the devices will be disposed of in an inappropriate manner. All countries have regulations regarding the disposal of access devices. These regulations protect the environment and provide for a consistent manner to address toxic materials and plastics. Businesses bear this risk to a high degree even when the disposal is assigned to a contracted partner.

To mitigate the risk in this area, businesses may test the processes and observe the actual disposal activities. It is important to understand, however, that even if contractually the risk is mitigated, depending on the violation, there may be negative press and legal issues that may occur in disposition. One of the ways to hedge this risk is by the selection of global disposition partners that scale appropriately to the business operations.

Global disposal is a complex business model, and there are many regulations, many of them local, that need to be adhered with to be compliant.

DATA INTEGRITY

The disposal of the access devices presumes that the data stored on those devices has been cleansed. Risk mitigation suggests that the cleansing of the information contained on the devices be done in-house whenever possible, and if not, inventoried in such a manner that is reasonable.

Part of the rigor for risk in many businesses is a period of quarantine during which the information is backed up remotely in case of a recovery scenario. In certain industries, this is required by regulation. The risk in disposal is that these processes need to be audited and reviewed to be effective.

PERSONAL PRIVACY

With all the information contained on access devices, personal privacy is paramount. Risk occurs when there are gaps in the transition from decommissioning to disposition. During the period the device is stored ready for transit, it should be secured in such a way that no personal information can be obtained from the device. If the device is mobile and not encrypted, this presents a significant risk.

Many businesses control the devices until the devices are released to a carrier to the disposition agent. This presents risk in the transit of the devices. With tools available to perform a DoD type of cleansing on-site, businesses could consider this process for personal privacy types of situations. If this is not performed, the risk assignment may be high.

INTELLECTUAL PROPERTY

Protecting intellectual property may be a critical issue when examining off-site or offshore development of software; for example, how the disposal of a remote access device should be handled when a technology refresh occurs. Today, because offshoring has recently become more aggressively adopted, this is an issue that has not arisen at a high degree. However, as the timing for refresh approaches, you can understand that this should have been an initial consideration. This is an excellent example of a lifecycle decision that should be a part of the initial acquisition decision.

PDAS

Few businesses have disposition processes defined for PDAs. The technology refresh cycle for PDAs may very well be 18 months or less. With this in mind, how to dispose of the assets and, as important, how to ensure that the information contained on the devices is secured may present the next significant risk to operations.

Just as with laptops, look for new generations of PDAs to have encryption included as an embedded feature. There is also the environmental issue to deal with regarding PDAs, which is often overlooked, too.

NOTE: Many businesses have not determined the governance model for handheld devices beyond the acquisition portion of lifecycle. From both a cost and risk perspective, this situation is likely to change rapidly, driven by regulations and policy.

INVENTORY

If a business is maintaining a client device inventory outside of the asset-management software, risk increases. Management by "spreadsheet" is not effective to mitigate risk because it is not proactive in its design. The control and ad hoc reporting simply does not scale to the requirements of most businesses, and the reporting is not reliable because it generally does not poll and access what is on the business network.

Inventory outside of the asset-management process is generally finished goods, work in process, or staged awaiting deployment, spares, and other types of transactions. Risk is created because some of the devices may not be cleansed and may contain information prepared for the next user or retained from the previous user. In many businesses, inventory is retained quite informally. This informality increases exposure because accurate inventories are difficult to determine and, more important, it is difficult to understand precisely what information is on the system inventoried.

TECHNOLOGY-REFRESH CYCLE

The technology-refresh cycle should be partially driven by the determination of risk, perhaps to a high degree depending on the business model. Technology refresh is mitigation representing a movement toward more current standards. The standards include a standard image that would include a current version of antivirus software and firewall software. Older devices might not be able to be as current as businesses would like the devices to be.

Older operating systems represent significant exposure and risk. In many cases, the antivirus software is not available; or if it is, it is patched and potentially at an extra cost. Viruses can more easily access older devices. Older operating systems suggest that there are simply more images to maintain. There is a point when the quality of support declines and exposure can occur. Downtime is often a result of risk and exposure.

NOTE: A technology-refresh program represents a compelling event. As access devices are refreshed, there will be challenges that businesses encounter as the number of access devices must be accounted for while the exposure is the highest. Those businesses that have not embraced strong asset-management philosophies may incur significantly more expense and exposure.

HOME OFFICE

More and more businesses have employees who work at home with corporate equipment or have access from home on their home PC. It is important from a risk perspective to understand that retention of information accessed is easy on the home PC. Therefore, businesses must decide whether it is appropriate for this information to reside on a home PC.

Although mail can be read on the home PC through a company's intranet site, for example, the question is whether the business would want that information to be available outside of the company. Home PCs generally do not have the disposal rigor that an enterprise client device will have associated with it. Businesses generally do not have administrative or effective control over the lifecycle disposal practices of the home PC, including how information may be retained.

This represents exposure and risk and must have a well-defined governance model associated with it. For example, as the privilege for accessing information on the home PC is supported, the employee must agree to dispose and cleanse the PC according to business policy. This would be a condition for use. However, few businesses have implemented this policy, but it will most likely be a critical next step in the risk cycle.

PRINTING

As more and more businesses support teleworkers and home office workers as a viable alternative, the risks associated with printing should be explored. It is interesting to note that many businesses have standards for home printing, including fax, scanning, and multipurpose devices, but few have standards for shredding documents that are produced through hard copy. For example, many businesses do not have a standard shredder profile or related policy to address this with the employees. This element of the risk cycle represents an exposure in risk that must be addressed.

It might seem to be common sense, but many home offices that produce reports, and potentially print out sensitive information, do not have a shredder available or a governance model that requires one. In our personal lives, many of us have shredders to destroy unused (or unwanted) credit cards and other correspondence, but this has not translated to businesses as of this writing.

A shredder on a small scale represents an extraordinarily small cost. It is difficult to imagine businesses encrypting laptops and tracking assets but failing to protect information that may appear on printed output.

PERSONNEL

Many businesses have engaged personnel (also known as human resources) to assist in mitigating the risk cycle. Personnel can mitigate risk in several ways. One way is to prepare an asset report that identifies the business assets assigned to an individual within a business.

When the end user and the access devices assigned to the end user are identified, personnel sends a form to the end user validating that he or she does indeed have this equipment. The form indicates that the devices are solely for the conduct of business under certain guidelines. In addition, the form can request that if there is any other equipment assigned to the end user, the process to return the equipment be provided.

In providing this request, personnel can leverage their position to assist in the governance model. Personnel can establish the guidelines that the home PC can be used for only certain access, too.

To best leverage personnel in lifecycle, the governance model needs to be thoroughly defined and communicated to senior management.

STEWARDSHIP

A large number of businesses still rely on the stewardship of their employees to assist in risk mitigation. Although this is a reinforcement of the confidence in human nature and the positive expression of support, it is likely not sufficient as a risk-mitigation plan or strategy.

Many risks occur not from end users or IT doing something wrong, they often derive from an implication from something that may have been performed correctly. Stewardship suggests that there is a right and a wrong way of doing something, and that if faced with a choice, the correct thing would be done. Risk often comes from doing the right thing but not thoroughly understanding the implications.

The point of stewardship is fundamentally correct. There is protection from those who seek to perform or act in an inappropriate manner. Governance is often ignored in those scenarios anyway. Stewardship reflects the company's adherence to the policy and cultures that makes the business a good place to work as an employee.

Stewardship also implies the proverbial 80/20 rule, that in the vast majority of the time, the right things will be performed.

Stewardship, however, is not a solid risk-mitigation strategy, nor does it reduce exposure. The process, policies, and procedures must still be defined and followed with periodic audits for compliance.

CASCADING

As stated elsewhere in this book, cascading is not typically a best practice. In terms of risk and exposure, cascading rarely achieves its ultimate goal of cost reduction, and moreover dramatically increases risk.

Risk is increased in cascading by moving a device from point A to point B within a business when the device contains end-user information. During this period of time, the access device is not on the network and often is not tracked effectively. In many cases, the device is in transit and not truly accounted for in general.

This is the moment of the greatest exposure if the device is lost, or in many cases informally retained as a backup device within a business. These devices could be retained in unsecured areas, offline, for an extended period of time. Stealth IT may consider the device as a part of the informal infrastructure. During this period of time, the device is not cleansed, and information remains on the drives.

If the device is lost or stolen, it would be challenging to report it as missing because the records would not reflect the destination.

The other scenario that occurs is when the device is returned to inventory but is not cleansed until it is readied for redeployment. In this example, the device is stored with information residing in the drives until it is reused.

In both scenarios, the risk is high, which is why cascading, if it is to be practiced, needs to have an appropriately high level of inventory management and cleansing of the information contained. When the risk in the case of cascading is combined with the set of economics, there is a compelling case from both perspectives to seriously consider alternatives carefully.

INTERNET DOWNLOADS

The Internet presents yet another element of risk to the access devices. Not only can information be accessed through the Internet, but, as we all know, so can programs and executables. Although governance models exist, and there is the ability to view what is being accessed, the scale and effort required is not insignificant. Spyware is quite common, as are viruses associated with accessing the Internet.

Many sites are safe and appropriate for business. Others are more casual and require monitoring or suggest that the content be outside of the governance model.

This is an area where stewardship does play a role, and most businesses are quite confident that there is appropriate access. However, even reasonable usage, which is the standard of most of the governance models, is subject to interpretation. Is music, for example, permissible? Is wallpaper from a favorite television show? The question is this: At what point do the business computers become personal computers?

The risk associated with this approach is that when the devices are refreshed, many personal preference items are migrated. Moreover, it is assumed that all the personalization is appropriately copyrighted and approved. The business retains the risk because it is a business computer. This has led many businesses to restrict Internet access to specific end-user segments and increase the monitoring of activities.

NOTE: Businesses in the near term are developing strategies that will permit the enterprise to monitor end-user Internet activities. This action is in place today in many policy statements, but the rigor in enforcement and monitoring is still in the early, developmental stages.

CAMERAS AND PERIPHERALS

Many businesses have a price-list approach, as discussed earlier in this book. This approach permits an end user to acquire components and peripherals from an approved set of items. Often, among these items are cameras, speakers, and other components.

Although this might be appropriate, there are certain scenarios where the need for using a business computer to develop electronic imaging may not seem to be a business use. Some of this may again seem like common sense, but the liability is upon the business to ensure that the usage is appropriate and the expense is a business expense. More important is that the usage of the device is correctly a business use.

An example is a business that approved its workforce to use cell phones and PDAs that could take electronic pictures. The businesses' customers did not permit such devices in their manufacturing plants or its facilities. The business use for this feature has clear limitations, and in this case was not appropriate. However, other applications, of course, make sense.

The key in examining the features is to ensure that there is not risk and exposure associated with the inclusion of this technology in the installed base.

NOTE: One of the key decisions that a business needs to make very clear is whether the PC is a business or personal device. The addition of components that may not be driven by specific business needs weakens the governance model in place.

SUMMARY

Risk and security issues surround lifecycle management in every lifecycle element. The same bill of material that is the foundation for the closed loop lifecycle planning drill-down should be reviewed and analyzed by the risk and security teams for exposure.

This creates the "risk cycle" that is akin to lifecycle management, except that instead of seeking cost reduction, cost avoidance, and impacts to service levels, this strategy seeks to assess risk and exposure from the decisions made in delivering lifecycle management.

The benefit of using and leveraging the same approach in the bill of material is that the data collection and the use of the information collected are similar and will be more easily understood by all interested constituencies within a business.

Each lifecycle element as identified in this chapter can result in a risk matrix similar to the quantification matrix that on a single page could assist in identifying the risks and exposure associated with lifecycle.

16

Global Lifecycle

INTRODUCTION

Global lifecycle is a requirement for many businesses today. It is no longer optional to have multiple strategies globally, each unique in its architecture and construct. Although the global aspects of lifecycle are beginning to be well understood, the fact remains that global lifecycle remains unique to every business. It is quite challenging to establish governance, policy, process, and procedures in one location, but add to that all the variables that a business needs to address globally in lifecycle, and the complexity becomes quite daunting. It is so daunting, that many businesses may ignore or oversimplify the impact.

Global lifecycle management is frequently underestimated in its complexity, scope, and support requirements. One reason it is underestimated is that assumptions are made during the goal-setting process. Another reason is the reluctance to "drill down" deeper in a due-diligence process to ensure that the details are clear. The old expression that the "devil is in the details" was never more accurate than in global lifecycle management.

NOTE: As with other parts of an enterprise, IT organizations can be organized independently by regions or business units, creating different and competing lifecycle strategies across the globe.

Although there are many businesses, third parties, consultants, and others professing expertise in global lifecycle management, the discipline is new enough that few can seamlessly deliver global lifecycle management. This is not because the infrastructure and core competency does not exist; it is more likely due to the maturity required by all participants in the practice levels. Lifecycle requires a collaborative relationship that only develops over time.

When global lifecycle is driven through requests for price (RFPs) and requests for information (RFIs), as is the case today, the learning is not immediately available. Therefore, there are a number of "starts and stops" in implementing lifecycle management. This is to be expected, and likely not different from other global business operations.

Generally, a gap exists between perception and reality. In lifecycle management, the gap is not readily observable. As mentioned previously in this book, lifecycle management is often reduced to a trust level. This is particularly true in global lifecycle management. Businesses must realize that one of the key success factors is not only the core competency to deliver, but the sharing of core values and experience in delivering the solution, which is paramount.

The menu of considerations for global lifecycle management is critical to understand when selecting whether to insource, out-task, or outsource. It is equally important that the service providers, resellers, and manufacturers understood these issues, too. In global lifecycle management, one of the keys to success is the proper setting of expectations regarding cost, risk, and service levels. This just cannot be provided unless the experience and relationship exist at the practitioner level.

It is equally important that, as a business, the enterprise is ready for an integrated, global solution. Readiness is a critical element for a business to adopt the practices required to deliver the service, regardless of who delivers the actual solution.

It is important to understand that the services that global lifecycle delivers are indeed already being delivered locally by the business in some manner. This is true even in nonglobal lifecycle solutions. Although there may be a level of best practice and economies of scale to consider, the existing process, which may be suboptimized, works according to the perception of the end users or the enterprise delivering the solution today. A business case must be developed to demonstrate that the environment is better served under a globalized lifecycle strategy. It is not unusual for initial conflict to arise when it is assumed that all parties understand and agree on the underlying business rationale.

In exploring global lifecycle management, the following represents a brief listing of some of the considerations that add complexity to the approach and literally make each solution unique at some level. These considerations include the following:

- Countries and regions participating (North America, South America, Canada, Europe, Middle East, Asia [EMEA], Asia Pacific [AP], Latin America) and all countries and states within these geographies
- Labor laws in countries, states, and provinces
- Environmental laws and regulations for disposal of assets
- Global and local regulations and laws
- Personal privacy laws
- Copyright and patent laws
- Intellectual property laws
- Value added taxes (VAT)
- Duties and tariffs
- Invoicing regimens required by country or by province
- Billing in local currencies
- Languages for support and help desk
- Country kits for access devices
- Time zone differences, including changes in daylight savings time
- Support expectations and service levels
- Sales and use taxes
- Reporting requirements
- Unique cultural characteristics
- Product delivery service levels
- Standard in country part numbers (global SKUs)
- Standardized pricing and pricing methodology
- Customs processes
- In-country manufacturing or reseller requirements
- Existing local relationships
- Remote sites
- Sites not covered by a direct or indirect channel
- Sites lacking density, but in the overall lifecycle scope

This list identifies just some of the characteristics of a global lifecycle-management scenario. Depending on the number of countries involved, the variations could be considerable. It is this uniqueness that creates the complexities in global lifecycle management.

Based on this menu of attributes, the fundamental question then is why global lifecycle management is desirable? The answer lies in the response of many businesses that suggest that without the higher-level governance model, business growth and agility is constrained. The result is investing in areas where the payback and return on investment are significantly slowed.

Many businesses refer to a non-lifecycle-management scenario as a loose confederation of businesses. There is little synergy to be gained through this approach. However, in many businesses this may be the optimal alternative if the issues discussed in this chapter cannot be overcome.

If global acquisition and expansion into global markets is the vehicle for market share, global lifecycle management is a requirement, not an option. An enterprise cannot commit to all the regulations and laws under a loose confederation; there must be an overriding governance model. Otherwise, a business cannot commit to the various topics covered in the preceding list.

Because global lifecycle management is a requirement, closed loop lifecycle planning is one of the key methodologies that can assist a business in addressing the issues confronted by it today.

Each point presented in the bulleted summary could become a chapter or section by itself in terms of the detailed understanding required to become effective at global lifecycle management. However, a few key points can be made to embellish on some of the critical areas.

NOTE: As this chapter and others present the issues that global businesses face, remember that the details and complexities of conducting business impact the success or failure of lifecycle management. Experience is the key and must always include the local teams from the business and its suppliers to make the solution work effectively.

GLOBAL SERVICE LEVELS

Many businesses assume that the service levels for product and services should be the same country by country. Intuitively, this seems to be a logical assumption; however, it is not. Due diligence is required to assure that service levels identified are in fact deliverable.

To understand the implications, let's drill down into a product and a service level agreement (SLA).

Many businesses decide that the product globally should be delivered in x number of days. The days are the same worldwide. The reality is that the ability to deliver the product is widely variable in each of the geographies. During a selling cycle or a buying cycle, often triggered by an RFP or RFI, suppliers will commit to aggressive SLAs, understanding that the delivery may require a stocking level or other strategies to consistently achieve the service level. This is totally appropriate.

From the business' perspective, the focus is on what can consistently be delivered without incurring more complexity in the product-fulfillment discipline. It has always seemed peculiar that client devices are often referred to as commodities, and yet the very groups that deem the devices commodities are the first to become concerned about the lead time to deliver that commodity device.

For product, the answer lies in the middle ground. What is the overall service level that covers the majority of countries and sites, and is there another that can address the remainder? The "one size fits all" product-delivery service level globally ignores the reality of the business problem that is trying to be addressed. This scenario is correct when the devices are replacement devices. In the case of net new employees, alternative strategies should be developed to consistently achieve the service levels.

For services such as warranty, the first question is this: What is the warranty coverage, and is it adequate for the device being covered? After this question has been answered, the next question is this: Who will deliver the warranty service? Depending on the location, it might be a reseller, the manufacturers, or a service partner providing the warranty coverage (unless the business is a self-maintainer). The warranty is a contractual service, so the SLA will most likely be achieved. The question is, however, for the portion that is not attainable, can it be identified early in the process to set expectations? More importantly, it is necessary to establish the optimal service-delivery strategy.

GLOBAL PROGRAM MANAGEMENT

When a transaction for lifecycle becomes global, a program manager and a program management office (PMO) is the single most important factor for success. An experienced practitioner, supported by the correct teammates, can deliver global lifecycle management. Without an experienced PMO in place, global lifecycle management will be a less-than-satisfactory experience for the business.

As you can understand from the issues identified in the bulleted summary, which are above the day-to-day lifecycle activities, global lifecycle-management solutions add a dimension of complexity that is extraordinary.

Many businesses have issues with the overall size of robust program offices and believe it is not required. Often, there is impetus to reduce the size of the PMO. If the relationship with the lifecycle provider is mature and collaborative, the size should reflect what the provider believes is necessary to deliver the solution. Do not confuse a pricing objection with staffing considerations.

One of the key deliverables expected from the PMO is the seamless (as much as possible) delivery of the global lifecycle solution. If the first objection is the size of the PMO, the program itself might be heading in the wrong direction initially. The staffing plan is the key. Businesses should fully understand the experience and logic behind the roles and responsibilities of the PMO and how the deliverables are accomplished.

From this understanding will develop an understanding of the costing out of the resources and skill sets required. Although there may remain pricing issues, it is highly probable that the staffing plan will be reasonable. Global, experienced lifecycle providers understand the effort it takes to achieve the results in the most complex of environments.

It is equally important for the business to understand its responsibilities in the PMO, where it is likely that a similar infrastructure may be created to complement the service provider. The staffing relationships, although not one to one, would have some relative positioning that must be determined.

There may very well be multiple PMOs or project managers in the delivery of global lifecycle. Although there will always be only one true program manager, it is highly probable that that person would have counterparts in the various geographies if the volumes and complexities dictate that level of support. This does not mean that there is not a single point of contact. This does mean that local issues may require locally available program manager talent and skill sets.

Programs often are not successful when there are multiple and equal program offices. The reason for this is simple: There can be only one team setting strategy and accountable. Multiple PMOs could work when the environment is collaborative and the mission objectives and charters are defined and clearly articulated.

NOTE: Pursuing global lifecycle without a PMO and an experienced program manager is not endorsed by closed loop lifecycle planning. Based on experience and research, the single point of contact and program planning are essential in delivering lifecycle management across multiple regions.

For all enterprises, certain locations, regions, or geographies will present a challenge to deliver lifecycle solutions consistently. The challenge to deliver a lifecycle solution globally (or an element of lifecycle globally) should not be seen an exception, but as a normal part of service delivery. The global program manager is generally the experienced and logical single point of contact to address these types of issues. These unique situations might not necessarily be the small or less-dense locations, but could represent a logical challenge regardless of scale.

CENTRALIZATION OF SPECIFIC LIFECYCLE-MANAGEMENT OPERATIONS

In certain respects, some elements of lifecycle should be consistent globally under closed loop lifecycle planning. Aside from the PMO, which was discussed previously, the lifecycle elements that should be consistent are the help desk and asset management (and the related management tools).

In many circumstances, global lifecycle participation is considered an alternative or optional for business units. When this is established as a possibility, it is often perceived that enterprisewide IT restricts business unit flexibility, and change by its very nature is uncomfortable. If an enterprise is to adopt the best practices and sincerely address the consistency in lifecycle management, participation should not be optional.

If the help desk and asset management are viewed in a global perspective, it is easily seen that the economics favor centralization and the overall control by the enterprise to be compliant to global rules and regulations.

Let's assume that a business is seeking to consolidate multiple help desks that today are handled business unit by business unit on a global basis. Although the enterprise has a standard product and image, each business unit has invested in its own geographically oriented help desk. The tools and volumes are unique to that business, and the headcount is retained by that business unit. Adopting an enterprise help desk may require lowering the headcount or redeploying the existing headcount.

Given this, the issue is how this business unit compares to other business units within the enterprise. Moreover, what are the volumes and help desk statistics that enable a comparison? Typically, Stealth IT also plays a role in the discussion because there are generally local resources that assist in day-to-day support. This makes it difficult to compare "apples to apples" in the help desk solution globally.

Often, the benefits for centralization simply do not accrue to a specific business unit, but to the global enterprise in total. This might create metrics issues. Just as with pricing objectives, businesses should not confuse metric issues and budget issues with business objections. The cost per call is best when there is simply a larger installed base population to amortize the costs to establish the infrastructure. The more business units that may opt out, the more the enterprise as a whole could be penalized.

If it is assumed in an example that a business unit has 10,000 access devices, and the enterprise has 50,000 access devices, and the infrastructure to create a help desk infrastructure approaches $2,000,000, the cost per call for the enterprise is $40 per call. By adding 10,000 incremental seats, assuming some incremental headcount, but likely nominal, the cost per call becomes $33, or a 17 percent reduction.

Exiting a business operation is never an easy thing to do, particularly if the compelling rationale requires adoption of an enterprise portfolio. However, to develop the best practice for a help desk solution, a global help desk is the key.

One of the indicators that the scaling of the help desk will be a challenge is the sheer number of help desks that exist in an enterprise. Many businesses overlook the politics and dynamics of this infrastructure and do not relate it back to the practice levels.

The business case for a global asset management solution should be far less controversial than the global help desk. To comply with regulations and to have a reasonable technology-refresh strategy, it is necessary to have asset management at a reasonable level globally. Many disparate systems, including spreadsheets and other reporting tools, simply are not integrated enough to deliver the results required for the governance models.

Globally, the regulations and laws require a higher level of asset management to comply with the myriad regulations. Businesses are, therefore, finding that the global asset management for hardware and software is much less contentious than for other lifecycle elements.

Asset management, similar to the help desk, is most effective when the scale is enterprisewide. There can be process, policy, and procedures that apply globally that can be consistent regardless of geography. Most businesses would adopt the asset-management strategy if it were properly communicated and the risk and exposure explained. There is also the benefit of the compliance with local regulations, which is challenging without more comprehensive tools.

Asset management is likely to occur on a global basis when as a part of the staging and integration script, a discovery agent is loaded that identifies all the client devices on the network. The identification of the hardware and software configuration becomes a by-product of the configuration effort. No incremental work is therefore required by the geographies other than to specify the content and format of the output reporting.

Although there might be a hesitancy to include the agent as a part of the script, the position is an emotional objection, not a business objection, because the information is still required. Although there are tools that do not require the agent to be loaded, at this time this approach remains the most viable to ensure that the client assets can be identified globally.

With help desk and asset management centralized on a global basis, the fundamental underpinnings of lifecycle management exist and can be appropriately leveraged.

GLOBAL PART NUMBERS

Much has already been written about global part numbers (SKUs). Businesses constantly seek on a global basis a standard part number that represents the corporate standard. Often, lost in the process is the understanding that the baseline configuration will need to be customized for the local geographies. Because of this, the global SKU frequently becomes modified, and an in-country part number is created.

The dilemma occurs when that particular part number has a limited use. As mentioned previously, density plays a key role is establishing infrastructure processes. If there are locations with minimal density, or that have an infrequent order schedule, establishing unique part numbers often complicates the ordering process by creating a larger-than-required number of parts. Errors in ordering can occur more frequently in this scenario.

Increasingly, businesses are migrating to an order catalog approach in which the configuration alternatives are designed. In some cases, these might be driven by a part number scheme, in others it might be a "drop and drag" approach to creating the configuration desired. Having a high number of part numbers globally is similar to the situation where the standards become a price list, except this price list is global. Of course, configurations would be modified for country kits, adapters, and other items; but the requirement for a unique part number may limit the effectiveness of the strategy on a global basis. This might be the case where the marketing of the lifecycle solution exceeds the benefits desired.

RFPS AND RFIS

As business becomes more and more global, the RFPs and RFIs related to lifecycle are becoming quite common. Basically, the requirements appear to be similar to the North America RFP and RFI, with questions or commentary that relate to the global capabilities of a supplier.

Such documents miss the point of being global: the ability to scale and retain the uniqueness of the local geography while delivering the appropriate levels of service. Many RFPs and RFIs ask for a single service level for product delivery globally (with some exceptions) and for service levels that are somewhat generic. Although not "boilerplate" in the construct, many documents lack the due diligence to arrive at conclusions about how global lifecycle can be delivered.

In some cases, the lack of specificity is a conscious strategy. The business desires respondents to provide the content and direction. This becomes more of an educational process, but what is missing from the business perspective is the knowledge of whether what is being transferred will be optimal for the business.

In closed loop lifecycle planning, the RFP should not be the discovery document. The RFP or RFI should not be the first step in the process. The initial step is a drill-down by the business to understand the requirements of the business at some specific level of detail. Many businesses respond to this suggesting that global lifecycle is not their core competency, so the RFP/RFI process will provide that bridging.

If a business suggests that global lifecycle management is not a core competency, and therefore the specifications are vague, the question becomes this: Are the review and decisions related to the RFP/RFI similarly outside of the core competency? This becomes the challenge of global lifecycle management: making optimal decisions while understanding that there are many unknowns.

The preceding scenario explains to a high degree why the contracts for global lifecycle are so complicated and why the first step in the process is the due diligence by the suppliers.

EMOTIONS OF GLOBAL LIFECYCLE

Change is unsettling. Therefore, many of the objections, concerns, issues, and perspectives are not necessarily business related, but emotional. Executing global lifecycle management is extraordinarily challenging. The sheer number of unique issues is daunting.

It is easy to oversimplify global lifecycle and suggest that the premise is merely one of scale. The issue is really one of complexity.

An example may illustrate the point. In many lifecycle solutions, there are countries of high density with ease of access, and there are remote locales. Remote locations do not equate to less important. Businesses often do not understand or appreciate that it could be the remote locations with low density that may become the critical factor. Establishing service-level expectations for these geographies that mirror the other geographies may be a part of the problem.

Because of the inability to address an issue, a business might think that although the overall volumes are significant, a supplier needs to address all locations at the same priority, and thus meet or exceed service parameters. This is the moment that the emotional element is initiated. The issue framed is not a "what service level can be attained," but "why is the service level defined not being achieved."

Suppliers generally do not sign up for service levels that they cannot attain. Typically what occurs is that the complexities exceed expectations. The behavior should be to bring all the parties back to the definition stage of the service level; however, more often the conversation tends to be aggressive with regard to the service level that is a problem.

The problem is that after the issue has been addressed, the root cause, the difficult service level, might not be addressed at all. Businesses, just like individuals, avoid conflict whenever possible. Therefore, emotions remain in the situation, and the collaborative relationship is tested. This is one of the key areas where the PMO adds the value of ensuring that the emotions do not exceed the norm.

To be clear, however, any business planning to implement global lifecycle management should be prepared for issues beyond the day-to-day business issues.

With business trending becoming more multinational in scope, the emotions of change will become a critical success factor.

NOTE: Global lifecycle requires a full embracing of each unique way in which that business is conducted. This does not mean that standardization cannot occur, but does imply that flexibility and consideration are vital to solicit participation from the regions impacted by global lifecycle management. In some regions, the strategies *will be* unique.

SUMMARY

Perhaps the issue with global lifecycle is that it *seems* straightforward. It is not. There are many factors associated with global lifecycle, and each participating region or country may have a different practice level with regard to the lifecycle elements.

In addition, many fundamental aspects do not impact each region in the same manner. Product fulfillment appears straightforward, for example, until the entire list of potential action items is formally captured and presented.

Global lifecycle is equally challenging for businesses and for their partners. The complexities do not diminish by assigning the uniqueness to another party. In global lifecycle, closed loop lifecycle planning cautions against the tendency for businesses and their partners to define how the lifecycle will be delivered not by assessing the reality, but by how the businesses would like the reality to become.

This disconnect described partially explains why, in many instances, global lifecycle depends on the initial expectations. Experience in identifying what cannot be performed is as important, if not more so, than what can be performed across various regions.

17

Disaster Recovery and Business Continuity

INTRODUCTION

When discussing client lifecycle management, the dialogue would not be complete without a review of disaster recovery. As a strategy, discipline, and deliverable, disaster recovery has been recognized for quite a while. In many circumstances, a disaster recovery plan is required by law. If a catastrophic event occurs, businesses need to be able to continue operations and report on the existing set of information (for example, financial reporting).

The definition of *disaster recovery* remains the backup, restoration, and continuation of business operations. The disaster could be natural or man made. Regulations require that businesses test, including through simulation, the strength of the disaster recovery planning periodically.

Disaster recovery is a logical follow-up step to the risk cycle, in which each process is assessed to determine actual risk. As mentioned previously, the importance of disaster recovery planning has long been recognized, typically with regard to the data center. As businesses consolidate data centers, disaster recovery is one of the basic building blocks of that strategy. Therefore, policies, practices, and service providers available to deliver such services are mature in the industry.

Disaster recovery also has a companion strategy: business continuity. Often these terms are used interchangeably. Closed loop lifecycle management differentiates the terms by defining *business continuity* as the lifecycle solution that addresses the availability of information. Unlike disaster recovery, business continuity is more localized and does not necessarily become triggered by an enterprisewide or widespread catastrophic event.

Both disaster recovery and business continuity are important because of the impact on the business and the need to continue business-as-usual operations.

DISASTER RECOVERY

Disaster recovery implies a widespread catastrophic event that requires moving operations from one site to another. However, it can also mean storing data in new servers to protect against severe crashes and other potentially damaging events. To effect disaster recovery, businesses apply their own data center strategies, where possible, and sometimes use third parties that specialize in such services. In many scenarios, both alternatives serve as vital components defined in the disaster recovery plan. And regulatory guidelines apply to both internal and external disaster recovery planning.

The ability to recover and restore service levels is fundamental to a business. Customers, employees, management, and stakeholders expect nothing less. But a cost is associated with protecting information and the capacity to deliver it. IT must balance the capacity and capability, with the requirements to continue operations with the least interruption of service.

As businesses consolidate servers and data centers, the technology profiles that can be leveraged today differ from the profiles only a few short years ago. With blade servers, multiple applications residing on servers, and more management tools to direct workload, many businesses can now self-sufficiently transfer work from one data center to another internally (without invoking a full disaster plan). To a significant degree, the available technologies have enabled this improvement.

More important, a consolidated approach can reduce costs by changing the way work is performed. After all, consolidated data centers help address the issue of server sprawl, and therefore the full disaster recovery location could logically have and require a smaller footprint.

The goal of an off-site disaster recovery is to continue the provision of services at acceptable service levels to the relevant constituencies. And, because more end users and customer interfacing is being performed online, the failure to recover (hence downtime) is measurable.

When a business is global, disaster recovery planning is more complex. Global businesses must consider not only logistics, but also differences in support and cultures. And, as offshore support is contemplated, the implications for disaster recovery strategies are more pronounced because the capability to provide such support might not exist internally. Therefore, businesses that include outsourced functions must ensure that the outsourced business also has an effective disaster recovery plan. Global disaster recovery requires a significant level of due diligence, and all the practices and policies relevant to data center and server consolidations.

For many years, disaster recovery represented just a duplication of the existing environment. Today, because of access device diversity, disaster recovery has a different focus. The data center is still the predominant concern, as before, but there is perhaps less concern about access devices because access is now more flexible than ever before.

BUSINESS CONTINUITY

Business continuity differs from disaster recovery in many respects, including the scope. Business continuity as a part of overall lifecycle management can refer to a service level. The goal of business continuity is to make access and information available to end users. (Business continuity is the lead-in strategy for user segmentation, the focus of the last part of this book [online].)

Local events can trigger the invocation of a business continuity plan, as can medical quarantines or the inability to meet in person for any reason. Recent experiences with SARS and the potential of a bird flu pandemic have raised business awareness of the importance of business continuity.

Business continuity is more than a marketing term defining specific service levels. Business continuity is reflective of a new direction in access approaches, a direction that addresses end-user requirements with regard to information acquisition when the impediment is localized or otherwise not on the scale of a traditional disaster recovery scenario.

Business continuity may be threatened by any number of issues, including the following:

- Bird flu or other pandemic
- Terrorist acts
- Natural disasters

- Computer viruses or significant outage
- Network/localized connectivity issues

We're not discussing a disaster in the traditional sense here. A traditional disaster is widespread and impacts many. In contrast, business continuity may be a personal type of outage that impacts only a few.

Many businesses have developed essential-personnel plans, in which vital personnel are identified and workarounds defined so that service levels may be maintained in the event of a disaster. In contrast to just a few years ago, technology and management tools available today enable businesses to plan (and simulate) their responses to potential business continuity crises. It is difficult to imagine the manner in which such issues could have been addressed in even the recent past.

Because "disasters" can be local, regional, or widespread, reasonable contingency planning is that much more difficult. However, businesses must specifically define the scope of their disaster plans (including business continuity). The corollary is that businesses must acknowledge in their plans those situations (at least in general terms) for which they are not planning.

Business continuity requires an awareness of which constituencies require which types of access. User segmentation is therefore required to define service levels (relating to both access and collaboration capacity) that end users may require during periods of crisis (potentially extending for long periods of time). About access devices, businesses must decide whether mobility is essential (so that, perhaps, end users can move from room to room if quarantined). Is a desktop most desirable because its reliability is so high, or is this a business case in which thin clients make sense because there would be no moving parts whatsoever? This type of business continuity discussion should occur when assessing the strategy.

For an example of access device business continuity, imagine a medical quarantine situation. In this scenario, end users are at home and cannot go to a business facility. In this situation, access device issues must be fully planned for. Remember, it's not just that the end users cannot come into the office, it is also that support cannot go to them either. Therefore, support is remote and must be planned for accordingly. To facilitate operations (business continuity), the devices leveraged in this scenario must be highly reliable and provide access to high-speed networking. Business continuity service levels might suggest hot backup devices or certain technologies as a bundle. These are discussed in detail in the Bonus Section, "User Segmentation: A Complement to Closed Loop Lifecycle Planning" (online).

As mentioned previously, business continuity strategies must address collaboration. Here again, current technology is our friend, enabling business to maintain significantly higher collaboration service levels than was possible just a few short years ago. Help desks and support teams can now provide support online (that is, remote support). In addition, Webcasts and other streaming capacities are now common, enhancing the full range of "distance" business presentations. Videoconferencing is just one example enabled by this technology.

Business continuity is a part of lifecycle management and focuses on access to information. At what point does the lack of access to information become a business continuity issue? This is one of the basic triggering questions. In business continuity strategies, various user segments will certainly require different service levels. Business continuity cannot be implemented effectively without this approach; it would simply be cost-prohibitive.

Unlike a global disaster recovery strategy, the global business continuity planning is less about servers and data centers and more about end user access to information. Business continuity service levels vary and are even more diverse when examining the proposition on a global basis because organizationally the models may differ. However, the primary focus is to provide the requisite access to information necessary to perform work responsibilities. It is here that the first user segment is introduced: essential personnel. In this user segment, the work requirement is aligned with service levels, access devices, and overall access to information.

SUMMARY

Lifecycle management, in response to the "new norms" in disaster recovery and business continuity, embraces new technologies to address requirements in these areas of potential risk and security.

Enhanced product features and technical innovations will make it easier for businesses to adopt disaster recovery/business continuity policies and practices that go beyond just duplicating or replicating the current-state environment (as most historic plans called for). Virtualization, for instance, which can provide back-up and recovery capabilities, is just one by-product of centralizing computing support in the data center.

Many of the solutions in place today for both disaster recovery and business continuity will likely evolve in the near term as management tools and the capabilities of the service suppliers to provide remote support are enhanced.

18

End-User Downtime

INTRODUCTION

In the Quantification table, end-user downtime was not listed among the elements in our example. It certainly could be, however, if downtime could be measured in an objective manner and related to cost-reduction and cost-avoidance dollars. Historically, downtime was perceived as a "soft" cost. Everyone recognized it as existing, but it could not be traced into the balance sheet or income statement. Therefore, downtime has been relegated to somewhat of a marketing term. Downtime has been associated with productivity and efficiency, too, which has added to the desire to list downtime as a "footnote" to traceable costs.

As businesses become more and more reliant on access devices to complete job requirements, downtime is becoming a critical part of the overall discussion of lifecycle. Downtime *can be* quantified and is not a soft cost. Like risk, downtime is not often considered real until it occurs. However, downtime occurs with enough frequency that it should become a day-to-day metric that lifecycle management relies on for validation.

In the IT service marketplace, downtime is a fundamental metric that IT and the manufacturers, resellers, and partners promote. Uptime is expressed in terms of 99.999 percent uptime and so on. Mission-critical service levels with failover and zero downtime are an often-discussed metric. In client lifecycle management, however, the discussion of downtime is considered quite subjective. End users basically base their perception of IT on downtime.

Downtime results from any of several events. Often, IT does not consider an event as a driver of downtime, so perhaps a definition is in order to establish the premise. Closed loop lifecycle planning defines *downtime* as the inability of an end user to use the access devices provided to perform the responsibilities of his or her job. Under this definition, any event that does not permit end users to perform their work is downtime.

The following list identifies situations (both hardware and software related) that, although prevalent in business environments, may inhibit end users' ability to perform their work. Consciously omitted from these scenarios is the impact of disaster recovery and business continuity. The downtime that is most important in this section is the downtime that occurs in the business-as-usual environment.

- Older technology
- Technology refresh
- Help desk calls
- Patch and release management
- Desk-side support calls
- Data corruption
- Repair and restore issues
- System server crashes

OLDER TECHNOLOGY

Some businesses struggle to eliminate older devices from their installed base, believing that because the equipment is still functional, they have no compelling reason to replace older devices. But remember, when supporting the installed base, network capacity can define failure or success. From an end-user perspective, "waiting" for information to be processed (staring at the "hourglass") is downtime.

To quantify the impact of this form of downtime, consider this example. An end user has a loaded salary and fringe of $50,000 annually. At 50 weeks per year (allowing 2 weeks for vacation), this calculates to $1,000 per week. Hourly this calculates to $25 per hour on a basis of 40 hours per week. (Note that this baseline assumption is used throughout this downtime discussion.)

If the end user must wait five minutes per hour (8 percent of each hour) while information is processing (most end users would suggest a longer time), the "hourglass" represents $2 of the end-user's hourly rate. From the business' perspective, this is time that the end user cannot work; it is downtime.

To extend the logic of the calculation, $2 per hour multiplied by a 40-hour work week, and then multiplied by 50 weeks yields $4,000. Of course, these numbers are just representative of loss in general as a result of processing time required because of older devices; each company doing this analysis may calculate a different cost. That said, even if the number here is inaccurate by 50 percent, the downtime resulting from the use of older technology might cost more than the actual cost of a new client device. Many businesses fail to identify this trade-off as a justification (and cost driver) for the refresh.

NOTE: Many help desks and dispatched support fail to track older equipment separately. For effective closed loop lifecycle planning, however, support databases should identify the older equipment in their captures so that its impact on downtime (and other financial aspects) can be measured.

TECHNOLOGY REFRESHES

The term *technology refresh* refers to the replacement of access devices, typically desktops and laptops. Although technology refreshes are completed for any number of reasons, the principle one (the business driver) is to increase end-user productivity.

When newer technology improves performance, the end user does not have to wait for the hourglass to complete a particular function or operation. Because the hourglass is seen at the end-user level, it is frequently not tracked, but it does represent downtime for the end users.

Some businesses believe (albeit incorrectly) that this impact is nominal in terms of financial impact and that end users just adjust to slower speeds. The opposite is true. End users become dissatisfied, and frequently seek alternatives to a slow device, which might explain why many standards are not adhered to in a business.

Businesses should think of the hourglass not as a timer but as an "ATM" into which they deposit real resources. Obviously, even an hour of downtime per month across an end-user base adds up to a significant amount. And yet, many businesses question this rationale for technology refreshes.

TECHNOLOGY REFRESH TIMING

As technology refreshes are happening, end users cannot process information. Therefore, many businesses perform technology refreshes after hours to minimize their impact on end users. However, this is not always feasible.

Planned technology refreshes occur one third annually; this is a baseline assumption for purposes of this calculation. A typical technology refresh of a client device takes approximately 90 minutes to 2 hours. Because a total technology refresh event occurs once every three years, and each year impacts one third of the installed base, the best way to present the downtime cost of the total refresh is to divide the impact by 30 percent, to represent the impact on the installed base.

A technology refresh that takes 90 minutes "costs" $37.50 per technology refresh under these assumptions as downtime impact. Now divide that by one third to reflect the three-year cycle, and we have $12.50.

Often, technology refreshes and calls to support are measured just as service-delivery costs, not in terms of downtime. As you can understand from this section, however, the downtime dimension is significant.

NOTE: If a technology refresh plan is not well planned and executed, more downtime will be required than might be necessary otherwise. This will lead to end-user dissatisfaction and negatively color their perception of IT. Therefore, businesses should consider a metric to track downtime as a part of the technology refresh metric.

HELP DESK CALLS

Help desk calls are generally not considered in the context of downtime. The help desk event is measured by the cost of the call, and in many cases by the cost of any escalation required.

An often-overlooked aspect is the downtime associated with the event itself, which is end-user downtime. The IT metric focuses on the resources and effort required to solve the problem, not on how the problem affects the end user in the first place. To determine the financial impact of help desk calls, we must make further reasonable assumptions, including the following:

- Each end user places 1 help desk call per month, 12 annually.
- The duration of the help desk call is five minutes.
- The annual time spent by an end user with the help desk is one hour.

Based on these assumptions and the hourly rates defined previously in this chapter, the cost of downtime related to help desk calls is estimated at $25. This is over and above, again, the cost to deliver the support service. (Note that the assumptions in this section are conservative and might significantly understate actual financial impact.)

PATCH AND RELEASE MANAGEMENT

Remote-access and management tools enable the delivery of patches and security updates throughout the day. Delivery of such is a *critical* function required to sustain the security of the installed base. There is no question as to whether function should or should not occur.

For our discussion here, assume that businesses deliver patches at least once each month (and more often based on virus and hacking attacks). If patch implementation takes five minutes (a conservative estimate) and occurs only one time each month (again conservative), the impact on downtime is $25 annually for each end user.

Patches are often bundled and sent out for the end-user to execute via a predefined script. In some cases, end users must then restart the access device for the patch to take effect. Therefore, the impact on the end user may occur while the patch is executing, but also when the end user restarts the device, if required. In such scenarios, the end user halts work that must be reinitiated later.

DESK-SIDE SUPPORT CALLS

Desk-side support calls typically occur in a campus or centralized environment, and so an established downtime metric generally applies only to those who are in that installed base. Mobile users require a different scenario. Instead of a desk-side support call, the support service level for mobile users might be express mail, and so the downtime metric associated with the mobile profile differs fundamentally from the desk-side support metric.

A desk-side support event is estimated to last two hours. This quantification assumes that the end user cannot use the access device while work the device repair, upgrade, or even restore is being performed. The two-hour downtime financial impact is $50, based on the hourly rate identified for this discussion. Further, it is assumed that this scenario occurs only once a year.

The laptop or mobile user has a more pronounced problem in that downtime generally lasts one full business day (with express shipping, these end users can usually receive alternative devices overnight). As a reasonable assumption for scaling, let's say that across an installed base the number of events occurring is .3 of the overall population. The financial impact from mobile-user downtime is 8 hours at $25 per hour multiplied by the .3 factor for scaling, or $60 for the installed base.

QUANTIFICATION OF DOWNTIME

Downtime is a normal part of lifecycle management and is an expected consequence of some decisions. Typically, however, downtime is an unintended consequence. Expected or unintended, downtime can be measured and not confined only to critical events such as disaster recovery, business continuity, network outages, or server outages. Table 18.1 summarizes the results of a downtime quantification for the example scenario used throughout this chapter.

Table 18.1   Quantification Results

End-User Downtime Events	Annual Downtime (in $)	Annual Downtime (in hours)
Older technology	1,000	40
Technology refresh	12.50	.5
Help desk calls	25	1.0
Patch and release management	25	1
Desk-side support	60	2.4
Total	1,122.50	44.9

Although the numbers will differ for any business, the important point is to remember that even if lifecycle management practice levels are high, you can still quantify the impact of end-user downtime. The calculations could influence technology refresh cycles, customer satisfaction levels, and other aspects of lifecycle.

Businesses that ignore the impact of downtime on end users, or that perhaps consider downtime costs to be "soft" and focus instead on just the cost to deliver, may draw wrong conclusions about costs, customer satisfaction, and practice levels.

The example presented in this section suggests that even when practice levels are high, at least one week of downtime occurs because of support. Note that in the "older technology" calculation for this quantification, the results were not listed at the $4,000 level but scaled back to $1,000.

The lower the lifecycle management practice level, the greater the impact of downtime on end users. An important point to remember is that this downtime is not driven by events but is a part of the business-as-usual, service-delivery model.

The basic conclusion is that each end user will likely experience the equivalent of one week of downtime per year in the lifecycle management. And this conclusion assumes that the lifecycle management processes are integrated and delivered as part of a methodology such as closed loop lifecycle planning. When there is no underlying integration, or if the services are delivered in a "stovepiped" manner, businesses can expect the end user to experience more downtime than just one week per year.

In our example, we estimated the employee cost to the business (salary and benefits) at $50,000 annually. With one week defined as the expectation of downtime, the cost of downtime is estimated at $1,000 per end user per year. The financial impact becomes much more meaningful as businesses customize the information by user segmentation or by end-user pay/service levels.

Downtime is significant. Put into perspective, and discounting customer satisfaction levels, examine the financial impact based solely on the number of end users, understanding that these estimates are quite conservative (see Table 18.2). The question becomes this: Would a business modify any lifecycle elements if the calculations presented in this chapter were part of their overall financial analysis? Closed loop lifecycle planning holds that this is certainly the case.

Table 18.2 Impact Summary

Number of End Users	Range of Downtime Quantified
2,000 to 5,000	$2,000,000 to $5,000,000
5,000 to 10,000	$5,000,000 to $10,000,000
10,000 to 20,000	$10,000,000 to $20,000,000

Even if the numbers were divided by half in this example, the material impact would remain significant and should factor in many other decisions. This quantification suggests a strong link beyond direct costs associated with service delivery only.

A frequent observation is that many IT organizations and businesses focus inward (with regard to lifecycle). However, focus should be on end users. Many businesses have adopted this approach in dealing with end users, as if the end users are, in effect, the customers of internal IT. The overall management and relationship is similar to the customer-business relationship.

Sometimes it is difficult for an IT organization to align itself in this manner. In many cases, IT is not collaborative, but is instead just service delivery oriented only. Such a scenario represents a potentially missed opportunity for the enterprises to engage in day-to-day interaction with constituencies and thus synergize.

SUMMARY

Downtime is an important and frequently overlooked aspect of lifecycle management. But, many businesses still hold that downtime is a "soft" cost, not one that can be quantified when assessing the impact on the business of other "hard" costs. However, closed loop lifecycle planning requires the quantification of downtime. At a minimum, downtime should be considered as a cost avoidance in assessing financial impact.

End users inherently understand downtime (and its impact) and may express that understanding in any customer satisfaction scoring. Even so, in many businesses, downtime has become routine, which may indicate suboptimal lifecycle practices.

Although a correlation exists, loss of productivity is not the same as downtime. Downtime is best calculated based on actual impact, not being able to conduct or complete a specific business transaction or task.

19

Lifecycle Management: Business Observations

INTRODUCTION

This chapter discusses a number of lifecycle-management principles that are important to remember as a business moves forward with a lifecycle-management plan. The information in this chapter focuses on business drivers that impact lifecycle management. Many are just factors that must be addressed, such as legal requirements. Other business drivers might be potential obstacles to the success of lifecycle management (for instance, enterprise readiness, the political nature of decision making, and the desire for change).

Rules, regulations, laws, and so on seldom, if ever, become simpler. As time moves forward, therefore, we can expect that intellectual property rights, personal privacy rights, and a whole slew of other "rights" and responsibilities will increase compliance complexity. It might not be enough to do the "right" thing; the execution process might be all that is important. In this context, client lifecycle management is not optional. In fact, it may be one of the few alternatives that address the overall regulations/requirements. The time to determine whether lifecycle management is a fit in an organizational model is now; there is no good reason to defer that determination.

Although regulations and enforcement of such have changed over time, the business drivers that created the need for the regulations in the first place have not changed materially. Businesses adapt to comply with rules and regulations, and over time these adaptations reach a comfort level that might seem to indicate a lessening of the rules.

NOTE: Notwithstanding any legal ramifications, PR and consumer-confidence damage that results from a security breach could clearly outweigh the actual financial impact.

Client lifecycle management will almost invariably be reduced to a "who do you trust" proposition. Regardless of whether internal or external solutions (or a combination) are selected, the issue will be reduced to the point where the core competencies at the highest levels will likely appear similar. Not until the due diligence phase will differentiation become evident. Do not confuse higher-level marketing with subject matter expertise, however.

An enterprise must be ready to adopt best practices. This readiness implies that the organizational, political, and operational aspects are all aligned under the executive sponsor to deliver the solution. Readiness also implies an ability to change. It is important to assess as an initial step whether the contemplated changes (and the implications of their full scope) can be internalized organizationally and managed.

Conflict is inevitable. Professional maturity is required to overcome emotional objections. It is important to continually remind the team that there are no right or wrong answers, only conscious decisions. "Tree hugging" to obtain a comfort level is human nature but must be carefully approached. Value the various perspectives. Consensus may or may not be possible.

In and of itself, lifecycle management is not an emotional topic. However, I have found it fascinating at times to watch various issues surface. Many of the issues are not, at an empirical level, associated with lifecycle at all; instead, they tend to relate to the organization or structure of a business.

From an architectural perspective, determine whether the scope is enterprisewide, comprehensive client lifecycle management, or a phased subset of the approach. The scope of the client lifecycle transaction will be the instrumental part that will create the overall vision. Do not focus solely on tactics; ensure that the overall strategy is articulated. If the client lifecycle plan is to be scoped, identify the various stages and timelines.

Understand that incremental implementation of client lifecycle management is making a conscious decision to suboptimize the economics.

Client lifecycle management is all about process. An extraordinary level of detail is required to provide the best practice level. Although some people might not find this exciting, it is a fundamental requirement to ensure best practice levels. The process, workflows, policies, and procedures should be well documented. It is important for any business to be very cautious. By its nature, lifecycle management is complex, and there should be concerns if the processes are simplified and presented as "easy" or "simple" to achieve.

Much has been written about comprehensive lifecycle management and related topics. Much of the research is protected by copyright, but much of it is syndicated and available. Businesses should access relevant material when establishing a lifecycle-management plan. After all, due diligence has *no* substitute. Part of the due diligence is to assign a focal point to conduct research. Often the RFI/RFP process substitutes for the business performing research. As a part of the rigor, educating the business about the market is a reasonable expectation. (I hope that this book serves in some way to facilitate this process.)

Lifecycle management is a collaborative effort that requires effective teamwork and partnership. Partners should be selected carefully based on the knowledge and experience they bring to the process.

After the specifications have been developed, it is the time to address the service-delivery strategies available to the business. The discussion of service-delivery strategies is frequently an emotional conversation. The perspectives from all sides need to be articulated and understood before the decisions are made. Determining the service-delivery strategy earlier in the process may presume optimization. In many cases, decision makers believe that internal support can deliver lifecycle management at less cost than an external provider. Often, they are correct. Decision makers who hold a contrasting view might be questioning whether a service area is one that the business wants to declare a core competency and continue to invest in. To make this important decision, a full analysis of investment and cost is vital to the deliberation.

Lifecycle management should be considered a long-term program, not a short-term "fix." Businesses that view client lifecycle management in this way can allocate internal resources (always finite, and often limited) to projects that truly require the internal expertise that only the business can deliver. Lifecycle may, in fact, be one of those projects, but that decision must be made holistically.

In client lifecycle management, go for the "low-hanging fruit"—those quick wins that can assist in building momentum. These early successes will provide a framework to build on. It is important to remember, however, that all wins must be quantified to count.

In the lifecycle drill-downs, the results are packaged as considerations, not suggestions or recommendations. Basically, the process is intended to provide alternative ideas and best practices that might allow the business to close existing gaps in practice levels. It would be presumptuous for any consultant or expert to make recommendations before considerable time has been spent on due diligence.

The output and considerations are expressed in terms of themes, tactical and strategic. The tactical themes relate to lifecycle elements that can be framed and addressed with minimal impact on other lifecycle elements. In addition, tactical themes are those lifecycle considerations that could produce the quick wins mentioned previously in this section. Strategic themes include those that require a broader consensus. The strategic themes require more in-depth discussion and the establishment of longer-term objectives. In terms of the lifecycle suites, the strategic themes revolve around these topics and the implications that result from those decisions.

It is important to cover the consumer experience element before we move forward with a discussion about user segmentation. End users expect the flexibility, service levels, and even form factors that they enjoy as personal consumers. End users also want to be able to use what's "in" their business client devices (downloaded data, music, proprietary information, and so on) on their home computers; because of this, businesses must be aware of and adopt policies that deal with copyright and intellectual property issues.

An important point to emphasize here is that client lifecycle management, best practices, and process optimization are not just academic exercises. Businesses of various shapes and sizes have done all this before. The suppliers, service providers, and other partners have likely delivered comprehensive solutions before.

The fundamental point to remember from this discussion is to *enjoy* the process. Although this might seem unlikely, nothing gratifies more than presenting ideas, debating them, and then implementing them to make a business work better, more efficiently, and more competitively.

Client lifecycle management can increase end-user satisfaction. The more content the end user, the more focused the end user becomes (at least this is true for me and most of the businesses I've worked with on this subject). Eliminating uncertainty makes the environment more predictable; ancillary issues that end users are concerned about today (Where is my support is coming from? When will I get a new access device? How do I dispose of my old device?) become predictable and their solutions well communicated. Expectations are important.

One other benefit of client lifecycle management should not go unstated in this summary. Becoming a subject matter or content expert in client lifecycle management, or any one of the lifecycle elements, enhances the skill set of the employee and is highly marketable both internally and externally.

At the time of this writing, many businesses are considering a curriculum that would create a portfolio of content experts who will, in effect, become lifecycle practitioners. These IT personnel become the trusted advisers to the business on matters of lifecycle management. This is similar to the tactic that many businesses adopted when total cost of ownership (TCO) was all the rage.

Closed loop lifecycle planning focuses on a strategy that is practitioner oriented, and a subject matter expert on staff is an invaluable asset for any business. A practitioner's perspective is an experienced point of view that focuses on what can realistically be completed and executed as a part of the client lifecycle plan. This approach is results oriented and can deliver specific financial metrics when executed.

NOTE: Closed loop lifecycle planning is driven by the enterprise to optimize the bill of material required to support client devices. In this manner, end-user satisfaction can be increased, cost minimized, security improved, risk lessened, and most important, a continuous process improvement plan can be developed.

"LANDMINE AVOIDANCE": WHAT DOESN'T WORK

A final concluding point in closed loop lifecycle planning is an understanding of what *does not* work. Again, this is one of the benefits of the practitioner and experience perspectives. Somewhat humorlessly referred to as "landmine avoidance," this philosophy defines those ideas and tactics that, although they might sound reasonable, usually do not work. The following short list identifies the types of objections typically articulated in the field:

- Senior manage will dictate that client lifecycle management will be implemented.

- Global lifecycle, and lifecycle in general, is easy to implement; consultants present this as more complicated than is necessary because it is in their interest to do so.

- Here are the reasons that client lifecycle management will not work in my business unit.

- Let me tell you how it should be done.
- Lifecycle is pure marketing hype.
- Senior management simply does not understand what work we do in the field.
- We are unique; standards simply will not work.
- Client lifecycle management is just not my priority.
- When I worked at Company X, here is how we did it.
- *We* will show *them* how to do this particular function.
- They just don't understand my business.
- We can do it at significantly less cost than anyone else, corporate or third party.
- Why should we change if what we have is working for us?

In all these statements, the tone is emotional. It is quite challenging to go from this emotional level to a level of collaboration.

An old adage suggests that one needs to "pick your battles carefully." This is a true in client lifecycle management as in any other scenario. The difference in this scenario is that in most cases, change is inevitable—not because one idea is better than another, but because regulations and cost drivers require consistency between businesses.

As a practitioner, one of the behaviors that you need to be prepared to consider is this: Perhaps, despite any bias, the person(s) providing feedback do represent a pocket of best practices. Do not be too eager to dismiss input just because of the style or initial emotional positioning. Although this might be a challenge to do, it just might represent some level of opportunity. The previously listed statements are warning signs of emotion and bias, but that does not necessarily mean that the feedback is invalid.

This could be particularly true if a client lifecycle management solution is global in nature. Regardless of the practitioner's knowledge and experience, a local person in the field may be more attuned to any real-time changes in the environment that impact client lifecycle management.

Note that there are many businesses that can deliver client lifecycle management in North America. Decidedly fewer can provide global lifecycle management at a high competency level. This is why some of the objections previously listed might have merit beyond the emotional response to change.

In many businesses, client lifecycle management becomes optional. Many of the objections previously cited may not have specific compelling responses that can be delivered back to business units. Caution should be taken in this scenario. Typically, the issues are more related to control and funding models and to whom the benefits accrue organizationally. By permitting client lifecycle management to be an option, the element of competition is introduced, to prove that one solution may work better than another.

The compromise is that if a business unit is indeed the funding model, the business should align the program so that business units are encouraged to participate. This might mean that IT needs to absorb incremental costs. In absorbing incremental costs, an objection is removed that represents an obstacle for enterprise adoption. Interestingly, when businesses have offered this and made it available to the business units, there is still hesitation. Perhaps part of the hesitation is that the absorption of costs might not be seen as a viable longer-term strategy.

More likely, the financial objection is only the first and perhaps the "excuse" not to participate in the client lifecycle program. If there are sequential objections, the issue is political and emotional, not business oriented. This then suggests alternatives for addressing the issues outside of the economics. If participation is optional, however, an enterprise will have a significant challenge in complying with all the regulations in place today and coming in the future. Therefore, multiple steps to validate alignment might be necessary. In the end, it still is the business that is liable for any breach, and this could in essence be the "tie breaker" in terms of participation in client lifecycle management.

NOTE: Many businesses focus on the future while discounting lessons learned in the past as significant indicators of that future. In closed loop lifecycle planning, lessons learned represent the experience level of the team chartered to address lifecycle management. Objections will definitely be raised during the closed loop lifecycle planning process, and the basis for them (most likely based on past experience) needs to be reviewed and understood; this is more important, or at least as important, as "new" knowledge that focuses only on the future.

NEVER CLOSE ON A NEGATIVE

One should never close a discussion on a negative note, such as "what doesn't work." A final point here can bridge the gap between this lifecycle section and the upcoming section on user segmentation.

Lately, more and more requests for proposals (RFPs), and other requests, are asking respondents for their perspectives on client lifecycle management. In many instances, the RFPs are quite detailed regarding product specifications, services desired, and service levels appropriate to the tender.

One clause that is becoming standard asks for the most comprehensive/creative alternatives that the respondents can suggest. A disclaimer always warns that responses to that clause will not be a determining factor in the bid, but the request is there nonetheless. In other cases, the request asks for, among other things, the approach that a supplier might take to reduce the TCO for client computing. In addition, most teams that receive a product- and service-driven RFP generally include an unsolicited tender representing the client lifecycle management approaches to be taken.

Within a year, the vast majority of the RFPs will most likely request this information. In even more, templates will just request the client lifecycle management overview that can be applied to the overall environment. In fact, suppliers will most likely provide the templates on their respective websites, with relative pricing, to facilitate business inquiries.

In truth, some third parties provide such information in white papers. However, self-stated core competencies might differ from the reality of actual experience. Typically, a business can effectively make a determination only after at least one on-site visit or a comprehensive presentation.

As the price of a client device declines, the features and services aligned with the product become as important as the product. These services are the lifecycle elements discussed to this point in this book. The gap between products will narrow, and the differentiator will become the quality of the device, the features that are unique, embedded services, and the more comprehensive lifecycle services.

Not a lot of business strategies, even if implemented effectively, can become somewhat self-sustaining. Therefore, client lifecycle management, if implemented at a best practice level, should have an aggressive return on investment that could fund even further improvements in the client lifecycle environment. Client lifecycle management is now a hot topic, as evidenced by aggressive and increasing marketing and the recent proliferation of white papers and industry experts on the subject.

The overall lifecycle strategy has been extended from clients to the following:

- Servers
- Networking
- Printing
- Monitors

Each area listed here integrates with other service initiatives to take advantage of the economy of scale in sharing program office and program management office (PMO) resources.

Think about another situation that "proves" the points made in this section. Many consumers have multiple media devices (televisions, radios, DVD players, CD players, PCs, and even high-speed Internet). There is, therefore, market demand for a unified "entertainment center." In the old days, a remote control was *the* item to have! Now, however, consumers want as many devices as possible to work together in an easily managed environment (and not to have separate controllers for each). In addition, it is desirable that the lifecycle of each of the devices be co-terminus, if possible, to thus reduce complexity.

By analogy, this is the business case for enterprise client lifecycle management. As we move on to user segmentation, the business case will become even clearer, and an important question will be asked: Just how many of those devices do you really need?

SUMMARY

Lifecycle management in general and closed loop lifecycle planning in particular have become mainstream in businesses today. All the lifecycle elements have been available in one way or another to businesses, but what has been lacking is an overall framework and methodology that can integrate all the lifecycle elements in a straightforward, easily understood approach. An approach like this is warranted because lifecycle management is complicated, particularly when so many facets of the environment are constantly changing and evolving.

Lifecycle planning requires the integration of disparate offerings, strategies, and tactics into an enterprisewide approach that all involved believe is an actionable framework. Lifecycle management *must be* actionable, which differentiates lifecycle management from other disciplines and approaches.

Additional Detailed Lifecycle Management Content

NOTE: Part II and the Bonus Section are located online. Register your book at www.awprofessional.com to access these chapters. The index that follows this page begins on page 529 and includes these online chapters.

INDEX

NOTE: Pages beginning with "PDF" are located in the online chapters.

N

T

U

X-Y-Z

Register
Your Book

at www.awprofessional.com/register

You may be eligible to receive:

- Advance notice of forthcoming editions of the book
- Related book recommendations
- Chapter excerpts and supplements of forthcoming titles
- Information about special contests and promotions throughout the year
- Notices and reminders about author appearances, tradeshows, and online chats with special guests

Contact us

If you are interested in writing a book or reviewing manuscripts prior to publication, please write to us at:

Editorial Department
Addison-Wesley Professional
75 Arlington Street, Suite 300
Boston, MA 02116 USA
Email: AWPro@aw.com

Visit us on the Web: http://www.awprofessional.com